D1217468

Strategies for Teaching
WHOLE NUMBER COMPUTATION

Strategies for Teaching

WHOLE NUMBER
COMPUTATION

Using Error Analysis for Intervention and Assessment

David B. Spangler

CORWIN
A SAGE Company

For information:

Corwin
A SAGE Company
2455 Teller Road
Thousand Oaks, California 91320
(800) 233-9936
Fax: (800) 417-2466
www.corwin.com

SAGE India Pvt. Ltd.
B 1/I 1 Mohan Cooperative Industrial Area
Mathura Road, New Delhi 110 044
India

SAGE Ltd.
1 Oliver's Yard
55 City Road
London EC1Y 1SP
United Kingdom

SAGE Asia-Pacific Pte. Ltd.
33 Pekin Street #02-01
Far East Square
Singapore 048763

Printed in the United States of America.

Library of Congress Cataloging-in-Publication Data

Spangler, David B.
Strategies for teaching whole number computation: using error analysis for intervention and assessment/David B. Spangler.
        p. cm.
Includes bibliographical references.
ISBN 978-1-4129-8106-4 (pbk.: alk. paper)
    1. Arithmetic—Study and teaching (Elementary)—Activity programs. 2. Mathematics—Study and teaching (Elementary)—Activity programs. I. Title.

QA135.6.S568 2010
372.7'2—dc22   2009054002

This book is printed on acid-free paper.

10 11 12 13 14   10 9 8 7 6 5 4 3 2 1

Acquisitions Editor:	Jessica Allan
Editorial Assistant:	Joanna Coelho
Production Editor:	Cassandra Margaret Seibel
Copy Editor:	Adam Dunham
Typesetter:	C&M Digitals (P) Ltd.
Proofreader:	Scott Oney
Cover Designer:	Anthony Paular

Contents

Preface

Strategies for Teaching Whole Number Computation provides a practical intervention model with targeted hands-on materials for teachers to use when working with struggling learners. This book is a comprehensive resource—providing the "what," the "why," and the "how"—to guide and support classroom work with whole number computation *at whatever grades students may need intervention* for these skills and concepts.

This book addresses key concepts of the *Number and Operations* Content Standard recommended by the National Council of Teachers of Mathematics (NCTM; 2000) in their *Principles and Standards for School Mathematics*. In 2006, NCTM

> "Historically, number has been a cornerstone of the mathematics curriculum."
>
> —NCTM (2000, p. 32)

expanded upon those standards with its publication *Curriculum Focal Points for Prekindergarten Through Grade 8 Mathematics: A Quest for Coherence*. That document describes a new approach to curriculum development that focuses on areas of emphasis within each grade—recommending the most significant mathematical concepts and skills that should be taught at each grade level. *Strategies for Teaching Whole Number Computation* addresses the depth of coverage envisioned by the focal points with respect to number and operations for whole numbers for grades two through five.

NCTM Content Standard:
Number and Operations

Instructional programs from prekindergarten through grade 12 should enable all students to—

- understand numbers, way of representing numbers, relationships among numbers, and number systems;
- understand meanings of operations and how they relate to one another;
- compute fluently and make reasonable estimates.

—Principles and Standards for School Mathematics (NCTM, 2000)

NCTM Curriculum Focal Points:
Number and Operations—Whole Numbers

Grade 2: Develop quick recall of addition facts and related subtraction facts and fluency with multidigit addition and subtraction.

Grade 3: Develop understandings of multiplication and division and strategies for basic multiplication facts and related division facts.

Grade 4: Develop quick recall of multiplication facts and related division facts and fluency with whole-number multiplication.

Grade 5: Develop an understanding of and fluency with division of whole numbers.

—Curriculum Focal Points for Prekindergarten Through Grade 8 Mathematics: A Quest for Coherence (NCTM, 2006)

Communication

"Communication is an essential part of mathematics and mathematics education."

—NCTM (2000, p. 60)

Reasoning and Proof

"Teachers can understand students' thinking when they listen carefully to students' explanations."

—NCTM (2000, p. 126)

Representation

"Representing numbers with various physical materials should be a major part of mathematics instruction in the elementary grades."

—NCTM (2000, p. 33)

Content Knowledge

Knowledge of the subject

Pedagogical Knowledge

Knowledge of instructional practice

Pedagogical Content Knowledge

Knowledge of mathematical content for its use in the classroom

—Schulman (1987)

The instructional strategies described in this book are pedagogically aligned with all five NCTM process standards: problem solving, reasoning and proof, communication, connections, and representation. The following three process standards are especially embedded in the Intervention Activities of this book:

- *Communication:* Suggested questions that may be used directly with students are provided throughout the Intervention Activities; suggestions for student writing opportunities are also provided.

- *Reasoning and Proof:* Many of the suggested questions, along with the writing opportunities, require students to *explain their reasoning and thinking.*

- *Representation:* The concept development in the Intervention Activities utilizes manipulatives, number lines, grids, and other models and diagrams.

Three types of knowledge crucial for teaching mathematics at any level are described at the left. O'Donnell (2009) citing Hill and colleagues (2004) notes that teachers illustrate *pedagogical content knowledge* by "generating representations, interpreting student work, and analyzing student mistakes." *Strategies for Teaching Whole Number Computation* addresses all three types of knowledge in a concise, user-friendly way. With a focus on *how* to apply specific pedagogy to specific content, this resource is especially strong in the area of pedagogical content knowledge. Because this book develops *mainstream mathematics concepts in a way that is truly meaningful for students,* teachers should find this book to be an effective supplement to *any* textbook program—from those on the traditional end of the continuum to those that are based on reform.

RESEARCH BASE FOR THE BOOK

Strategies for Teaching Whole Number Computation is informed by academic research conducted and analyzed during the past 35 or more years. In developing this book, the author provides a mix of this extensive research base with his personal experience of about 40 years in mathematics education. The author's experience includes teaching at various levels, including classroom (grades five through eight), community college (in a remedial teaching lab), and university (methods courses).

Although some errors that occur in students' work with whole number computation are due to incorrect recall of number facts or carelessness, many are due to misconceptions and the use of incorrect strategies. According to Pincus and colleagues (1975), "too often, when teachers find errors in a child's work, they mark the example wrong, assume that the child did not master the basic facts, and prescribe further drill. *Careful analysis of errors through observation and interviews with individual children is essential*" (p. 581).

A key premise of this book is that if teachers (1) analyze student work for *error patterns* (revealed through diagnostic tests, practice, activities, and student discourse and oral interviews) and (2) then provide timely, targeted, and meaningful intervention, student errors will decrease in frequency—while at the same time student understanding of concepts will increase. By taking into account academic research on how students learn, the intervention strategies illustrated in this book should result in improved student performance and more positive student dispositions toward learning mathematics.

HOW THE BOOK IS ORGANIZED

The book begins with a substantial section, "A Look at the Academic Research: Intervention in the Mathematics Classroom." This academic research supports the goals and premises of the book, the pedagogical practices utilized in the Intervention Activities, and other aspects of intervention. These practices include activating prior knowledge, scaffolding, using representations, using estimation and mental math, introducing alternative algorithms, differentiating instruction, participating in instructional games, and more.

Next is a two-part section titled "Big Ideas in Computation and Problem Solving." The first part provides the principles on how our base-ten place-value system underpins multidigit computation. Much of this book's intervention work is based on those principles. The second part of this section is titled "Actions and Operations: Problem Structures for Addition, Subtraction, Multiplication, and Division." Here, illustrative models are provided for teachers to use with children to help them decide which operation to use to solve a given problem by thinking of *actions* that can be done with objects (or other representations) that relate to mathematical operations. By focusing on real-world contexts for the operations, key connections are made between *problem solving* and computation.

According to Kilpatrick, Swafford, and Bradford (2001), "Studies in almost every domain of mathematics have demonstrated that problem solving provides an important context in which students can learn about number and other mathematical topics" (p. 420). The author suggests that the problem structures described in this section be used with students as they study each operation. Students should then be asked to write their own word problems based on these structures to enhance their understandings of the operation. Because problem solving is not the major focus of this book, teachers are encouraged to integrate additional resources for problem solving when they teach computation.

Four main units then follow—one each for addition, subtraction, multiplication, and division of whole numbers. The units follow a predictable format. Each begins with a diagnostic test (in multiple-choice format), followed by an Item Analysis Table that keys student incorrect test responses to specific error patterns. (Each distractor on the tests is based on a specific error pattern.) A detailed section of error patterns with *step-by-step* Intervention Activities (the heart of the book) then follows. Initially for each operation, the Intervention Activities support student success with the "traditional algorithm" for that operation. However, because historically many students struggle with some of the traditional algorithms, instruction is also provided for the use of *alternative interventions* or *alternative algorithms*. It should be noted that the Intervention Activities (both for the traditional and for the alternative algorithms) may be used with students as part of the *initial instruction*—and are not just intended for use with students *after* they may have struggled with a concept.

A hallmark of this book is its strong focus on *teaching for understanding* in developing the Intervention Activities for each operation. Guided questions (with suggested student responses) and hands-on experiences—all with an emphasis on *place value* and the properties of operations—are used to achieve student understanding. It should be noted that the draft *Common Core State Standards for Mathematics* (2010) likewise places an emphasis on place value and the laws of arithmetic. Following the Intervention Activities for each unit is a short section of practice (keyed to the Item Analysis Table). Supplemental material (blacklines) for estimation, instructional games, and follow-up activities are also included for each unit.

Each main unit, along with the sections on academic research and "Big Ideas," concludes with a set of *Questions for Teacher Reflection*. These open-ended questions are intended to provide springboards for discussion among teachers or preservice teachers who may be using this book in a professional-development setting, workshop, or methods course.

INTENDED USES AND AUDIENCE FOR THE BOOK

Strategies for Teaching Whole Number Computation is intended to serve a wide audience of educators, and there are a variety of ways to use the book.

- **Intervention program for whole number computation in pullout or full-classroom situations:** The book may be used as a full-fledged intervention program for whole number computation. The book provides a comprehensive tool for quickly diagnosing and pinpointing trouble spots students are encountering—with specific Intervention Activities tailored to address the weaknesses identified.

- **Resource for elementary classroom teachers:** The book provides the types of errors struggling students frequently make with whole number computation. Teachers, especially those with limited experience teaching this content, should find this knowledge valuable as they teach computation concepts.

- **Resource for special education teachers:** These teachers—from the elementary level through high school—should find this material useful as they work with students individually or in small groups.

- **Resource for teachers and tutors working in developmental labs at the high school and community college levels:** The book provides fresh approaches to help students who have been struggling for years to learn how to compute.

- **Resource for instructional supervisors and curriculum coordinators:** These educators should find this book to be an important tool to use as they work with their teachers.

- **Text that may be used with teachers and preservice teachers in mathematics methods courses, workshops, and professional development programs (including online programs):** Educators at all grade levels should embrace this book as a key source of pedagogical content knowledge that they can directly use in their classrooms. The *Questions for Teacher Reflection* provide opportunities for teacher discussion and/or assignments in such settings.

- **Resource for educators interested in academic research on intervention:** This book provides a handy compilation of important research findings over the past 35-plus years related to intervention for whole number computation.

Acknowledgments

I would like to thank Jessica Allan, Anthony Paular, Joanna Coelho, Cassandra Margaret Seibel, and Adam Dunham of Corwin for their professional expertise on this project. I would also like to thank the many reviewers who provided much insight and direction in the development of the manuscript. Their contributions are greatly valued—and many of their suggestions were incorporated into the book. Finally, I would like to express gratitude to my wife, Bonnie, and children, Ben, Jamie, and Joey, for their encouragement for me to write this book.

Additionally, Corwin gratefully acknowledges the following peer reviewers for their editorial insight and guidance:

Donna Adkins
First-Grade Teacher
Perritt Primary
Arkadelphia Public Schools
Arkadelphia, AR

Roxie R. Ahlbrecht
Second-Grade Classroom Teacher/Math Teacher Leader
Robert Frost Elementary/Sioux Falls Public Schools 49-5
Sioux Falls, SD

Gloria Avolio DePaul
Elementary School Counselor
Hillsborough County School District
Tampa, FL

Judith A. Filkins
K–8 Math Curriculum Coordinator
Lebanon School District
Lebanon, NH

Barbara Fox
Teacher and Math Coach
Cambridge Public Schools
Cambridge, MA

Jean L. Krsak
Faculty
CalStateTEACH
California State University, Fullerton

Katharine Olson, EdD
Assistant Superintendent for Curriculum, Instruction, and Assessment
Northbrook Elementary School District 27
Northbrook, IL

Cathy Patterson
Assistant Principal
Evergreen Elementary
Diamond Bar, CA

Joyce Stout
Elementary School Counselor
Redondo Beach USD
Redondo Beach, CA

About the Author

 **David B. Spangler** has devoted his entire professional career of more than 35 years to mathematics education. After graduating from Northern Illinois University with BS and MS degrees, he began his career as a middle school mathematics teacher where he taught in an individualized setting. Later he taught at Triton Community College where he gained direct experience interacting with struggling students in a developmental math laboratory. Currently, he teaches mathematics methods courses through National-Louis University and *Active*Math Workshops, a professional-development company that he cofounded in 1994 (www.activemath.com). Some of the methods courses and workshops he facilitates address special-needs students, intervention, computation, and error analysis at the elementary level. David has literally worked with thousands of students and teachers during his career.

For many years, David has worked as a mathematics textbook editor at the K–12 level for major publishers. He has also authored several mathematics books and has written numerous articles for mathematics journals, such as *Mathematics Teaching in the Middle School*. Based on his extensive experience in mathematics education, David is uniquely qualified to write this book.

As a mathematics educator, David's goal has always been to teach mathematics for meaning rather than in a way that promotes rote memorization. This book was written to help teachers achieve that goal. David's other professional goals include exploring ways to teach mathematics through engaging, real-world applications and to explore humorous aspects to mathematics—especially mathematical blunders that illustrate mathematics illiteracy. David is a frequent speaker at conferences of the National Council of Teachers of Mathematics and other professional organizations where he addresses teaching mathematics for meaning, teaching mathematics through real-world applications, and teaching mathematics through humor. He also delivers after-dinner talks on the subject of mathematical humor.

David lives with his wife, Bonnie, in Northbrook, Illinois. They have three grown children, Ben, Jamie, and Joey. He would like to thank all of them for their love, support, and encouragement throughout his entire career.

A Look at the Academic Research

Intervention in the Mathematics Classroom

INTRODUCTION TO THE ACADEMIC RESEARCH

This book provides a model for diagnosing errors in computation and providing *meaningful instructional strategies for timely, pinpointed intervention.* The book begins with a two-part section called "Big Ideas in Computation and Problem Solving." That section is included because before students consider specific algorithms, they should have an understanding of the role our base-ten place-value system plays in multidigit computation—along with the types of *actions* and *problem structures* that are suggested by each operation.

Each unit on computation begins with a diagnostic test (in multiple-choice format), followed by an Item Analysis Table that keys student incorrect test responses to specific error patterns. Each distractor on the tests is based on a specific error pattern. A comprehensive section, "Error Patterns & Intervention Activities," then follows. This section provides detailed analysis of error patterns with supporting Intervention Activities for each operation. The items used on the diagnostic tests are drawn from this section. Each unit ends with a short section of supplemental practice.

Beattie and Algozzine (1982) note that when teachers use diagnostic tests to look for error patterns, "testing for teaching begins to evolve" (p. 47). And because diagnostic testing is just one of many tools to analyze student understanding, with each Item Analysis Table are additional suggestions to delve into the rationale of student errors.

According to Thanheiser (2009), "To help their students learn about numbers and algorithms, teachers need more than ability to perform algorithms. They need to be able to explain the mathematics underlying the algorithms in a way that will help children understand" (p. 277). Research by Hill, Rowan, and Ball (2005) found that this type of knowledge, known as mathematical knowledge for teaching (or pedagogical content knowledge), positively predicted mathematics student achievement gains in Grades 1 and 3.

The Intervention Activities in this book are based on instructional practices supported by academic research that teach for *meaning.* The activities place a strong emphasis on using *place value* as a way to develop this understanding. The practices employed include activating prior knowledge, using representations, using estimation and mental math, introducing alternative algorithms, and participating in instructional games.

According to Kilpatrick, Swafford, and Bradford (2001), "when students practice procedures they do not understand, there is a danger they will practice incorrect procedures, thereby making it more difficult to learn correct

Lack of Conceptual Understanding—Error Patterns

"[Children frequently] either fail to grasp the concepts that underlie procedures or cannot connect the concepts to the procedures. Either way, children who lack such understanding frequently generate flawed procedures that result in systematic patterns of errors. . . . The errors are an opportunity in that their systematic quality points to the source of the problem and this indicates the specific misunderstanding that needs to be overcome."

—Siegler (2003, p. 291)

Linking Research and Practice

"The call for a better linking of research and practice has been echoed in the mathematics education community for some time."

—Arbaugh et al. (2010, p. 4)

ones. . . . Further, when students learn a procedure without understanding, they need extensive practice so as not to forget the steps" (pp. 122–123).

A common subtraction error is shown at the right. Fuson and Briars (1990) found that students who learn to subtract with *understanding* rarely make this error.

An important premise of this book is that when teachers analyze student work for conceptual and procedural misconceptions—and then provide timely, targeted, and meaningful intervention—the probability of the errors repeating in the future decreases. Hill, Ball, and Schilling (2008), citing the research of others, found when teachers investigated how students learn particular subject matter, such as whole-number operations, "their classroom practices changed and student learning was improved over that of teachers in comparison groups" (p. 376). According to Cox (1975), systematic errors (errors that occur in at least three out of five problems for a specific algorithmic computation) are potentially remediable, "but without proper instructional intervention the systematic errors will continue for long periods of time" (p. 152).

It is important to emphasize that class or individual discussions of the errors should be conducted as part of a *positive* learning experience—one that allows for students to use reasoning and problem solving to explore why an erroneous procedure may not yield the correct answer.

Finally, any discussion on intervention would be incomplete without addressing key factors that affect the entire child, such as the principle of equity, student dispositions, and differentiating instruction. These areas are addressed in this research chapter.

EQUITY AND QUALITY IN THE MATH CLASSROOM

Equity and *quality* in the math classroom often imply providing every student with both an equal and a quality learning experience. Hiebert and colleagues (1997) define equity such that "every learner—bilingual students, handicapped students, students of all ethnic groups, students who live in poverty, girls, and boys—can learn mathematics with understanding. In order to do this, *each* student must have access to learning with understanding" (p. 65).

The research of Campbell (1995) and others has shown that *all* children, including those who have been traditionally underserved, can learn mathematics when they have access to high-quality instruction and instructional materials that promote their learning.

A Common Subtraction Error Pattern

$$\begin{array}{r} 92 \\ -28 \\ \hline 76 \end{array}$$

The student subtracts the lesser digit from the greater digit in each place-value position, ignoring order (and renaming).

"As we teach computation procedures, we need to remember that our students are not necessarily learning what we think we are teaching; we need to keep our eyes and ears open to find out what our students are *actually* learning. We need to be alert for error patterns!"

—Ashlock (2010, p. 14)

The Equity Principle

"Excellence in mathematics education requires equity—high expectations and strong support for all students."

—NCTM (2000, p. 12)

The Curriculum Principle

"A curriculum is more than a collection of activities: it must be coherent, focused on important mathematics and well articulated across the grades."

—NCTM (2000, p. 14)

Since the passage of Public Law 94-142 in 1975 and its reauthorization as the Individuals with Disabilities Education Improvement Act (IDEA) in 2004, students with a variety of disabilities are increasingly being taught mathematics in inclusive classrooms. In fact, the majority of students with disabilities are now in regular classrooms for at least a portion of each school day. According to the work of Truelove, Holaway-Johnson, Leslie, and Smith (2007), when teachers implement instructional strategies designed to help those with learning disabilities, *all students*—not just those with disabilities—will likely benefit.

STUDENT DISPOSITIONS

During the elementary grades, students often acquire individual views and dispositions toward the learning of mathematics that last for the rest of their lives.

> "Students who have developed a productive disposition are confident in their knowledge and ability. They see that mathematics is both reasonable and intelligible and believe that, with appropriate effort and experience, they can learn."
>
> — Kilpatrick, Swafford, and Bradford (2001, p. 133)

Such dispositions as curiosity, cooperation, and perseverance are personal habits that play a key role in future success with mathematics both in school and beyond.

An important question to ask is, "Why is it important to take student dispositions into account?" The answer may lie in the work of Dossey, Mullis, Lindquist, and Chambers (1988), based on various national assessments. They found that students who enjoy mathematics and perceive its relevance have higher proficiency scores than students with more negative perspectives. They also found that students become less positive about mathematics as they proceed through school; both confidence in and enjoyment of mathematics appear to decline as students progress from elementary to high school.

> "When a child gives an incorrect answer, it is especially important for the teacher to assume that the child was engaged in meaningful activity. Thus, it is possible that the child will reflect on his or her solution attempt and evaluate it."
>
> —Yackel, Cobb, Wood, Wheatley, and Merkel (1990, p. 17)

One implication of this research is that mathematics instruction should not only enable students to learn skills and understandings but also promote the *desire* to use what has been learned. According to Lannin, Arbaugh, Barker, and Townsend (2006), "Part of the process of learning and solving problems includes making errors that, if examined, can lead to further mathematical insight" (p. 182). Lannin and colleagues, and others, believe that teachers should guide students to think and reflect about their errors through a process of recognizing, attributing, and reconciling.

This book—based on a philosophy of using error analysis with targeted interventions that are meaningful, along with follow-up instructional games and activities—is designed to promote *positive* learning experiences and favorable student dispositions toward mathematics.

> "If the student is misbehaving out of frustration with an activity, assisting the child with the activity will be more effective than punitive measures in correcting the behavior."
>
> —Truelove, Holaway-Johnson, Leslie, and Smith (2007, p. 339)

Finally, children with emotional and behavioral disorders (EBD) often present a variety of challenges to educators. EBD students are especially prone to frustration when performing complex tasks. Guetzloe (2001) and others suggest that *nonaggressive* strategies be used with EBD students to encourage them to stay in class and in school.

ACTIVATING PRIOR KNOWLEDGE

According to Steele (2002) and many others, teachers should review prerequisite skills or concepts no matter how long ago they were taught. Such review is even more important for students who have memory deficits, because they may quickly forget previously mastered skills, or they may have significant gaps in their knowledge.

According to the TIMSS (Trends in International Math and Science Study), teachers in the United States tend to do most of the mental work of introducing, explaining, and demonstrating new concepts—and 60% of the time, they do not link new ideas with other concepts and activities. In Japan, where students scored near the top on the TIMSS, *teachers made explicit connections* in 96% of the lessons (U.S. Department of Education, 1996).

The Intervention Activities in this book build on students' prior knowledge by using familiar concepts and tools to develop new content. For example, familiar *place value* concepts are embedded as a key vehicle to develop the algorithms for each operation. Familiar *addition and multiplication tables* are used to reinforce subtraction and division facts, respectively.

> "One of the most reliable findings from research is that students learn when they are given opportunities to learn. Providing an opportunity to learn means setting up the conditions for learning that take into account students' entry knowledge, the nature and purpose of the tasks and activities, and so on."
>
> —Hiebert (2003, p. 10)

REPRESENTATIONS

"The term representation refers both to process and to product" (National Council of Teachers of Mathematics, 2000, p. 67). As a process, it refers to creating in one's mind a mental image of a mathematical idea. As a product, it refers to a physical form of that idea, such as a manipulative, an illustration, or even a symbolic expression. Why is the idea of representation so important? Simply stated, *the more ways a student can think about a mathematical concept, the better that student will understand the underlying mathematical idea.*

A Concrete → Semiconcrete → Abstract Model of Instruction: A number of studies suggest that concept development is strong when students begin with a tactile, hands-on model (concrete), move to the use of illustrations of those objects (semiconcrete), and finally move

> **The Representation Standard**
>
> "Instructional programs from prekindergarten through grade 12 should enable all students to
>
> - create and use representations to organize, record, and communicate mathematical ideas;
> - select, apply, and translate among mathematical representations to solve problems;
> - use representations to model and interpret physical, social, and mathematical phenomena."
>
> —NCTM (2000, p. 67)

to a symbolic algorithm (abstract). Psychologist Jerome Bruner (1966) referred to those stages as *enactive, iconic,* and *symbolic.* Through his research, Bruner theorized that students learn mathematics better when their lessons progress through those three stages. Miller and Hudson (2007) found that such a three-stage model helps students with learning disabilities master concepts involving whole numbers, fractions, and algebra. Many of the intervention activities in this book are designed so that students first encounter manipulatives, then refer to drawings of those objects, and finally develop computational proficiency by connecting those representations to an abstract algorithm.

Research: Hands-On Activities; Manipulatives; Diagrams

In a study of over 7,000 students, Wenglinsky (2000) found that students whose teachers conduct hands-on learning activities outperform their peers by more than 70% of a grade level in math on the National Assessment of Educational Progress (NAEP).

In a meta-analysis of 60 research studies, Sowell (1989) found that for students of all ages, math achievement is increased and students' attitudes toward math are improved with the long-term use of manipulative materials.

Goldin (2003), in analyzing many research studies, concluded that "bonna fide representational power does not stand in opposition to formal proficiency, but, rather, strengthens it" (p. 283).

Ferrucci, Yeap, and Carter (2003) found, from their observations of Singapore schools and curricula, that modeling with diagrams is a powerful tool for children to use to enhance their problem-solving and algebraic reasoning skills.

ESTIMATION AND MENTAL MATH

Estimation involves a process of obtaining an approximate answer (rather than an exact answer).

Mental math involves a process of obtaining an exact answer in your head.

"Estimation relates to every important mathematics concept and skill developed in elementary school."

—Reys and Reys (1990, p. 22)

Traditionally, estimation and mental math have been thought of as supplemental skills. However, based on surveys of adults, Carlton (1980) found that most of the mathematics used in everyday living relies far more on estimation and mental computation than on traditional computation.

Also, traditionally, mental math and estimation have been taught *after* students master pencil-and-paper computation. However, Kilpatrick and colleagues (2001) found not only that children can learn to compute mentally and to estimate *before* learning formal pencil-and-paper computational procedures but also that mental math and estimation activities prior to formal work with computation actually enhance the learning of computation.

This book describes and integrates a variety of strategies to use for estimation. Front-end (with adjustment), rounding, and compatible numbers are all suggested as ways to check for the *reasonableness* of results. Because some teachers may not be as familiar with front-end estimation as, say, with rounding, this book provides instructional material on using front-end estimation for each operation. Front-end estimation focuses on the "front-end" digit of a number—the digit in the place-value position that contributes the most to the final answer. This method often provides better estimates than the rounding method because numbers that are close to the "middle" of a range (such as 352 or 349) are not dramatically rounded up (400) or down (300). Such an example is illustrated at the right.

Although many struggling students find the *rounding* method to be difficult, most traditional textbooks teach that method as the primary way to form estimates. To make rounding accessible to more students, this book includes a lesson titled "Roller Coaster Rounding." The roller coaster model provides a way for students *visualize* the rounding process. This book also provides instruction for using *compatible* (nice) *numbers* to estimate results. Students should be allowed to use the estimation strategy with which they are most comfortable, and they should be given ample opportunities to discuss those strategies with one another.

To promote fluency with mental math for addition and subtraction, this book provides Intervention Activities that use an "empty (open) number line" as a model. A growing body of research has reported on an international trend toward its use. According to Bobis (2007), students using the empty number line concluded that it is "easier to learn and remember than the pencil-and-paper method" essentially because the actions performed on an empty number line represent the *student's* thinking (p. 411).

According to O'Loughlin (2007), "Some children need a model like the open number line to keep a record of their counting and help them think while experimenting with patterns and relationships and thus developing number sense" (p. 134). Further, many students have difficulty learning the standard subtraction algorithm. The standard algorithm, shown at the right, is often the *starting point* of subtraction instruction. The following section addresses the benefits of using alternative algorithms with struggling students.

Estimation by Rounding (to the Nearest 100)

$$253 + 455 \rightarrow 300 + 500 = 800$$

Front-End Estimation

$$253 + 455 \rightarrow 2 + 4 = 6$$

Add the front-end digits. Since 2 hundreds + 4 hundreds = 6 hundreds, the sum is at least 600.

Now adjust: Since 53 + 55 is about 100, an estimate would be 600 + 100, or *about 700*.

Exact Answer

253 + 455 = 708

So, the estimate produced by front-end estimation (about 700) is closer to the exact answer than the estimate produced by rounding (800).

"When students have regular opportunities to estimate, share orally, evaluate, compare their approaches, and transfer strategies to new settings, they feel challenged and, ultimately, empowered."

—Rubenstein (2001, p. 443)

Using an Empty Number Line
Add: 26 + 57

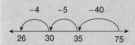

Think: 26 + 4 = 30;
30 + 50 = 80; 80 + 3 = 83

Subtract: 75 − 49

Think: 75 − 40 = 35;
35 − 5 = 30; 30 − 4 = 26

Standard Subtraction Algorithm

$$\begin{array}{r} 6\ 15 \\ \cancel{7}\ \cancel{5} \\ -\ 4\ 9 \\ \hline 2\ 6 \end{array}$$

History of the Word *Algorithm*

Around 780–850 C.E., Muhammad ibn-Musa al-Khwarizmi wrote *Book on Addition and Subtraction After the Method of the Indians* (title translated from the Arabic). In his book, solutions to problems are given in steps, or recipes. The word for these recipes, *algorithm*, is derived from the Latin that begins with *Dixit Algorismi*, or "al-Khwarizmi says."

—Pickreign and Rogers (2006, pp. 42–47)

ALTERNATIVE ALGORITHMS

An *algorithm* is "a precise, systematic method for solving a class of problems" (Maurer, 1998, p. 21). In school mathematics, students generally learn a traditional algorithm for each operation that is quite efficient. However, according to Van de Walle (2001), "Each of the traditional algorithms is simply a clever way to record an operation for a single place value with transitions (trades, 'borrows,' or 'carries') to an adjacent position" (p. 171). Although many students experience success using traditional algorithms, some students do not.

Unfortunately, some teachers give struggling students *more* instruction and practice using the same algorithms for which those students have already demonstrated failure. According to Ellis and Yeh (2008), "the traditional algorithms used for subtraction and multiplication are very efficient but not very transparent—they do not allow students to see why the methods work. When students learn traditional algorithms by rote, they often come to think of this as *the* way to do arithmetic rather than as *one* way among many" (p. 368).

These students often continue to struggle with the following kinds of questions:

- When multiplying with renaming, why do you multiply the next digit in the multiplicand before you add, rather than after?

- When multiplying by a 2-digit number, why do you move the second partial product one space to the left?

- In long division, why do you multiply and subtract as part of the process?

- In long division, what is the reason for the use of the phrase "bring down"?

> "The depressing thing about arithmetic badly taught is that it destroys a child's intellect and, to some extent, his integrity. Before they are taught arithmetic, children will not give their assent to utter nonsense; afterwards they will. Instead of looking at things and thinking about them, they will make wild guesses in the hopes of pleasing the teacher."
>
> —Sawyer (1943)

This book provides extensive, step-by-step Intervention Activities to address the traditional algorithms. However, the Intervention Activities also include *alternative algorithms* for each operation. According to Lin (2007/2008), alternative methods help students "understand how other algorithms work and prompt them to think more deeply about numbers and equations" (p. 298). It should be noted that alternative algorithms not only are effective with students who struggle with traditional algorithms but are also effective with *all* students up front—and may be used *instead* of those algorithms (or in addition to them). Many textbook programs include alternative algorithms with their materials because they benefit *all* students.

> "The standard algorithms used in the United States are not universal. . . . As our schools become more and more diverse, it is important that students' knowledge from their home cultures is valued within the classroom. Having students share alternative methods for doing arithmetic is one way to do so and honors the knowledge of their parents and community elders."
>
> —Ellis and Yeh (2008, p. 368)

One such alternative algorithm is for two-digit multiplication that uses grids to help find partial products. Englert and Sinicrope (1994) noted that "although the time spent in developing the multiplication algorithm using this visual approach is greater than the time needed to use a more traditional approach, less time is needed for review and reteaching. Students are able to attach meaning to the multiplication algorithm" (p. 447).

An important premise of this book is that for each operation, the dual benefits of *teaching for understanding* and *saving time* can be achieved by using meaningful alternative algorithms.

DIFFERENTIATING INSTRUCTION

According to Stiff, Johnson, and Johnson (1993), "if all students were the same, a teacher's job would be simple—and boring. Researchers would develop one comprehensive theory of learning; teachers would simply follow the recipe to produce high levels of success for 'all' students. The challenge is to find the combination of strategies that enable all students to reach their full potential" (p. 12).

> **More Than One Way to Perform an Operation**
>
> "Most people have been taught only one way, so they quite naturally assume that there is only one way. The realization that there are many possible procedures to follow when operating on numbers can change the way that people think of mathematics."
>
> —Sgroi (1998, p. 81)

Scaffolding

Scaffolding refers to assistance provided to students (temporary supports that are gradually removed) to allow them to engage at a higher level than they would be able to without the assistance. Kilpatrick and colleagues (2001) concluded that by offering a subtle hint, posing a similar problem, or asking for ideas, students are assisted in their ability to reason.

One Size Doesn't Fit All

"The idea of differentiating instruction to accommodate the different ways that students learn involves a hefty dose of common sense, as well as sturdy support in the theory and research of education."

—Tomlinson and Allan (2000)

Gardner's (1991) Multiple Intelligences

- Verbal/Linguistic
- Mathematical/Logical
- Visual/Spatial
- Musical/Rhythmic
- Bodily/Kinesthetic
- Interpersonal
- Intrapersonal
- Naturalistic

Student Writing

"By writing we find out what we know, what we think. Writing is an extremely efficient way of gaining access to that knowledge that we cannot explore directly."

—Smith (1982, p. 33)

One way to differentiate instruction is to use *scaffolding*. The Intervention Activities in this book are presented through *step-by-step instruction* with *guided questions* to pose to students—thus providing effective scaffolding.

According to Martin (2006), "to meet the needs of all students and design programs that are responsive to their intellectual strengths and personal interests, we must explore alternatives to traditional mathematics instruction. We need to examine not only what is taught, but how it is taught and how students learn" (p. iv).

Tomlinson (1999) advocates that teachers make accommodations to *content* (what you want students to learn), *process* (the way students make sense out of the content), and *product* (student outcomes at the end of the lesson) because, as she is known for saying, "one size does not fit all." According to Pierce and Adams (2005), differentiating instruction involves first determining which of those parts of the lesson you want to tier. This decision is based on students' readiness and learning styles. According to Little, Hauser, and Corbishley (2009), "Through tiering, mathematics teachers can give all students challenging tasks while ensuring sufficient scaffolding for struggling students and reducing repetition for more advanced students" (p. 36).

Cognitive research on multiple intelligences (Gardner, 1991) provides strong evidence demonstrating the need for children to experience a variety of pedagogical methods. Gardner concluded that students "possess different kinds of minds and therefore learn, remember, perform, and understand in different ways" (p. 11). As Martin (2007) puts it, "consider trying to learn to dance by reading a book and memorizing the steps. We learn when we are actively involved in the learning process and use a variety of learning modalities. Not all students have the same talents, learn the same way, or have the same interests and abilities" (p. iv).

Through the use of questioning, mathematical reasoning, and representations, this book tiers "process" while addressing the verbal/linguistic, mathematical/logical, and visual/spatial intelligences outlined by Gardner.

The verbal/linguistic intelligence is also addressed through student writing. This book provides suggestions for students to (1) write about procedures used in algorithms, (2) compare different algorithms for a given operation, and (3) write word problems that can be solved using a given operation. The writing may be viewed as a form of alternative assessment—providing a way for teachers to tier "product." According to Fello and Paquette (2009), "Writing in mathematics classrooms is imperative for students to describe their thinking processes, their methodology for solving problems, and their explanations for solutions" (p. 413).

According to the LdPride Web site, www.LdPride.net, "information about learning styles and multiple intelligences is helpful for everyone, but especially for people with learning disabilities and attention deficit disorder. Knowing your learning style will help you develop coping strategies to compensate for your weaknesses and capitalize on your strengths" (para. 1).

> **Interactive Instruments at the LdPride Web Site**
>
> - Find out your dominant intelligence.
> - Find out your learning style.
>
> (See www.LdPride.net; there may be a fee to obtain the test results.)

INSTRUCTIONAL GAMES

A number of studies suggest that the use of instructional games has the simultaneous goals of improved learning outcomes and increased student motivation for learning mathematics. Good instructional games provide "authentic" experiences for the construction and reinforcement of concepts—while ensuring that every child has an opportunity to participate.

Holton, Ahmed, Williams, and Hill (2001) reported that it is often difficult to convince students to check their answers: "In the context of a game, however, checking conjectures has a clear purpose—if the conjecture is wrong, then the child is likely to lose. In this regard, games provide an opportunity for teachers to question students about their thinking. One of the inhibiting factors in learning new concepts is the fear of failure and of getting wrong answers. Incorrect strategies within game situations are not recorded for later correction and so the stigma of failure does not exist" (p. 406).

> "When teachers use appropriate mathematics games, both student learning and motivation are strengthened. . . . Mathematics games can and should be used before, during, and after instruction to help students develop higher-level thinking skills. . . . Games can stimulate children to be alert, curious, and critical, and to see themselves as problem solvers."
>
> —Thornton and Wilson (1993, pp. 288–289)

The domino-type games *Balance the +/− Number Sentence!* and *Balance the ×/÷ Number Sentence!* are included in this book to promote memorization of the facts, mental math, and trial-and-error thinking to balance number sentences. By balancing number sentences, students develop the concepts of *variable* and *equality*—thus bridging arithmetic skills with algebraic reasoning.

In the *Balance the Number Sentence!* games, the unknowns appear in different positions in the sentences to foster the thinking described above. In particular, the research of Knuth, Stephens, McNeil, and Alibali (2006) and others suggests that many students at all grade levels have an inadequate understanding of what the equal sign means. Behr, Erlwanger, and Nichols (1980) found that young students often think the equal sign separates "the problem" from "the solution." They see the equal sign as a signal to perform an operation—rather than as a symbol of *equality* and *balance*.

Number Sentences Where the Unknowns Are in Different Positions

$\square + 3 = 11$

$12 = \square \times 4$

$4 + 7 = \square + 5$

"The problem is, kids get to eighth grade and they don't like math because it's not taught in an interesting manner."

—McGee (Rossi, 2009), former Illinois Superintendent of Schools, commenting on how to attack the math gap

Behr found that children do not change this thinking as they get older. Students who do not understand the meaning of the equal sign may conclude that the solutions for the number sentences at the left are 14, 48, and 11, respectively. Such erroneous thinking is especially common among students who are only exposed to number sentences where the unknown is alone on one side of the equation, as in $8 + 7 = \square$.

A key goal of this book is to provide material for teachers to use to make their math classes more meaningful and engaging. The instructional games, along with the other activities in the book, are designed to serve that purpose.

Research: Instructional Games in Mathematics

Bright, Harvey, and Wheeler (1979) found that games are effective for helping students acquire, practice, and transfer mathematical concepts and problem-solving abilities.

Klein and Freitag (1991) found that the use of instructional games increases student interest, satisfaction, and continuing motivation.

Allen and Main (1976) found that including instructional gaming in a mathematics curriculum helped to reduce the rate of absenteeism in inner-city schools.

RESPONSE TO INTERVENTION

Response to Intervention (RtI) is a multitier approach to the early identification and support of students with learning needs. Rather than testing students for learning disabilities after achievement failure has occurred, RtI identifies students whose performance does not match that of their peers early in the learning process so that they can receive assistance before they fall behind. RtI provides appropriate, increasingly intense research-based interventions to match each student's needs. Core features include differentiated instruction, guided and independent practice, and frequent progress monitoring with data-driven decision making (the use of student-performance data to continually evaluate the effectiveness of teaching and to make more informed instructional decisions).

RtI frequently is implemented as a three-tiered model. The three tiers generally used are similar to those described on page 13. Students who are participating in intervention programs at *any* of these tiers are part of the target audience for the instructional strategies provided in this book. As such, the material in this book may be delivered to the full classroom, to small groups, or to individuals.

De Corte, Greer, and Verschaffel (1996) found that learning is enhanced when teachers have access to the knowledge that learners bring to the lesson, use this knowledge as part of instruction, monitor students' changing conceptions as the lesson proceeds, and provide appropriate intervening instruction. According to Safer and Fleischman (2005), "Research has demonstrated that when teachers use student progress monitoring, students learn more, teacher decision making improves, and students become more aware of their own performance" (p. 82). According to Fisher and Kopenski (2007/2008), the use of *item analysis* is an effective way for teachers to diagnose student misconceptions, to improve and adjust instruction, and to prevent or reduce errors. Teachers using this book should find the error-analysis approach to be a valuable progress-monitoring tool. The sets of practice exercises at the end of each unit provide an additional progress-monitoring tool because they may be used as posttests (due to the fact that they are broken into parts that align with the parts of the diagnostic tests).

Meaningful practice is another aspect of RtI. Sutton and Krueger (2002) found that sufficient practice is essential for learning mathematics, but it is also essential that students *understand* the skill being practiced—so that they do not inadvertently practice incorrect procedures.

This book builds on the evidence cited in this chapter on academic research by providing a model of assessment or diagnosis (that is manageable and ongoing), intervention activities (delivered early in the process and that teach for understanding with multiple approaches), and practice or follow-up activities—enabling teachers to use real-time data to meet the needs of individual students.

Tier 1: Universal Interventions
Universal interventions occur in the classroom for all students; they are preventative, proactive, and differentiated.

Tier 2: Targeted Group Interventions
Targeted group interventions provide additional interventions to Tier 1 instruction for at-risk students who demonstrate a specific need; they involve frequent assessment.

Tier 3: Intensive, Individual Interventions
Intensive, individual interventions are individually administered; they are assessment-based, of high intensity, and of longer duration.

—Adapted from Batsche and colleagues (2005)

Web Sites That Provide Information and Resources About RtI
- National Center on Response to Intervention: www.rti4success.org
- RTI Action Network: http://www.rtinetwork.org

"Without information about [our] students' skills, understanding, and individual approaches to mathematics, teachers have nothing to guide their work."

— Mokros, Russell, and Economopoulos (1995, p. 84)

"We teach children to look for patterns in dealing with numbers; these patterns help children discover the structure of our number system. Similarly, teachers must look for patterns in the data they collect from children who are experiencing problems in computational skills. Recognizing patterns in the errors a child is making—that the child is, in other words, making a systematic error—is the initial step toward remediation of the error."

—Cox (1975, p. 156)

QUESTIONS FOR TEACHER REFLECTION

1. Consider the quote below from W. W. Sawyer. Explain how this quote relates to the type of computation instruction some students unfortunately experience. Use citations from this research section to support the importance of teaching for understanding. (This quote is used on page 9 of this book.)

   "The depressing thing about arithmetic badly taught is that it destroys a child's intellect and, to some extent, his integrity. Before they are taught arithmetic, children will not give their assent to utter nonsense; afterwards they will. Instead of looking at things and thinking about them, they will make wild guesses in the hopes of pleasing the teacher." (Sawyer, 1943)

2. Why is the promotion of positive student dispositions toward mathematics important? Include any personal experiences in your discussion.

3. What are representations? Why is it important for students to experience a variety of representations for a mathematics concept?

4. Why should students learn how to estimate, and why is estimation more than just a "supplemental skill"? How do you use estimation in your instructional strategies?

5. What is an algorithm? Discuss why the use of alternative algorithms is often recommended for whole number computation.

6. Why is it so important to activate prior knowledge before beginning a new topic—especially for the struggling student? Choose one of the operations. Discuss what prerequisite skills you would address with your students prior to instruction on the operation per se.

7. What is meant by *differentiating instruction?* How can differentiating instruction serve to achieve equity in the mathematics classroom?

Big Ideas in Computation and Problem Solving

THE BASE-TEN PLACE-VALUE SYSTEM AND MULTIDIGIT COMPUTATION

The following seven "big ideas" in computation underpin much of the intervention work that is developed in this book.

1. Our numeration system is called a *decimal system* because it is a system that uses ten digits (0–9), based on groups of 10.

2. It is also called a *base-ten place-value system* because it is a positional system, where each place-value position is 10 times as great as the position immediately to the right. So, a digit's position in a numeral (along with what the digit is) determines its value. For example, since the 7 in 4,739 is in the hundreds position, its value is 7×100, or 700.

3. The concept of 0 as a *placeholder* and a *value* is a major underpinning of the base-ten system. Zero does *not* mean "nothing." In numbers such as 203 or 540, the 0 is used as a placeholder and has a value of 0.

4. A number can be represented in *equivalent* ways. Another name for 17 is $10 + 7$. When you get 10 or more in a place-value position, you can rename and move to the next position. So *17 is renamed as 1 ten and 7.*

5. Most algorithms involve breaking apart numbers so that calculations involve just basic facts. The partial results are then "put back together" to obtain the final answer. So, instead of subtracting, say, $408 - 179$ all at once, you rename 408 as 3 hundreds, 9 tens, and 18 ones. Then, you subtract basic facts in each successive place-value position.

6. The properties of operations are the *rules* that govern arithmetic. The following properties apply to all real numbers:

Commutative Property of Addition	$a + b = b + a$
Commutative Property of Multiplication	$a \times b = b \times a$
Identity Property of Addition	$0 + a = a + 0 = a$
Identity Property of Multiplication	$1 \times a = a \times 1 = a$
Associative Property of Addition	$(a + b) + c = a + (b + c)$
Associative Property of Multiplication	$(a \times b) \times c = a \times (b \times c)$
Distributive Property ($\times$ over $+$)	$a \times (b + c) = a \times b + a \times c$
Distributive Property ($\times$ over $-$)	$a \times (b - c) = a \times b - a \times c$
Transitive Property of Equality	If $a = b$ and $b = c$, then $a = c$

7. Calculations can be *estimated* (approximated) by replacing the original numbers with numbers that are close in value to them. Using such round or "nice" numbers makes computation easier—while producing answers that are in the ballpark (close to the exact answers).

ACTIONS AND OPERATIONS
Problem Structures for Addition, Subtraction, Multiplication, and Division

To help themselves decide which operation to use to solve a given problem, students can think about *actions* that can be done with objects that relate to mathematical operations. These actions provide *problem structures* and *contexts* to help students *visualize* what is going on in a problem. The visualization process provides students with an important tool to help determine if a computational result is *reasonable*.

Although the examples used in this section may appear elementary in nature, these basic problem structures are the same regardless of the types of numbers used in a given problem. Knowledge of these actions and problem structures should help students write their own word problems for a given operation—and explain why the given operation can be used to solve the problems.

Addition

There is basically one type of addition problem, the "putting together" type.

Putting Together

- You know how many are in one group and how many are in another group.
- You are to find how many objects there are in all.

Example 1: Able has 7 small Fuddy-Duddies, Gable has 8 medium Fuddy-Duddies, and Mable has 9 large Fuddy-Duddies. How many do the 3 children have in all?

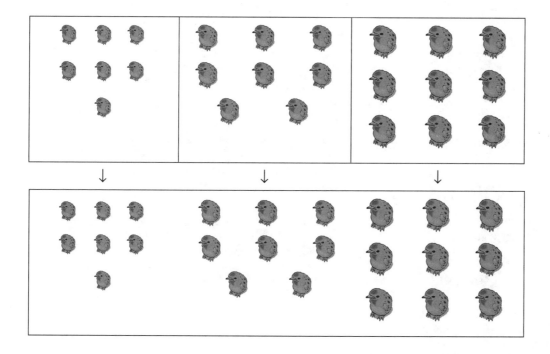

(The model shows that when the Fuddy-Duddies are combined, there are 24 in all. Some students erroneously add the 3 in with the total—essentially because they do not carefully read the problem.)

Example 2: After spending $125, Penny Nichols had $55 left. How much did Penny have at the start?

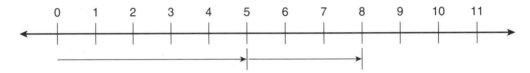

Money at Start		?	
Amount Spent	Amount Left	$125	$55

(The model suggests that to find how much Penny had at the start, you add. So, she began with $125 + $55, or $180. Some students erroneously subtract— perhaps because they focus on the word *left* rather than on the action suggested by the problem.)

Example 3: The temperature goes up 5 degrees and then goes up another 3 degrees. What was the total increase?

```
     0   1   2   3   4   5   6   7   8   9   10  11
  ←──┼───┼───┼───┼───┼───┼───┼───┼───┼───┼───┼───┼──→
```

(As you "slide" across the number line, you can see that the temperature rose 5 + 3, or 8, degrees.) Example 3 is often referred to as *the slide model of addition.*

Subtraction

There are four basic types of subtraction problems.

(1) Take-Away

- You know how many there are in all and how many are taken away.

- You are to find how many are left.

Example: Kent Read had 10 books. He gave away 7 books. How many books did he have left?

(The model shows that when 7 books are taken away, 10 − 7, or 3, are left.)

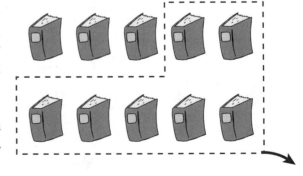

(2) Comparison

- You know how many are in one group and how many are in another group.

- You are to find how many more (or how many fewer) are in one group than the other. Essentially you are finding how far apart the two numbers are.

Example: Hy Rise lives in a building that has 16 floors. Ellie Vator's building has 9 floors. How many more floors are in Hy Rise's building?

(The model shows a one-to-one correspondence for the first 9 floors. As such, Hy's building has 16 – 9, or 7, more floors.)

(3) Additive (Missing Part)

- You know how many are needed in all and how many you have.

- You are to find how many more are needed.

Example: 16 hot dogs need to be roasted for a picnic. So far, Frank Furter has roasted 9 hot dogs. How many more does he need to roast?

(After finding a one-to-one correspondence for the first 9 hot dogs—using the same model—you can count on 7 more hot dogs to be roasted, until you reach 16.)

(4) Separation

- You know how many are in a group in all and how many of a certain kind are in that group.

- You are to find how many in the group are *not* of that kind.

Example: There are 27 animals in a room. Of them, 12 are dogs. The rest are cats. How many cats are in the room?

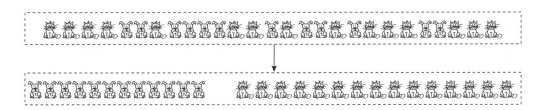

(When the animals are separated by type, you can see that there are 27 – 12, or 15, cats.)

Multiplication

There are three basic types of multiplication situations.

(1) Putting Together Same-Size Groups (Multiples)

- Find the total when you join groups of the same size.

Example: There are 6 basketball teams in the league. Each team has 12 players. How many players are in the league?

x x x x x x x x x x	x x x x x x x x x x	x x x x x x x x x x	x x x x x x x x x x	x x x x x x x x x x	x x x x x x x x x x

(When 6 teams are formed, each with 12 players, you can see that there are 72 players in all.)

Multiples can also be modeled in a linear fashion.

Example: Each rod is 5 feet long. How far would 6 rods extend?

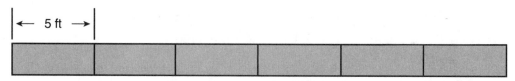

(There are several ways to use the model to find the result as described below.

- ❖ You can count by 5s: 5, 10, 15, 20, 25, 30.
- ❖ You can use 5 as an addend 6 times: $5 + 5 + 5 + 5 + 5 + 5 = 30$.
- ❖ You can find the product 6×5 to show 6 groups of 5 each.)

(2) Comparison

Find how large something is when it is so many times as large as another quantity.

Example: During a basketball game, "Airball" Brick scored only 3 points. Scott Swoosh scored 8 times as many points. How many points did Scott score?

(When 8 groups of 3 each are formed, you can see that Scott scored 8×3, or 24, points. It should be pointed out that in describing a situation such as this, some people erroneously say, "Scott scored 8 times *more* points than

Airball." This is erroneous because "8 times more points" would mean that Scott scored 8×3 *more* points than Airball. If this were true, Scott would have scored 3 + 24, or 27, points. So, "8 times more" really means "9 times as many.")

(3) Area

Find how many objects are in an array when there is a certain number of rows (or columns) of the same size.

Example: How many mailboxes are in this array?

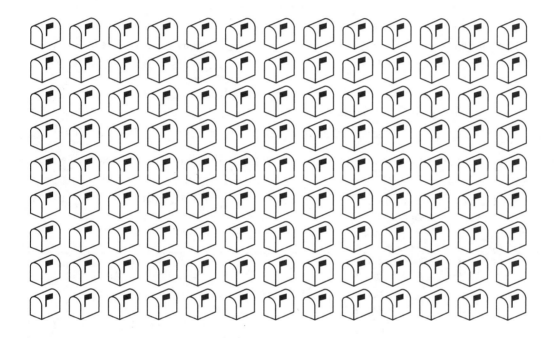

(By displaying the mailboxes in an array, students see that there are 9 rows of 13 mailboxes each, or $9 \times 13 = 117$ mailboxes in all. Students should conclude that using multiplication to find how many objects are in an array is clearly more efficient than, say, attempting to count each object.)

Division

There are four basic types of division situations.

(1) Equal Sharing (Partitioning a Set of Objects): "How many are in each group?"

- You know how many there are in all, and you know how many groups of the same size will be formed.

- You are to find *how many will be in each group.*

Example: There are 12 players to be distributed to 3 teams. Each team will have the same number of players. How many players will be on each team?

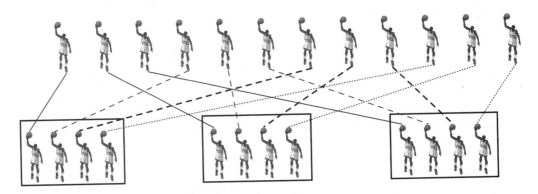

(The diagram shows how 12 players can be equally distributed to 3 teams. After the players are distributed, there are 12 ÷ 3, or 4, players on each team.)

(2) Separating a Quantity Into Equal Sets (Repeated Subtraction): "How many groups can be formed?"

- You know how many there are in all and how many will be in each group.

- You are to find how many groups there will be of the same size.

Example: There are 40 players in all. Each team will have 5 players. How many teams will there be?

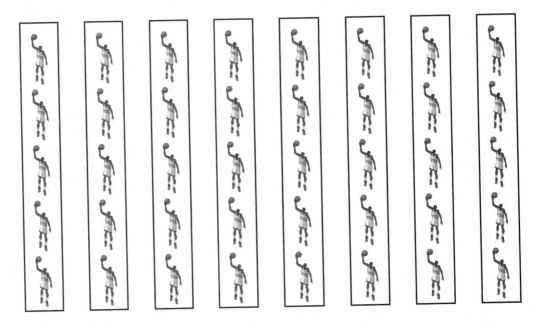

(After 5 players are placed on each team, you can see that 40 ÷ 5, or 8, teams are formed. This is akin to beginning with 40 and finding how many times you can subtract 5.)

(3) Comparison (Ratio): "How many times as large is one group than another?"

- You know the size of each of two groups.

- You are to find how many times as large one group is than the other.

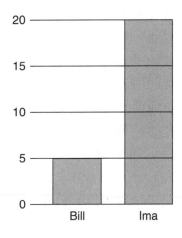

Example: Bill Boards painted 5 signs. Ima Painter painted 20 signs. How many times as many signs did Ima paint?

(The horizontal rules show that the bar for Ima is 4 times as tall as the bar for Bill. So, Ima painted 20 ÷ 5, or 4 times, as many signs.)

(4) Comparison: "How large is the other group?"

- You know how large a group is and how many times as large that group is when compared with another group.

- You are to find the size of the other group.

Example: Ima Painter painted 20 signs. This is 4 times as many signs as Bill Boards painted. How many signs did Bill Boards paint?

(A similar model can be used. Begin with Ima's bar, which is 20 units tall. When her bar is segmented into 4 equal parts, you can see that each part will be 5 units tall. So, Bill painted 20 ÷ 4, or 5, signs.)

Interpreting Remainders

In each problem below, you compute 30 ÷ 8. However, note that the quotient may *not* always provide the answer to the problem.

1. Tickets cost $8 each. You have $30. How many tickets can you buy? (3 tickets)

2. For a field trip, one parent is needed for every 8 students. If 30 students go on the field trip, how many parents are needed? (4 parents)

3. If 30 pennies are shared equally by 8 students, how many pennies are left over? (6 pennies)

QUESTIONS FOR TEACHER REFLECTION

1. One of the "big ideas" in computation is that a number can be represented in equivalent ways. Name the six ways you can represent $53 using any combination of $10 bills and $1 bills. Explain how one of these representations for 53 can help you perform this subtraction: 53 – 27.

2. Explain how you would determine if your students understand the pattern of place values in multi-digit numerals. Then choose one of the operations. Discuss how prior understanding of the base-ten place-value system aids in learning an algorithm for that operation.

3. Explain why there are no commutative and associative properties for subtraction and for division. Include numerical examples to illustrate why those properties do not exist.

4. Discuss how knowledge of problem structures based on "actions and operations" aids students in computational fluency.

5. Write a word problem for the putting together model of addition. Also write a word problem that illlustrates the slide model of addition. For each problem, indicate what the model is, and explain why the model applies.

6. Write a word problem for each of the models for subtraction: take-away, comparison, additive (missing part), and separation. For each problem, indicate what the model is, and explain why the model applies.

7. Write a word problem for each of the models for multiplication: putting together same-size groups (multiples), comparison, and area. For each problem, indicate what the model is, and explain why the model applies.

8. Write a word problem for each of the models for division: equal sharing (partitioning a set of objects); separating a quantity into equal sets (repeated subtraction); comparison (ratio): "How many times a large is one group than another?"; and comparison: "How large is the other group?" For each problem, indicate what the model is, and explain why the model applies.

Unit 1

Addition of Whole Numbers

The 20-question Diagnostic Test for Addition of Whole Numbers, in multiple-choice format, consists of four parts: addition facts, addition without renaming, addition with renaming, and addition with more than two addends. The test allows you to pinpoint specific skills and concepts that require more student work. For information on how to use this test to help identify specific student error patterns, see pages 28 through 30.

Throughout their work with addition, students should be encouraged to use estimation to check to see if their answers are reasonable. A visual model to aid students with the concept of rounding ("Roller Coaster Rounding") is on pages 143 and 144. (Answers are on page 194.) Reproducible lessons for estimating sums using front-end estimation and for estimating using compatible numbers (for all operations) are on pages 145 and 176, respectively. (Answers are on pages 194 and 199, respectively.)

Pages 139 through 149 provide instructional games and follow-up activities (reproducible) to support addition concepts.

Diagnostic Test
Addition of Whole Numbers

Multiple Choice: Circle the correct answer. If your answer is not given, circle *Not here.*

Part 1

1. $9 + 7 = \square$ **A** 15   **B** 16   **C** 17   **D** 18   **E** Not her

2. $8 + \square = 16$ **A** 6   **B** 8   **C** 10   **D** 24   **E** Not her

3. $14 = \square + 6$ **A** 6   **B** 7   **C** 8   **D** 20   **E** Not her

4. $\square = 8 + 9$ **A** 1   **B** 9   **C** 16   **D** 17   **E** Not her

5. $0 + 8 = \square$ **A** 0   **B** 7   **C** 8   **D** 9   **E** Not her

Part 2

6.
$$\begin{array}{r} 3\ 2 \\ +\quad 4 \\ \hline \end{array}$$
   A 9   **B** 76   **C** 63   **D** 36   **E** Not her

7. $5,210 + 6$ **A** 14   **B** 11,210   **C** 5,210   **D** 5,216   **E** Not her

8. $527 + 30$ **A** 557   **B** 827   **C** 550   **D** 558   **E** Not her

9.
$$\begin{array}{r} 5\ 0 \\ +\ 4\ 0 \\ \hline \end{array}$$
   A 900   **B** 90   **C** 91   **D** 09   **E** Not her

10.
$$\begin{array}{r} 2\ 0\ 0 \\ +\ 1\ 7\ 0 \\ \hline \end{array}$$
   A 3,700   **B** 300   **C** 370   **D** 381   **E** Not her

1.
```
    9  0  8
 +        9
```
A 917   **B** 26   **C** 1,907   **D** 17   **E** Not here

2.
```
    4  8  3
 +  5  8  2
```
A 966   **B** 1,065   **C** 965   **D** 9,165   **E** Not here

3.
```
    6  5
 +  8  7
```
A 142   **B** 413   **C** 152   **D** 242   **E** Not here

4.
```
    9  2  3
 +     8  9
```
A 1,012   **B** 902   **C** 91,012   **D** 2,902   **E** Not here

5.
```
    6,  7  3  5
 +  1,  6  4  5
```
A 8,480   **B** 7,370   **C** 713,710   **D** 8,380   **E** Not here

16.
```
    9
    5
    8
 +  7
```
A 9
B 19
C 29
D 27
E Not here

17.
```
    5  0
    6  4
 +  3  9
```
A 315
B 153
C 414
D 143
E Not here

18.
```
    6  8
    5  7
    8  2
 +  6  3
```
A 160
B 260
C 2,520
D 270
E Not here

19.
```
          7
    5  4  9
    9  3  5
 +  5  2  4
```
A 2,015
B 2,195
C 2,005
D 19,925
E Not here

20. 82 + 5,908 + 4,299

A 9,179   **B** 10,289   **C** 18,407   **D** 91,820   **E** Not here

ITEM ANALYSIS FOR DIAGNOSTIC TEST
Addition of Whole Numbers

Using the Item Analysis Table

- The correct answer for each item on the Diagnostic Test is indicated by a ✓ in the Item Analysis Table on page 30.

- Each incorrect answer choice is keyed to a specific error pattern and corresponding Intervention Activity found on pages 31 through 46. Because each item on the Diagnostic Test is an item that is analyzed in one of the error patterns, teachers may be able to use the Intervention Activities with identical problems that students may have missed on the test.

- Students should be encouraged to circle *Not here* if their obtained answer is not one of the given answer choices. Although *Not here* is never a correct answer on the Diagnostic Test, the use of this answer choice should aid in the diagnostic process. The intention is that students who do not see their obtained answer among the choices will select *Not here* rather than guess at one of the other choices. This should strengthen the likelihood that students who select an incorrect answer choice actually made the error associated with the error pattern.

- The Item Analysis Table should only be used as a *guide*. Although many errors are procedural in nature, others may be due to an incorrect recall of facts or to carelessness. A diagnostic test is just one of many tools that should be considered when assessing student work and making prescriptive decisions. Before being certain that a student has a misconception about a procedure or concept, further analysis may be needed (see below). This is especially true for students who frequently select *Not here* as an answer choice.

- A set of practice exercises, keyed to each of the four parts of the Diagnostic Test, is provided on page 47. Because the four parts of the set of practice exercises match the four parts on the Diagnostic Test, the set of practice exercises could be used as a posttest.

Using Teacher-Directed Questioning and Journaling

Discussions and observations should be used to help distinguish misconceptions about concepts and procedures from student carelessness or lack of fact recall. This should be done in a *positive* manner—with the clear purpose being to "get inside student thinking." The Intervention Activities are replete with teacher-directed questioning, frequently asking students to *explain their reasoning*. Students should also be asked to *write* about their thinking as they work through an algorithm—and, when alternative algorithms are used, explain why they may prefer one algorithm over another. You may also want students to write word problems based on *addition*—and then explain why addition can be used to solve them. This would be a good time to discuss with students the various actions and problem structures for addition (see pages 17–18).

Additional Resources for Addition

- A lesson providing a visual model for *rounding* is on pages 143 and 144. A lesson on using *front-end estimation* to check sums for reasonableness is on page 145; a lesson on using *compatible numbers* for estimation (for all operations) is on page 176. These lessons may be used at any point in the instructional process. When students engage in estimation activities, they should discuss why they believe a computed answer may or may not be reasonable. Students should also compare and contrast estimation strategies.

- Instructional games and follow-up activities designed to promote addition concepts are on pages 139 through 149. This material may be used at any point in the instructional process. (Specific points of use for this material are suggested within the Intervention Activities and on pages 139 and 140.) The activity *Next Number, Please* provides students an opportunity to discuss place value and mental math concepts. The game *Keeping Score in Bowling* provides another opportunity for students to discuss strategies for mental math.

ITEM ANALYSIS TABLE

The correct answer for each item on the Diagnostic Test is indicated by a ✓ in this table.

	Item	Answer Choices				Topic	Practice Exercises
		A	B	C	D		
	1	Error 1a	✓	Error 1a	Error 1a	Addition facts	Part 1, p. 4?
	2	Error 1a	✓	Error 1a	Error 1a	Addition facts	Part 1, p. 4?
	3	Error 1a	Error 1a	✓	Error 1a	Addition facts	Part 1, p. 4?
	4	Error 1a	Error 1a	Error 1a	✓	Addition facts	Part 1, p. 4?
Part 1	5	Error 1b	Error 1b	✓	Error 1b	Addition facts	Part 1, p. 4?
	6	Error 2a	Error 2b	Error 3	✓	Addition without renaming	Part 2, p. 4?
	7	Error 2a	Error 9	Error 6a	✓	Addition without renaming	Part 2, p. 4?
	8	✓	Error 9	Error 6a	Error 6b	Addition without renaming	Part 2, p. 4?
	9	Error 5	✓	Error 6b	Error 3	Addition without renaming	Part 2, p. 4?
Part 2	10	Error 5	Error 6a	✓	Error 6b	Addition without renaming	Part 2, p. 4?
	11	✓	Error 2a	Error 2b	Error 2c	Addition with renaming	Part 3, p. 4?
	12	Error 4	✓	Error 7	Error 8a	Addition with renaming	Part 3, p. 4?
	13	Error 7	Error 4	✓	Error 8b	Addition with renaming	Part 3, p. 4?
	14	✓	Error 7	Error 8a	Error 8b	Addition with renaming	Part 3, p. 4?
Part 3	15	Error 8c	Error 7	Error 8a	✓	Addition with renaming	Part 3, p. 4?
	16	Error 10a	Error 1a or 10a	✓	Error 1a or 10a	Addition with more than two addends	Part 4, p. 4?
	17	Error 3	✓	Error 4	Error 7	Addition with more than two addends	Part 4, p. 4?
	18	Error 1a or 10a	Error 1a or 10a	Error 8a	✓	Addition with more than two addends	Part 4, p. 4?
	19	✓	Error 10b	Error 10a	Error 8b	Addition with more than two addends	Part 4, p. 4?
Part 4	20	Error 7	✓	Error 9	Error 4	Addition with more than two addends	Part 4, p. 4?

ERROR PATTERNS & INTERVENTION ACTIVITIES
Addition of Whole Numbers

Error Pattern 1

Error Pattern 1a: Some students have difficulty recalling basic addition facts (through $9 + 9$).

Error Pattern 1b: When one addend is 0, some students write 0 for the sum. Others think they have added something and increase the other addend by 1.

Intervention

Have students use objects with the strategies described below to help them make an addition table. (A blank addition table is provided on page 188.) Students may need to refer to the table, as necessary, until the facts are mastered.

+	0	1	2	3	4	5	6	7	8	9
0	0	1	2	3	4	5	6	7	8	9
1	1	2	3	4	5	6	7	8	9	10
2	2	3	4	5	6	7	8	9	10	11
3	3	4	5	6	7	8	9	10	11	12
4	4	5	6	7	8	9	10	11	12	13
5	5	6	7	8	9	10	11	12	13	14
6	6	7	8	9	10	11	12	13	14	15
7	7	8	9	10	11	12	13	14	15	16
8	8	9	10	11	12	13	14	15	16	17
9	9	10	11	12	13	14	15	16	17	18

The "make a ten" strategy is effective in helping students learn and master the facts. With this strategy, students use objects to represent each addend. Then, they complete a ten-frame to make a group of 10 from those objects. They find the sum by beginning with 10 and then adding on the number of objects that remain. Provide students with two types of small objects and exercises prepared as shown on page 32. The first one is completed.

1.

$$\begin{array}{r} 9 \\ + 7 \\ \hline ? \end{array}$$

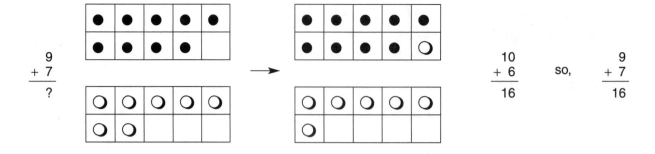

$$\begin{array}{r} 10 \\ + 6 \\ \hline 16 \end{array}$$ so, $$\begin{array}{r} 9 \\ + 7 \\ \hline 16 \end{array}$$

2.

$$\begin{array}{r} 8 \\ + 6 \\ \hline ? \end{array}$$

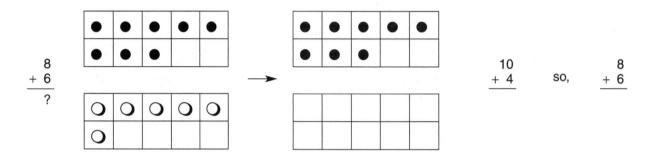

$$\begin{array}{r} 10 \\ + 4 \end{array}$$ so, $$\begin{array}{r} 8 \\ + 6 \end{array}$$

Another strategy is for students to use objects to form the largest possible two groups of "doubles" or "doubles plus one" as shown below.

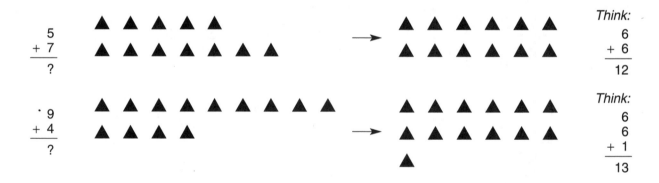

$$\begin{array}{r} 5 \\ + 7 \\ \hline ? \end{array}$$

Think:
$$\begin{array}{r} 6 \\ + 6 \\ \hline 12 \end{array}$$

$$\begin{array}{r} \cdot \ 9 \\ + 4 \\ \hline ? \end{array}$$

Think:
$$\begin{array}{r} 6 \\ 6 \\ + 1 \\ \hline 13 \end{array}$$

Have students use the completed addition table to observe patterns. For example, they should observe that when you change the order of the addends, the sum is the same. Point out that facts such as 5 + 8 and 8 + 5 are called "turn-around facts" (based on the *Commutative Property of Addition*). Advise students that if they are aware of the "turn-around facts," they will have fewer facts to memorize. Students may also notice that the sum of two even numbers is even; the sum of two odd numbers is even; and the sum of an odd and an even number is odd. Students may also use the addition table to help find all combinations that produce a given sum. For example, the addition facts for 12 are 3 + 9 and 9 + 3; 4 + 8 and 8 + 4; 5 + 7 and 7 + 5; and 6 + 6.

Error Pattern 1b: When one addend is 0, some students write 0 for the sum. Others think they have added something and increase the other addend by 1. To correct this error, have students display 8 counters. **Ask,** "Suppose we add 0 counters to the 8 we have. How many counters would we have in all? Is adding 0 counters the same as adding no counters?" Students should realize that if they add 0 counters they will still have 8 counters. Then **ask,** "What is the sum of 8 and 0?" Guide students to write the corresponding number sentence, 8 + 0 = 8.

Error Pattern 2

Error Pattern 2a: When adding a one-digit number to a multidigit number, some students add all the digits together.

```
    3  2              6  5              9  0  8
 +     4           +     7           +        9          5,210 + 6 = 14
 ─────────         ─────────         ────────────
       9           1  8                    2  6
```

Error Pattern 2b: Some students add the one-digit number to each digit of the other number.

```
                          1                      1  1
    3  2              6  5                  9  0  8
 +     4           +     7               +        9
 ─────────         ──────────          ──────────────
    7  6           1  4  2              1,  9  0  7
```

In the tens place, the student computes 7 + 6 + 1 = 14.

In the tens place, the student computes 9 + 0 + 1 = 10. In the hundreds place, the student computes 9 + 9 + 1 = 19.

Error Pattern 2c: Some students fail to add in the positions where the "extra" digits occur.

908 + 9 = 17

The student adds in the ones position only and computes 8 + 9 = 17.

473 + 25 = 98

The student adds in the ones and tens positions only and computes 73 + 25 = 98.

Intervention

Note: Base-ten blocks may be used instead of play money.

Supply an addition exercise on a place-value grid, a place-value mat on tagboard, and play money. (See pages 184–186 for play money, mat, and grids.) To add 65 and 7, guide students in placing play money on the mat to represent the first addend. Then, have them use play money to represent the second addend.

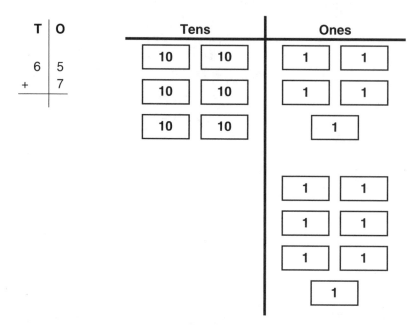

Ask, "How many one-dollar bills are there in all?" (12 one-dollar bills) Ask, "Does it make sense to combine the one-dollar bills with the ten-dollar bills? Explain." (No. Sample: The ten-dollar bills are worth more than the one-dollar bills, so you cannot combine them.)

Emphasize that sets of ones are joined with sets of ones; sets of tens are joined with sets of tens. Point out that we start with the ones and trade bills (regroup) if we can. Ask, "How can you use the play money to display the 12 one-dollar bills with the fewest possible bills?" (Trade 10 one-dollar bills for 1 ten-dollar bill.) Have students trade the bills and show the renaming of the sum of the ones in the addition exercise, stressing that 12 ones = 1 ten + 2 ones. The ten-dollar bill is placed in the tens column of the place-value chart.

Then, have students complete the addition by adding the tens.

```
    T | O
    1 |
    6 | 5
+     | 7
  ----|----
    7 | 2
```

Error Pattern 3

Some students write the digits for the sum in reverse order. For two-digit addition, they begin by adding in the ones positions, but they write the sum of the ones digits in the tens position. Then, they write the sum of the tens digits in the ones position.

```
          1            1              1
  7  1     2  9      5  0        9  3  7
+ 2  6   + 6  6      6  4     +     4  5
-------   -------   + 3  9      ----------
  7  9     5  9     ---------     2  8  9
                     3  15
```

Intervention

Use the remediation for Error 2 to emphasize that in a sum, the number of ones is recorded in the ones position, the number of tens is recorded in the tens position, and so on—and that only one digit is recorded in each place-value position.

Error Pattern 4

Some students add from left to right. (This error only becomes apparent in computations that involve renaming.)

```
         1                      1  1
  4  8  3              9,  5  0  7
+ 5  8  2            + 1,  6  8  7
---------            ---------------
  9  6  6              0  2  9  14
```

Intervention

Supply an addition exercise on a place-value grid with an index card, revealing only the digits in the ones place. Add in the ones position.

```
    H | T | O
    4 | 8 | 3
+   5 | 8 | 2
----|---|---
```

```
    | O
    | 3
    | 2
    |--
    | 5
```

Then, instruct students to move the card one column to the left, revealing the tens digits. Have students add in the tens column and record the result. Because renaming is involved, instruct students to move the card one more column to the left to reveal the hundreds place. Have them record the renaming and then add the hundreds.

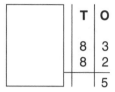

	T	O
	8	3
	8	2
		5

	H	T	O
		1	
	4	8	3
+	5	8	2
1,0	6	5

Error Pattern 5

When adding multiples of 10, 100, or 1,000, some students write too many zeros in the sum. Essentially, when 0 is added to 0, they record two 0s in the sum.

```
    5 0              2 0 0            8, 5 0 0
  + 4 0            + 1 7 0          +     4 0 0
  -------          ---------        -----------
    9 00            3, 7 00          8  9 00 00
```

Intervention

Have students use estimation to determine that answers such as those shown above are not reasonable. For 200 + 170, **ask,** "Can the sum of two numbers—each 200 or less—possibly be more than 3,000? Explain." (No. Sample: Using rounding, 200 + 200 = 400. This is much less than 3,000.)

Supply students with some base-ten blocks. Explain that each large cube represents 1,000, each flat represents 100, each rod represents 10, and each unit represents 1. Advise students that the blocks will help them represent the addends and the sum.

To find 200 + 170, have students display blocks for 200 and then for 170. **Ask,** "How many units do you have in all?" (0 units.) "How many rods do you have in all?" (7 rods.) "How many flats do you have in all?" (3 flats.) Then have students use the blocks to find the sum (370) by combing the units (ones), the rods (tens), and the flats (hundreds).

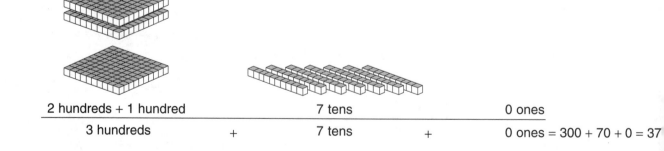

2 hundreds + 1 hundred		7 tens		0 ones
3 hundreds	+	7 tens	+	0 ones = 300 + 70 + 0 = 37

To illustrate that an answer such as 3,700 is not reasonable (for 200 + 170), you may want students to use blocks to represent such an incorrect answer:

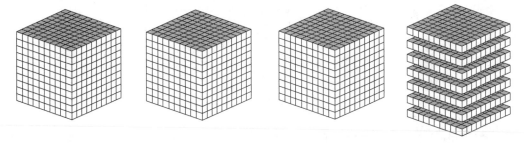

Have students discuss why the blocks represent a number that is much greater than the correct result. Help them use the blocks to conclude that the extra 0 in 3,700 results in a sum that is 10 times as great as the correct sum (370).

Follow-Up Activity: Next Number, Please
(See pages 141–142 for the activity. Answers are provided on pages 193–194. Students work in pairs.)

In this activity, students mentally decide what multiple of 10, 100, or 1,000 must be added or subtracted to obtain the next End Number. They use a calculator to check their results. In addition to promoting mental math skills, the activity relies heavily on students' ability to use place value to help them decide what number to add or subtract. In the sample round below, 90 must be added to 10 to obtain 100. Then, 400 must be added to 100 to obtain 500. Finally, 50 must be subtracted from 500 to obtain 450.

Start Number	To obtain the End Number, what must you *add* or *subtract*?	End Number
Enter 10	*Add 90.*	100
100	?	500
500	?	450

Error Pattern 6

Error Pattern 6a: When one of the digits in a place-value position is 0, some students record 0 as the sum for that position (illustrated in the first two examples below).

Error Pattern 6b: Some students think they have added something—and consequently add 1 rather than 0 (illustrated in the last two examples below).

$$
\begin{array}{r} 4\ 0 \\ +\ 2\ 6 \\ \hline 6\ 0 \end{array}
\qquad
\begin{array}{r} {\scriptstyle 1\ \ 1} \\ 2,\ 8\ 9\ 7 \\ +\ 5,\ 0\ 8\ 5 \\ \hline 7,\ 0\ 8\ 2 \end{array}
\qquad
\begin{array}{r} 3\ 7 \\ +\ 6\ 0 \\ \hline 9\ 8 \end{array}
\qquad
\begin{array}{r} {\scriptstyle 1} \\ 5\ 0\ 0 \\ 6\ 8\ 0 \\ +\ 3\ 5\ 3 \\ \hline 1,\ 5\ 4\ 4 \end{array}
$$

Intervention

Have students use play money to act out situations such as these to bring out the concept that the sum of any number and 0 is that number. (This is known as the *Identity Property of Addition*: $a + 0 = 0 + a = a$ for any number a.)

- "You have $3. Your friend gives you zero dollars. How much money do you now have, $0, $3, or $4?" ($3)
- "You have $40, and your friend gives you $26. How much money do you now have, $60, $66, or $67?" ($66)
- "You have $508, and your friend gives you $70. How much money do you now have, $500, $578, or $589?" ($578)

Error Pattern 7

When adding numbers with renaming, some students fail to write ("carry") the 1 ten, the 1 hundred, or the 1 thousand.

```
    3 9          6 5          9 2 3              8 2
  + 4 8        + 8 7        +   8 9         5, 9 0 8
  -----        -----        -------       + 4, 2 9 9
    7 7        1 4 2          9 0 2         ---------
                                           9, 1 7 9
```

The student fails to "carry" the 1 ten from 5 + 7, but records "14" for 6 + 8.

Intervention

Estimation: Determining If an Answer Is Reasonable

All students, especially those who obtain unreasonable answers, should be encouraged to use estimation either before or after computing. When students round 39 and 48 to the nearest ten, they should see that the answer to 39 + 48 should be about 40 + 50, or about 90. **Ask,** "If one number is close to 40, and the other number is close to 50, is it reasonable that their sum is just 77? Explain." (No. Sample: 40 + 50 = 90, so 77 cannot be correct.) For 923 + 89, **ask,** "Can the sum be less than 923? Explain." (No. Sample: When you add two whole numbers, the sum is larger than either of the whole numbers—not smaller.)

Some students have difficulty with the rounding process. The lesson "Roller Coaster Rounding" (pages 143–144) provides a model to help students *visualize* the rounding process. The use of this model should help students round numbers to make estimates.

Some students, especially those who find rounding to be difficult, may benefit from using *front-end estimation* as a way to determine if an answer is reasonable. Front-end estimation often provides a better estimate than rounding. The lesson, "Using Front-End Estimation to Check for Reasonableness: Addition" (page 145) teaches students how to use this strategy. A lesson on using *compatible numbers* to make estimates (for all operations) is on page 176.

Intervention: Using Play Money or Base-Ten Blocks

Supply an addition exercise on a place-value grid, a place-value mat on tag-board, and play money. (See pages 184–186 for play money, mat, and grids.) To add 923 and 89, guide students in placing play money on the mat to represent the first addend. Then, have them use play money to represent the second addend.

Th	H	T	O
	9	2	3
+		8	9

Hundreds	Tens	Ones
100 100	10 10	1 1
100 100		1
100 100		
100 100		
100		
	10 10	1 1
	10 10	1 1
	10 10	1 1
	10 10	1 1
		1

Emphasize that we begin with the ones and trade bills (regroup) if we can. **Ask,** "How many one-dollar bills do you have in all?" (12 one-dollar bills.) "How can you use play money to display the 12 one-dollar bills with the fewest possible bills?" (Trade 10 one-dollar bills for 1 ten-dollar bill.) Have students make the trade and record what they did in the algorithm. **Ask,** "Why must you record the 1 ten in the algorithm?" (Sample: 12 ones = 1 ten + 2 ones. If you do not record the 1 ten, you would be saying that 12 ones are equal to just 2 ones.)

Th	H	T	O
		1	
	9	2	3
+		8	9
			2

Hundreds	Tens	Ones
100 100	10	
100 100	10 10	1 1
100 100		
100 100		
100		
	10 10	
	10 10	
	10 10	
	10 10	

Now **ask,** "How many ten-dollar bills do you have in all?" Students should conclude that there are $1 + 2 + 8$, or 11 ten-dollar bills. **Ask,** "How much money is 11 ten-dollar bills?" ($110.) "How can you use your play money to display $110 with the fewest possible bills?" (Trade 10 ten-dollar bills for 1 hundred-dollar bill.) Have students make the trade and record the results in the algorithm. Then have them trade the resulting 10 hundred-dollar bills for 1 thousand-dollar bill and complete the addition.

Th	H	T	O	Thousands	Hundreds	Tens	Ones
	1	1					
	9	2	3				
+		8	9	**1000**		**10**	**1** **1**
1,	0	1	2				

Alternative Addition Algorithm: Partial Sums

Students who have difficulty with the renaming process may benefit from using this alternative algorithm. With this algorithm, students write partial sums based on place value rather than "carry" digits as they add from one place-value position to another.

Prepare addition exercises below. Have students add in each place-value position, recording each partial sum as shown. In the example on the left, students add 9 and 8, and directly record 17. (With the traditional algorithm, students record 7 and "carry" the 1 to the tens position). With the *partial sums* algorithm, students then add 3 tens and 4 tens, and record 70. (With the traditional algorithm, students just record 7.)

When students use this algorithm, you may want them to represent each addend with play money or base-ten blocks—and then combine the materials as they add in each place-value position. It should be noted that this algorithm prepares students for using an alternative algorithm for multiplication where they write *partial products* based on place value.

Two Examples Showing the Partial Sums Algorithm for Addition:

H	T	O
	3	9
+	4	8
	1	7
	7	0
	8	7

9 ones + 8 ones = 17 ones, or 17.
3 tens + 4 tens = 7 tens, or 70.
Add the "partial sums" in each place-value position.

Th	H	T	O
	9	2	3
+		8	9
		1	2
	1	0	0
	9	0	0
1,	0	1	2

3 ones + 9 ones = 12 ones, or 12.
2 tens + 8 tens = 10 tens, or 100.
9 hundreds + 0 hundreds = 9 hundreds, or 90
Add the "partial sums" in each place-value position.

Instructional Game: Keeping Score in Bowling
(See pages 146–149 for instructions on how to score in bowling and the instructions for how to play this tabletop bowling game. Students work in groups of 2, 3, or 4.)

In this game, students learn how to keep score in bowling. Then they play and score a bowling game by using number cubes to simulate each roll of the bowling ball. The game promotes mental math skills related to two-digit addition.

Error Pattern 8

Error Pattern 8a: When there is a sum of 10 or more in a place-value position, some students fail to rename the sum. Instead, they write the (entire) sum in the given place-value position.

```
   5  7          5  0  4           9,  7  8  5
 + 2  6        + 2  8  9         +      5  0  7
 ───────       ──────────       ──────────────
   7 13          7  8 13           9 12  8 12
```

Error Pattern 8b: When renaming is needed, some students write (or "carry") a 10 instead of a 1 (or they may "carry" a 20 instead of a 2).

```
  10            10 10             20  10 10
   5  7          6  0  4           9,  7  8  5
 + 2  6        + 3  8  9         +      5  0  7
 ───────       ──────────       ──────────────
  17  3         19  8  3          29   2  8  2
```

Error Pattern 8c: Some students write (or "carry") a 1 in each place-value position to the left of where a renaming occurs—whether such renaming is necessary or not.

```
     1  1              1  1  1
     5  0  4           6,  7  3  5
   + 2  8  9         + 1,  6  4  5
   ──────────        ─────────────
     8  9  3           8,  4  8  0
```

Intervention

Ask students to estimate the sums before they compute. **Ask,** "Does an answer of 713 (or 153) make sense when you add just 57 and 26?" (No.) For 504 + 289, **ask,** "When you add 500 and 300, could you possibly obtain 8,913 (or 1,883, or 893)?" (No.)

Supply an addition exercise on a place-value grid, a place-value mat on tagboard, and play money (or base-ten blocks). Use the intervention for Error Pattern 7 to emphasize that only *one* digit (0–9) is written in each place-value position. So, when you obtain 10 or more bills in a given place-value position, you trade 10 bills for *one* bill of the next denomination. A small "1" (renaming number) is recorded in the place-value position for that denomination to signify that 10 bills have been traded for the new bill. The new bill is then combined with the other bills of that denomination, and the process continues. When there are fewer than 10 bills of the same denomination, no trading occurs, and no renaming numbers are recorded in the algorithm.

Alternative Intervention: Using Mental Math on an Empty Number Line

Some students may gain fluency with addition by doing the computation mentally on an "empty (open) number line." By using an empty number line, students should (1) realize that answers such as those in the error patterns above are not reasonable and (2) obtain correct results without using an algorithm (that may have caused them difficulty).

Gravemeijer (1994) of the Freudenthal Institute, in the Netherlands, described some of the merits of using the empty number line:

1. The empty number line supports *informal solution procedures.*

   - Intuitive strategies such as counting on (or counting down) and compensation (adding or subtracting too much and then "compensating") are seen visually on a number line.
   - Marking on a number line allows students to see partial results. It shows which part of the operation has been carried out—and what remains to be done.

2. The empty number line promotes facility with counting by tens (on and off the decade), with bridging tens, and with splitting numbers.

   - Students gain facility with counting-on mental computations:

     On the decade: $50 + 10 = 60$; $60 + 10 = 70$.
     Off the decade: $57 + 10 = 67$; $67 + 10 = 77$.

   - Students gain facility with splitting the tens and ones—and addressing these separately:

     To find $57 + 26$, they may first find $57 + 20$. Then, they find $77 + 6$.
     $57 + 20 = 77$; $77 + 6 = 83$. So, $57 + 26 = 83$.

3. The empty number line provides a *linear representation.* Many applications, such as traveling distances, involve linear-type situations. It is important for students to be exposed to a linear model as well as to a set-type model (such as play money or base-ten blocks).

Use an empty number line to find 57 + 26:

To find $57 + 26$, begin by drawing an empty number line with 57 shown at the far left below the line.

To add 26, you could use the number line to first count on by 6 and then add 20. Or you could first add 20 and then count on by 6. Either way, you should obtain the sum 83.

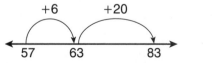

Think: $57 + 6 = 63$; $63 + 20 = 83$.

or

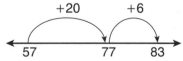

Think: $57 + 20 = 77$; $77 + 6 = 83$.

Another way to add 57 and 26 is to use the number line to add 57 and 30, obtaining 87. Because you added 4 too much, you compensate by subtracting 4 from 87, obtaining 83.

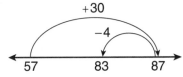

Think: 57 + 30 = 87; 87 − 4 = 83.

Using Student Journaling: Because the empty number line permits students to find sums in an individualized way—with students essentially making their own judgments to determine what steps to use—this method lends itself nicely to student journaling. Ask students to describe the steps they use to find various sums.

Error Pattern 9

When an addition exercise is posed in horizontal form, and there are more digits in the first addend than in the second addend, some students fail to align the digits correctly.

$$35 + 4 \quad \rightarrow \quad \begin{array}{r} 3\ 5 \\ +\ \ 4 \\ \hline 7\ 5 \end{array} \qquad\qquad 527 + 30 \quad \rightarrow \quad \begin{array}{r} 5\ 2\ 7 \\ +\ 3\ 0\ \ \\ \hline 8\ 2\ 7 \end{array}$$

Intervention

Supply play money, a place-value mat, and grid paper (see pages 184, 185, and 192). For 35 + 4, have students place 3 ten-dollar bills and 5 one-dollar bills on the mat to represent the first addend. Then have them use play money to represent the second addend. **Ask,** "Does each addend have one-dollar bills?" (Yes.) "Does each addend have ten-dollar bills?" (No.)

Guide students in recording the problem on the grid paper, aligning the ones with the ones, and so on. Have students join the one-dollar bills to conclude that there is $39 in all. Have students write the addition exercise on the grid paper, and record the sum. Emphasize that we add ones to ones, and since there are no tens to add to the 3 tens that we have, the result in the tens column is 3 + 0, or 3 tens.

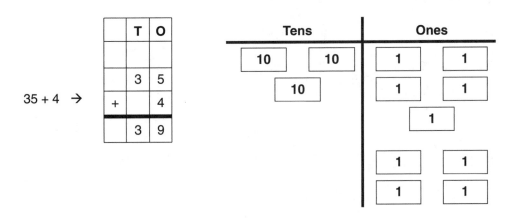

Alternative Intervention: Using Base-Ten Blocks

Supply students with grid paper and some base-ten blocks. Explain that each flat represents 100, each rod represents 10, and each unit represents 1. Advise students that the blocks will help them maintain the correct place-value positions for the digits as they convert an exercise set up in horizontal form to one set up in vertical form.

To find 527 + 30, have students begin by displaying blocks to represent 527. **Ask,** "How many units do you have?" (7 units.) "How many rods do you have?" (2 rods.) "How many flats do you have?" (5 flats.) "What number is represented by the blocks for the first addend?" (527.) Have students write 527 on the grid paper. (See diagram showing the display of the blocks and the grid for the algorithm below.)

Now, have students use the blocks to model the second addend (30). **Ask,** "How many units do you have?" (0 units.) "How many rods do you have?" (3 rods.) "How many flats do you have?" (0 flats.) "What number is represented by the blocks for the second addend?" (30.) Have students write 30 on the grid paper as shown in the diagram.

Ask, "When we combine the blocks to see how much we have in all, would it be correct to combine the rods with the flats? Explain." (No. Sample: Flats and rods contain different numbers of small cubes, so it would make no sense to try to combine them.) **Ask,** "So, why is it important to add ones to ones, tens to tens, and hundreds to hundreds?" (Sample: To find out how much you have, you have to combine like quantities with like quantities.) Have students use the blocks to find the sum by combing the units (ones), the rods (tens), and the flats (hundreds). Then, have students complete the addition on the grid paper.

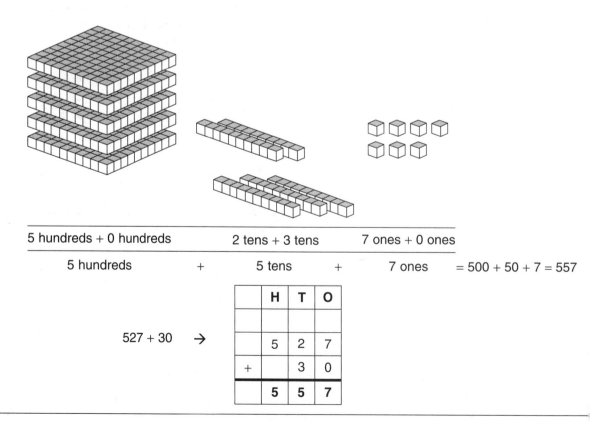

	5 hundreds + 0 hundreds	2 tens + 3 tens	7 ones + 0 ones	
	5 hundreds +	5 tens +	7 ones	= 500 + 50 + 7 = 557

527 + 30 →

	H	T	O
	5	2	7
+		3	0
	5	5	7

Error Pattern 10

Error Pattern 10a: In column addition, some students have trouble mentally finding the sums as they add in a column—especially when more than one renaming in a column is required. When the sum in a column is 20 or more, they may just "carry" a 1 to the next column. Others lose track of what they are adding and subsequently add the wrong numbers (illustrated in the first two examples that follow).

Error Pattern 10b: Some students "carry" a digit to the wrong column (third example below).

```
 1                     1                    2
     9                   6  8                       7
     5                   5  7                  5  4  9
     8                   8  2                  9  3  5
  +  7                +  6  3               +  5  2  4
 ---------            ---------             -----------
 1   9                1  6  0               2  1  9  5
```

Intervention

Remind students that it is generally easier to add when you can find sums of 10 within a given column. So, it often helps to regroup the digits in a column and/or change the order in which they are added. In the second example above, properties of operations could be used to rearrange the digits as follows.

$8 + 7 + 2 + 3 =$
$8 + 2 + 7 + 3 =$ Commutative Property of Addition (7 and 2 are commuted)
$(8 + 2) + (7 + 3) = 10 + 10 = 20$ Associative Property of Addition (8 and 2, and 7 and 3 are grouped)

Alternative Addition Algorithm: Low-Stress Addition

Hutchings (1976) developed this algorithm as a method to avoid the need for students to keep track of what they have previously added in a column. Students simply record each partial sum "as they go." As such, column addition essentially becomes a collection of addition facts. Although at first glance this algorithm may not look like it is low stress (due to all the "scratch" work involved), many students who struggle with the mental renaming needed in column addition find success with this algorithm (after they have been carefully guided through the process).

Prepare exercises in a place-value grid in large type with extra space at either side of each column as shown in the examples that follow. As students add pairs of digits in a column, they record each *partial sum* and then cross out the digits that have just been used.

Suppose you are adding in the ones column. If no renaming occurs in the partial sum, a small digit for the sum is recorded to the right of the digit that was added. If a renaming occurs, the tens digit of the sum is recorded *to the left* of the digit that was added; the ones digit is recorded *to the right*. Two examples are shown on page 46.

9 + 5 + 8 + 7			68 + 57 + 82 + 63		

Left example: 9 + 5 + 8 + 7

```
        T   O
  9        9
  5    1   5 4
  8  →     8
 +7    +   7
```

Step 1:
Add 5 + 9. Record the tens digit (1) of the partial sum to the left of the 5; record the ones digit (4) of the partial sum to the right. Cross out the 5 and 9 because they have now been used.

```
   T   O
       9
  1    5 4
  1    8 2
  +    7
```

Step 2:
Add 8 + 4. Record the tens digit (1) of the partial sum to the left of the 8; record the ones digit (2) of the partial sum to the right. Cross out the 4 and 8.

```
   T   O
       9
  1    5 4
  1    8 2
  +    7 9
```

Step 3:
Add 7 + 2. Because the sum is less than 10, there is no tens digit to record. Record the ones digit (9) of the sum to the right. Cross out the 7 and 2.

```
   T   O
       9
  1    5 4
  1    8 2
  +    7 9
  ─────────
   2   9
```

Step 4:
Determine the final sum: The ones digit is 9. (All other digits in the ones column have been used and crossed out.) The tens digit is 1 + 1 = 2.
   So the final sum is 29.

Right example: 68 + 57 + 82 + 63

```
        H   T   O
  6 8       6   8
  5 7       5 1 7 5
  8 2  →    8   2
 +6 3   +   6   3
```

Step 1:
Add 7 + 8. Record the tens digit (1 of the partial sum to the left of the record the ones digit (5) of the partial sum to the right. Cross out the 7 and 8 because they have no been used.

```
   H   T   O
       6   8
       5 1 7 5
       8   2 7
   +   6   3
```

Step 2:
Add 2 + 5. Since the sum is less than 10, there is no tens digit to record. Record the ones digit (7) o the partial sum to the right. Cross out the 2 and 5.

```
   H   T   O
       6   8
       5 1 7 5
       8   2 7
   +   6 1 3 0
```

Step 3:
Add 3 + 7. Record the tens digit (1 of the sum to the left of the 3; reco the ones digit (0) to the right of the 3. Cross out the 3 and the 7.

```
   H   T   O
   2
       6   8
       5 1 7 5
       8   2 7
   +   6 1 3 0
   ───────────
           0
```

Step 4:
The ones digit of the final sum is 0 (All other digits in the ones column have been used and crossed out.) Record the 0 in the ones column. Because there are 1 + 1, or 2 tens (resulting from the two renamings) record 2 above the 6 in the tens column (to show 2 tens). Cross ou the two 1s.

```
   H   T   O
   2
     6 8   8
   1 5 3 7 5
       8   2 7
   +   6   3 0
   ───────────
           0
```

Steps 5 & 6:
Add 2 tens + 6 tens. The partial su is 8 tens. Record the 8 to the right the 6. Cross out the 2 and the 6.
   Add 5 tens and 8 tens. The partia sum is 13 tens. Record the 1 to the left of the 5; record the 3 to the rig of the 5. Cross out the 5 and the 8

```
   H   T   O
   2
     6 8   8
   1 5 3 7 5
   1 8   2 7
   +   6 7 3 0
   ───────────
   2   7   0
```

Remaining Steps:
Add 8 tens and 3 tens. The partial sum is 11 tens. Record one 1 to th left of the 8; record the other 1 to right. Cross out the 8 and the 3.
   Add 6 tens and 1 ten. Record the to the right of the 6. Cross out the and the 1 (on the right).
   Determine the final sum: The tens digit of the final sum is 7. Record the There are 1 + 1, or 2 hundreds. Reco 2 in the hundreds position of the sum
   So, the final sum is 270.

ne _____ Date _____ Class _____

Practice Exercises
Addition of Whole Numbers

t 1

. $9 + 0 =$ _____

2. _____ $+ 9 = 10$

3. $6 + 6 =$ _____

4. $7 +$ _____ $= 14$

. _____ $+ 9 = 18$

6. _____ $= 9 + 8$

7. $15 =$ _____ $+ 7$

8. $4 +$ _____ $= 13$

t 2

.
```
    9 0
+     9
```

10.
```
    9 0 1
+       8
```

11.
```
    2 0
+   6 0
```

12.
```
    8 2 0
+   1 6 6
```

.
```
  7, 1 2 5
+ 2, 0 7 0
```

14.
```
  5, 0 0 0
+     5 5 5
```

15. $8,915 + 23$

16. $9,719 + 280$

t 3

.
```
    4 9
+     8
```

18.
```
    8 1 6
+       8
```

19.
```
    8 5 3
+     5 5
```

20.
```
    7 7
+   7 7
```

.
```
    6 9 8
+   3 0 5
```

22.
```
  5, 0 9 4
+ 4, 9 6 7
```

23. $298 + 58$

24. $6,987 + 188$

t 4

.
```
    8
    9
    0
+   1
```

26.
```
    4
    9
    6
+   7
```

27.
```
    2 6
    6 0
+   8 9
```

28.
```
    7 0 9
    4 9 6
    3 3 1
+     6 4
```

.
```
      9 5
    3 4 0
    8 0 0
+   8 9 7
```

30.
```
  9, 9 9 9
  9, 9 9 8
  1, 0 7 2
+ 8, 9 0 0
```

31. $29 + 137 + 6$

32. $555 + 1,090 + 26$

1. Compare and contrast the rounding method for estimating addition of whole numbers with front-end estimation for addition of whole numbers. Discuss any advantages or disadvantages of using either method.

2. Explain why play money and base-ten blocks are ideal manipulatives to use with students to support the teaching of addition of whole numbers. Discuss how other types of manipulatives could be used to teach addition of whole numbers.

3. Explain how you would teach the traditional algorithm for addition of whole numbers in a manner that should reduce the chances that your students develop error patterns.

4. Consider the quote below from Mokros, Russell, and Economopoulos (1995). Explain how you would gather information on student error patterns and then use that information as an instructional tool to improve student computational fluency in your classroom. (This quote is also used on page 13 of this book.)

   "Without information about students' skills, understanding, and individual approaches to mathematics, teachers have nothing to guide their work" (p. 84).

5. Choose one of the addition error patterns that you believe is practiced by many students. Explain what the student did and what mathematical concept or procedure was likely misunderstood. Provide a specific strategy you would use with students to correct that misunderstanding and error.

6. Explain how you would teach students how to use mental math to find $39 + 38$.

7. Many educators accept—and even encourage—the use of student-invented strategies or algorithms. For example, students using base-ten blocks to find the sum $497 + 326$ might use the blocks to add from left to right as shown below.

   $(400 + 300) + (90 + 20) + (7 + 6) = 700 + 110 + 13 = 823.$

   How may students benefit from constructing their own computational methods? Describe any downsides to the use of these methods. What sort of criteria would you use to evaluate a student-invented algorithm?

Unit 2

Subtraction
of Whole Numbers

The 20-question Diagnostic Test for Subtraction of Whole Numbers, in multiple-choice format, consists of four parts: subtraction facts, subtraction without renaming, subtraction with renaming, and subtraction with renaming involving 0s. The test allows you to pinpoint specific skills and concepts that require more student work. For information on how to use this test to help identify specific student error patterns, see pages 52 through 54.

Throughout their work with subtraction, students should be encouraged to use estimation to check if their answers are reasonable. A visual model to aid students with the concept of rounding (Roller Coaster Rounding) is on pages 143 and 144. Reproducible lessons for estimating differences using front-end estimation and for estimating using compatible numbers (for all operations) are on pages 153 and 176, respectively. (Answers are on pages 195 and 199, respectively.)

Pages 151 through 162 provide instructional games and follow-up activities (reproducible) to support subtraction (and addition) concepts.

Name _____ Date _____ Class _____

Diagnostic Test
Subtraction of Whole Numbers

Multiple Choice: Circle the correct answer. If your answer is not given, circle *Not here.*

Part 1

1. $14 - 8 = \square$ **A** 8   **B** 6   **C** 22   **D** 14   **E** Not here

2. $13 - 5 = \square$ **A** 8   **B** 18   **C** 12   **D** 7   **E** Not here

3. $15 - \square = 6$ **A** 21   **B** 11   **C** 8   **D** 9   **E** Not here

4. $\square - 8 = 6$ **A** 2   **B** 9   **C** 14   **D** 16   **E** Not here

5. Which addition problem can be used to find the value of $\square$ in $16 - 7 = \square$?

   A $\square + 7 = 16$ **B** $7 + 16 = \square$ **C** $16 + \square = 7$ **D** $\square - 16 = 7$ **E** Not her

Part 2

6.
$$\begin{array}{r} 8\ 7 \\ -\quad 7 \\ \hline \end{array}$$
   A 10   **B** 0   **C** 80   **D** 8   **E** Not here

7. $45 - 3$ **A** 15   **B** 42   **C** 12   **D** 32   **E** Not here

8. $648 - 40$ **A** 608   **B** 248   **C** 640   **D** 5,918   **E** Not here

9.
$$\begin{array}{r} 1\ 5\ 8 \\ -\quad 5\ 6 \\ \hline \end{array}$$
   A 912   **B** 102   **C** 1,112   **D** 12   **E** Not here

10.
$$\begin{array}{r} 8\ 6\ 7 \\ -\quad 5\ 0 \\ \hline \end{array}$$
   A 617   **B** 817   **C** 17   **D** 810   **E** Not here

          8   4
        − 3   6   **A** 52   **B** 58   **C** 28   **D** 48   **E** Not here

        821 − 63   **A** 842   **B** 868   **C** 758   **D** 191   **E** Not here

          8   5   2
        − 2   8   1   **A** 670   **B** 571   **C** 631   **D** 5,611   **E** Not here

          4   1   5
        − 1   9   3   **A** 322   **B** 222   **C** 321   **D** 2,112   **E** Not here

          9, 2   1   8
        − 7, 3   9   5   **A** 1,823   **B** 2,923   **C** 2,183   **D** 2,912   **E** Not here

          9   7   0
        −   6   **A** 304   **B** 964   **C** 970   **D** 854   **E** Not here

          8   7   0
        − 3   6   3   **A** 507   **B** 4,107   **C** 57   **D** 513   **E** Not here

          7   0   5
        − 2   8   9   **A** 326   **B** 584   **C** 416   **D** 506   **E** Not here

          5, 0   0   4
        −   6   1   0   **A** 394   **B** 5,000   **C** 3,494   **D** 4,394   **E** Not here

          6, 0   0   0
        − 1, 7   5   3   **A** 4,357   **B** 5,753   **C** 4,247   **D** 5,357   **E** Not here

ITEM ANALYSIS FOR DIAGNOSTIC TEST
Subtraction of Whole Numbers

Using the Item Analysis Table

- The correct answer for each item on the Diagnostic Test is indicated by a ✓ in the Item Analysis Table on page 54.

- Each incorrect answer choice is keyed to a specific error pattern and corresponding Intervention Activity found on pages 55 through 72. Because each item on the Diagnostic Test is an item that is analyzed in one of the error patterns, teachers may be able to use the Intervention Activities with identical problems that students may have missed on the test.

- Students should be encouraged to circle *Not here* if their obtained answer is not one of the given answer choices. Although *Not here* is never a correct answer on the Diagnostic Test, the use of this answer choice should aid in the diagnostic process. The intention is that students who do not see their obtained answer among the choices will select *Not here* rather than guess at one of the other choices. This should strengthen the likelihood that students who select an incorrect answer choice actually made the error associated with the error pattern.

- The Item Analysis Table should only be used as a *guide*. Although many errors are procedural in nature, others may be due to an incorrect recall of facts or to carelessness. A diagnostic test is just one of many tools that should be considered when assessing student work and making prescriptive decisions. Before being certain that a student has a misconception about a procedure or concept, further analysis may be needed (see below). This is especially true for students who frequently select *Not here* as an answer choice.

- A set of practice exercises, keyed to each of the four parts of the Diagnostic Test, is provided on page 74. Because the four parts of the set of practice exercises match the four parts on the Diagnostic Test, the set of practice exercises could be used as a posttest.

Using Teacher-Directed Questioning and Journaling

Discussions and observations should be used to help distinguish misconceptions about concepts and procedures from student carelessness or lack of fact recall. This should be done in a *positive* manner—with the clear purpose being to "get inside student thinking." The Intervention Activities are replete with teacher-directed questioning, frequently asking students to *explain their reasoning*. Students should also be asked to *write* about their thinking as they work through an algorithm—and, when alternative algorithms are used, explain why they may prefer one algorithm over another. You may also want students to write word problems based on *subtraction*—and then explain why subtraction can be used to solve them. This would be a good time to discuss with students the various actions and problem structures for subtraction (see pages 18–19).

Additional Resources for Subtraction

- A lesson providing a visual model for *rounding* is on pages 143 and 144. A lesson on using *front-end estimation* to check differences for reasonableness is on page 153; a lesson on using *compatible numbers* for estimation (for all operations) is on page 176. These lessons may be used at any point in the instructional process. When students engage in estimation activities, they should discuss why they believe a computed answer may or may not be reasonable.

- Instructional games and follow-up activities for subtraction concepts are on pages 151 through 162. This material may be used at any point in the instructional process. The games *Balance the Number Sentence!* and *Target Math* may be used as vehicles for observing student behavior in trial-and-error thinking, computation, and problem solving. The follow-up activity *Editor Error Search* provides a rich opportunity for students to play the role of editor to find and correct errors in a manuscript. Students also are asked to discuss the error patterns they observe in the manuscript.

ITEM ANALYSIS TABLE

The correct answer for each item on the Diagnostic Test is indicated by a ✓ in this table.

	Item	Answer Choices				Topic	Practice Exercises
		A	**B**	**C**	**D**		
	1	Error 1	✓	Error 1	Error 1	Subtraction facts	Part 1, p. 7
	2	✓	Error 1	Error 1	Error 1	Subtraction facts	Part 1, p. 7
	3	Error 1	Error 1	Error 1	✓	Subtraction facts	Part 1, p. 7
	4	Error 1	Error 1	✓	Error 1	Subtraction facts	Part 1, p. 7
Part 1	5	✓	Error 1	Error 1	Error 1	Subtraction facts	Part 1, p. 7
	6	Error 3	Error 6a	✓	Error 11b	Subtraction without renaming	Part 2, p. 7
	7	Error 4	✓	Error 3	Error 6b	Subtraction without renaming	Part 2, p. 7
	8	✓	Error 4	Error 11	Error 9	Subtraction without renaming	Part 2, p. 7
	9	Error 9	✓	Errors 2 & 9	Error 11b	Subtraction without renaming	Part 2, p. 7
Part 2	10	Error 6b	✓	Error 6a	Error 11a	Subtraction without renaming	Part 2, p. 7
	11	Error 2	Error 5	Error 10	✓	Subtraction with renaming	Part 3, p. 7
	12	Error 2	Error 5	✓	Error 4	Subtraction with renaming	Part 3, p. 7
	13	Error 7	✓	Error 2	Error 9	Subtraction with renaming	Part 3, p. 7
	14	Error 5	✓	Error 7	Error 9	Subtraction with renaming	Part 3, p. 7
Part 3	15	✓	Error 5	Error 2	Error 7	Subtraction with renaming	Part 3, p. 7
	16	Error 3	✓	Error 11a	Error 6b	Subtraction with renaming involving 0 or 0s	Part 4, p. 7
	17	✓	Error 10	Error 11b	Error 2	Subtraction with renaming involving 0 or 0s	Part 4, p. 7
	18	Error 8	Error 2	✓	Error 10	Subtraction with renaming involving 0 or 0s	Part 4, p. 7
	19	Error 6a	Error 11a	Error 8	✓	Subtraction with renaming involving 0 or 0s	Part 4, p. 7
Part 4	20	Error 8	Error 2	✓	Errors 5 & 8	Subtraction with renaming involving 0 or 0s	Part 4, p. 7

ERROR PATTERNS & INTERVENTION ACTIVITIES
Subtraction of Whole Numbers

Error Pattern 1

Some students have difficulty recalling basic subtraction facts (through $18 - 9$). A lack of understanding of the do/undo (inverse) relationship between addition and subtraction is often a contributing factor to making these errors.

Intervention

Have students "think addition" when they do subtraction by finding the missing part of a subtraction sentence. For example, for $14 - 6 = \square$, have students think (from right to left), "*What* plus 6 makes 14?" If students cannot recall that $8 + 6 = 14$, have them make or use an addition table to help them recall the facts. (A blank table and a completed table are provided on pages 188–189.)

Students could find 6 in the shaded column on the left in the table, then slide across (along the dashed arrow) to 14, and finally slide up to see that 8 (circled in the top row) answers, "*What* plus 6 makes 14?" Repeat the above for $14 - 8 = \square$. The solid arrows in the table show that 6 answers the question, "*What* plus 8 makes 14?"

+	0	1	2	3	4	5	⑥	7	⑧	9
0	0	1	2	3	4	5	6	7	8	9
1	1	2	3	4	5	6	7	8	9	10
2	2	3	4	5	6	7	8	9	10	11
3	3	4	5	6	7	8	9	10	11	12
4	4	5	6	7	8	9	10	11	12	13
5	5	6	7	8	9	10	11	12	13	14
6	6	7	8	9	10	11	12	13	14	15
7	7	8	9	10	11	12	13	14	15	16
8	8	9	10	11	12	13	14	15	16	17
9	9	10	11	12	13	14	15	16	17	18

Repeat with subtraction sentences where the missing part is *not* on the right-hand side of the equal sign, such as $14 - \square = 8$ or $\square - 8 = 6$. Such sentences encourage students to think of the equal sign as meaning equality and balance (rather than as "find the answer").

As you relate subtraction facts to the addition facts students already know, bring out the idea of fact families. Provide an addition sentence, and then have students write the three corresponding related sentences. For $9 + 7 = 16$, students should write all four facts in the family as shown below.

9 + 7 = 16	7 + 9 = 16
16 − 7 = 9	16 − 9 = 7

Instructional Game: Balance the +/− Number Sentence!
(See pages 154–157 for game instructions and game pieces. Students work in groups of 2 or 3.)

This "domino-type" game promotes memorization of the facts while having students use trial-and-error thinking to balance addition/subtraction number sentences. Students use playing cards as "dominoes" to match either a number sentence with its solution or a solution with its number sentence. (Shown below, the card with the white 14 was placed next to the card with $\square - 8 = 6$ because 14 makes that sentence true.)

17 − □ = 9	14	□ − 8 = 6	7

Most of the game cards involve the use of the basic facts. However, advise students that those game cards that are based on two-digit addition or subtraction can be solved using *mathematical reasoning* rather than by performing actual computations. For example, to solve $24 + 25 = \square + 24$, students can use the *Commutative Property of Addition* to determine that $\square = 25$. For $31 - 24 = 31 - \square$, students should think about the value for $\square$ that puts both sides in balance. The value for $\square$, of course, is 24.

Error Pattern 2

Some students subtract the lesser digit from the greater digit in each place-value position, ignoring order (and renaming).

$$
\begin{array}{r}
8\ 4 \\
-\ 3\ 6 \\
\hline
5\ 2
\end{array}
\qquad
\begin{array}{r}
8\ 2\ 1 \\
-\ \ \ 6\ 3 \\
\hline
8\ 4\ 2
\end{array}
\qquad
\begin{array}{r}
8\ 7\ 0 \\
-\ \ \ 7\ 6 \\
\hline
8\ 0\ 6
\end{array}
\qquad
\begin{array}{r}
9,\ 2\ 1\ 8 \\
-\ 7,\ 3\ 9\ 5 \\
\hline
2,\ 1\ 8\ 3
\end{array}
$$

Intervention

Note: Base-ten blocks may be used instead of play money in the Interventions for Error Patterns 2 through 6.

Supply a subtraction exercise on a place-value grid, a place-value mat on tagboard, and play money. (See pages 184–186 for play money, mat, and grids.)

To subtract 36 from 84, guide students to model the top number (the *minuend*) by placing 8 ten-dollar bills and 4 one-dollar bills on the mat to represent 84. Point out that the *subtrahend* tells us how much we are to *take away* in each place-value position. In terms of vocabulary, to help students connect "subtrahend" to "the bottom number of a subtraction exercise," have them think of *subway*.

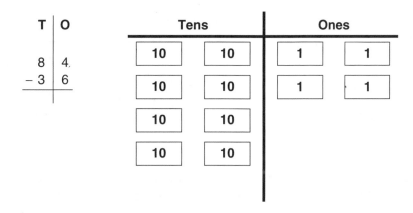

Emphasize that we start with the ones. **Ask,** "Are there enough one-dollar bills on the mat so that you can remove 6 one-dollar bills?" (No.) Note that when you ask whether there are enough one-dollar bills on the mat to remove 6 one-dollar bills, try to avoid language such as "Can you subtract 6 from 4?" To suggest that you *cannot subtract 6 from 4* could lead to later confusion when students study integers and learn that $4 - 6 = -2$.

Ask, "What can we do with the play money we have to get more one-dollar bills on the mat?" (Sample: Trade 1 ten-dollar bill for 10 one-dollar bills.) Guide students in trading 1 ten-dollar bill for 10 one-dollar bills, and record the renaming in the subtraction exercise. (See page 58.)

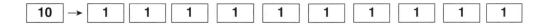

Ask, "Did this renaming change the total amount of money you have with your ten- and one-dollar bills? Explain." (No. Sample: Before the renaming, we had 8 ten-dollar bills and 4 one-dollar bills, or $80 + $4 = $84. After the renaming, we have 7 ten-dollar bills and 14 one-dollar bills, or $70 + $14 = $84.) Then, have students perform the subtraction in the ones position on the mat by removing 6 one-dollar bills. Instruct students to record the result in the exercise. Then, have them remove 3 ten-dollar bills and record the final result.

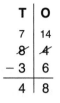

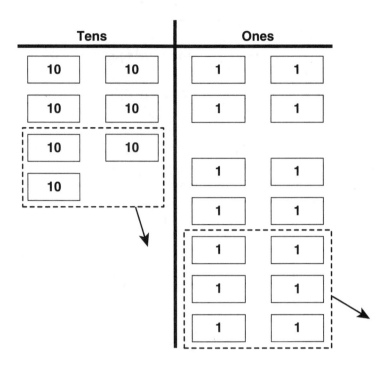

Alternative Intervention: Using Mental Math on an Empty Number Line

Some students may gain fluency with subtraction by doing the computation mentally on an empty (open) number line. By using an empty number line, students should (1) realize that answers such as those described in Error Pattern 2 are not reasonable and (2) obtain correct results without using an algorithm (that may have caused them difficulty).

Merits of using an empty number line are detailed in the unit on addition, on page 42. These benefits include the ability to see partial results, gaining practice with compensation (adding or subtracting too much and then compensating), and more. For subtraction, the empty number line also promotes facility with counting by tens (on and off the decade), with bridging tens, and with splitting numbers as described below.

- Students gain facility with counting-down mental computations:

  On the decade: 80 – 10 = 70; 70 – 10 = 60
  Off the decade: 54 – 10 = 44; 44 – 10 = 34

- Students gain facility with splitting the tens and ones—and addressing these separately:

  To find 76 – 9, they may first find 76 – 6 = 70. Then they find 70 – 3, obtaining 67.

Use an empty number line to find 84 – 36:

To find 84 – 36, begin by drawing an empty number line with 84 shown at the far right below the line.

84

Next, you can subtract 30 by counting down 30 units (to the left) all at once (to obtain 54). Or, you can count down 10 at a time from 84 to 54.

Think: 84 − 30 = 54

or

Think: 84 − 10 = 74; 74 − 10 = 64;
64 − 10 = 54

To subtract the remaining 6 from 54, you can first subtract 4 to obtain 50. Then subtract 2 to obtain 48.

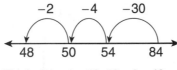

Think: 54 − 4 = 50; 50 − 2 = 48.

Another way to subtract 36 from 84 is to use the number line to subtract 40 from 84, obtaining 44. Because you subtracted 4 too much, you compensate by adding 4 to the 44, obtaining 48.

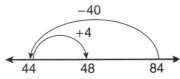

Think: 84 − 40 = 44; 44 + 4 = 48.

Using Student Journaling: Because the open number line permits students to find differences in an individualized way—with students essentially making their own judgments to determine what steps to use—this method lends itself nicely to student journaling. Ask students to write about the steps they use. Also, have them compare and contrast this algorithm with the traditional algorithm.

According to Carroll and Porter (1998), students' writing about their algorithms encourages them "to think through the steps of their algorithms and clarify and refine their ideas about the procedures used. . . . Written descriptions of the algorithm can help to clarify for the teacher whether the student merely made a careless slip or has a deeper misunderstanding of the procedure—something that may not be clear from the use of the algorithm alone" (p. 113).

Error Pattern 3

When subtracting a one-digit number, some students subtract the one-digit number from each digit of the minuend.

```
         7   12                         6  10
  8 7    8   2                      9   7   0
−   7   −    6                      −       6
─────   ──────                      ──────────
  1 0    1   6                      3   0   4
```

Intervention

Students should be encouraged to use estimation to check if their answer is reasonable. **Ask,** "Can 7 from 87 possibly be just 10?" (No.) "Can 6 from 970 possibly be 304?" (No.)

Supply a subtraction exercise on a place-value grid, a place-value mat on tagboard, and play money (or base-ten blocks). To subtract 7 from 87, guide students in placing 8 ten-dollar bills and 7 one-dollar bills on the mat. Instruct students to remove 7 one-dollar bills and record the result (0) in the subtraction exercise.

Ask, "Are we being asked to remove any tens?" (No.) Emphasize that because there are no tens to remove, you subtract 0 tens from 8 tens. Bring out that you subtract ones from ones, tens from tens, and so on.

T	O
8	7
−	7
8	0

Tens		Ones	
10	10	1	1
10	10	1	1
10	10	1	1
10	10		1

Error Pattern 4

When a subtraction problem is posed in horizontal form and there are more digits in the minuend than in the subtrahend, some students fail to align the digits correctly.

$$45 - 3 \quad \rightarrow \quad \begin{array}{r} 4\ 5 \\ -\ \ 3 \\ \hline 1\ 5 \end{array}$$

$$648 - 40 \quad \rightarrow \quad \begin{array}{r} 6\ 4\ 8 \\ -\ 4\ 0 \\ \hline 2\ 4\ 8 \end{array}$$

Intervention

Supply grid paper, a place-value mat on tagboard, and play money. For 45 – 3, have students place 4 ten-dollar bills and 5 one-dollar bills on the mat. **Ask,** "Are we subtracting ones or tens?" (Ones.) Guide students in recording the exercise on the grid paper, aligning the ones with the ones, and so on. Have students remove 3 one-dollar bills from the mat and record the subtraction on the grid paper. Emphasize that we subtract ones from ones, and since there are no tens to subtract, we have 4 – 0, or 4 tens, in the answer.

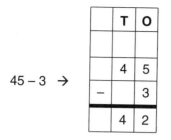

$45 - 3 \rightarrow$

	T	O
	4	5
−		3
	4	2

Tens	Ones

Alternative Intervention: Using Base-Ten Blocks

Supply students with grid paper and some base-ten blocks. Explain that each flat represents 100, each rod represents 10, and each unit represents 1. Advise students that the blocks will help them maintain the correct place-value positions for the digits as they convert an exercise set up in horizontal form to one set up in vertical form.

To find 648 – 40, have students begin by displaying blocks to represent 648. **Ask,** "How many units are there?" (8 units.) "How many rods are there?" (4 rods.) "How many flats are there?" (6 flats.) Have students write 648 in the minuend on the grid paper as shown below.

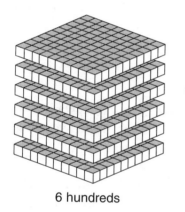

6 hundreds   4 tens   8 ones

Then, ask students to represent 40 with the blocks. **Ask,** "How many units are there? (0 units.) **Ask,** "Will we be writing a digit in the ones place of the subtrahend? If so, what digit?" (Yes; 0.) **Ask,** "How many rods are there?" (4 rods.) **Ask,** "Will we be writing a digit in the tens place of the subtrahend? If so, what digit?" (Yes; 4.) **Ask,** "How many flats are there?" (0 flats.) **Ask,** "Will we be writing a digit in the hundreds place of the subtrahend? If so, what digit?" (No.) Have them write 40 in the subtrahend on the grid paper.

$648 - 40 \rightarrow$

	H	T	O
	6	4	8
−		4	0

To complete the subtraction, refer students to the base-ten blocks representing the minuend. **Ask,** "When 0 ones are subtracted from 8 ones, how many ones are left?" (8 ones.) **Ask,** "When 4 tens are subtracted from 4 tens, how many tens are left?" (0 tens.) **Ask,** "Will we be subtracting any hundreds from the 6 hundreds that we have?" (No.) Have students complete the subtraction to determine that the difference is 608.

Error Pattern 5

When a subtraction involves renaming, some students do not record all of the renaming process. This generally involves "incomplete trades."

```
        11
   4    X   5
 - 1    9   3
 ─────────────
   3    2   2
```

The student adds 10 tens to the tens position, but no renaming is done to the hundreds.

Step 1

```
               10
    6    4    0
 -  3    5    9
 ──────────────
              1
```

Renaming occurs in the ones position, but not in the tens position

Step 2

```
        14   10
    6    4    0
 -  3    5    9
 ──────────────
    3    9    1
```

Then renaming occurs in the tens position only.

Intervention

Estimation: Determining If an Answer Is Reasonable

All students, especially those who obtain unreasonable answers, should be encouraged to use estimation either before or after computing. When students round 415 and 193 to the nearest hundred, they should see that the answer to 415 – 193 is about 400 – 200, or about 200 (and that, say, 322 is far from the exact answer). Some students, however, find rounding to be a difficult process. The lesson "Roller Coaster Rounding" (pages 143–144) provides a model for students to use to visualize the rounding process.

Some students, especially those who find the rounding process to be difficult, may benefit from using front-end estimation as a way to determine if an answer is reasonable. The lesson "Using Front-End Estimation to Check for Reasonableness: Subtraction" (page 153) teaches students how to use this strategy. A lesson on using *compatible numbers* to make estimates (for all operations) is on page 176.

Intervention: Using Play Money or Base-Ten Blocks

Three-digit subtraction with renaming is especially difficult for some students. As Thanheiser (2009) points out, "to explain regrouping from the hundreds to the tens in the (standard) algorithm, a student needs to see the hundred in terms of 1 hundred to explain why we are taking away 1, in terms of 10 tens to explain why we add 10 in the tens place, and in terms of 100 ones to explain the value of the regrouped digit in the tens place" (p. 262).

Activities with students should thus engage them in understanding (1) why renaming is necessary and (2) why the renaming does not change the value of the number.

Supply a subtraction exercise on a place-value grid, a place-value mat on tagboard, and play money (or base-ten blocks). To subtract 193 from 415, guide students in placing 4 hundred-dollar bills, 1 ten-dollar bill, and 5 one-dollar bills on the mat to represent 415.

H	T	O
4	1	5
− 1	9	3

Hundreds	Tens	Ones
100 100	10	1 1
100 100		1 1
		1

Emphasize that we start with the ones. **Ask,** "Can you remove 3 one-dollar bills?" (Yes.) Have students remove 3 ones and record the result in the subtraction exercise. **Ask,** "Can you remove 9 tens from the mat?" (No.) **Ask,** "What can we do with the play money so that we have more ten-dollar bills?" (Trade 1 hundred-dollar bill for 10 ten-dollar bills.)

| 100 | → | 10 | 10 | 10 | 10 | 10 | 10 | 10 | 10 | 10 | 10 |

Have students show this renaming by removing 1 hundred-dollar bill from the hundreds column and replacing it with 10 ten-dollar bills in the tens column. **Ask,** "Did this renaming change the total amount of money you have with your hundred- and ten-dollar bills? Explain." (No. Sample: Before the renaming, we had 4 hundred-dollar bills and 1 ten-dollar bill, or $400 + $10 = $410. After the renaming, we have 3 hundred-dollar bills and 11 ten-dollar bills, or $300 + $110 = $410.) Instruct students to show this renaming in the exercise as shown below. Now have students remove 9 ten-dollar bills and then 1 hundred-dollar bill. Then have students record the results in the exercise.

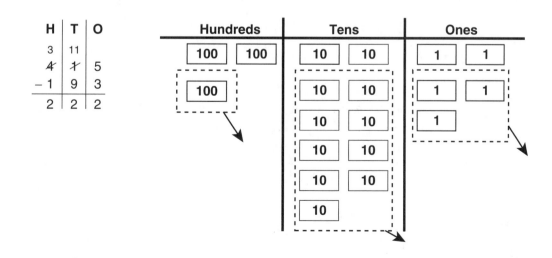

Error Pattern 6

Error Pattern 6a: When there are more digits in the minuend than in the subtrahend, some students fail to subtract in the positions where the "extra" digits occur (illustrated in the first two examples below).

Error Pattern 6b: When there are more digits in the minuend than in the subtrahend, some students may correctly subtract in the ones position, but "subtract" 1 from each of the "extra" digits (illustrated in the final two examples below).

```
                      7  12                              6  10
    9  7              8   2            6  8           9  7   0
 -     4           -      6         -     7        -         6
 ─────────         ─────────        ───────        ──────────
       3                  6          5  1           8  5   4
```

The student subtracts 4 from 7 but fails to record anything in the tens position.

The student fails to subtract in the tens position.

The student subtracts 7 from 8 but subtracts 1 from the tens digit (rather than 0).

The student correctly subtracts in the ones position but subtracts 1 in each of the other positions.

Intervention

Ask students to estimate the differences before they compute. **Ask,** "Does an answer of 3 make sense when you take 4 from 97? Explain." (No. Sample: There are no tens to subtract off. The answer should be close to 90.) Use the Intervention for Error Pattern 3 to emphasize that when no bills are to be removed from a place-value position, you are subtracting 0 from a number.

Error Pattern 7

Some students subtract from left to right. (This error only becomes apparent in computations that involve renaming.)

```
                                              9
     15  1                       14  10   1
  8   5   2                   7,  4   0   2
- 2  8   1                  - 5,  6   8   0
 ──────────                 ──────────────
  6  7   0                    2,  8   1   1
```

Intervention

Supply a subtraction exercise on a place-value grid with an index card, revealing only the digits in the ones place. Subtract in the ones position.

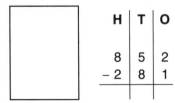

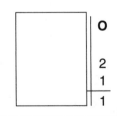

Then instruct students to move the card one column to the left, revealing the tens digits. Because renaming is necessary before subtracting the tens, instruct students to move the card one more column to the left to reveal the digits in the hundreds place. Have them record the renaming and subtract the tens and then the hundreds.

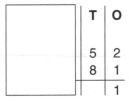

	T	O
	5	2
	8	1
		1

	H	T	O
	7	15	
	8̸	5̸	2
−	2	8	1
	5	7	1

Error Pattern 8

Some students rename incorrectly when they have to "cross 0s" in the minuend.

5	10	10	10
6̸,	0̸	0̸	0̸
− 1,	7	5	3
4,	3	5	7

The 1,000 that is "borrowed" from the 6 thousands is spread across three place-value positions as 10 hundreds, 10 tens, and 10 ones.

Step 1

6		15
7̸	0	5̸
− 2	8	9
		6

Renaming is done directly from hundreds to ones. The student renames 7 hundreds as 6 hundreds and 10 ones.

Step 2

5		
6̸	10	15
7̸	0̸	5̸
− 2	8	9
3	2	6

Renaming from the hundreds is then done a second time—this time to the tens.

Intervention

Many students find subtracting "across 0s" to be one of the most difficult tasks they experience at this point in their mathematics careers. Some students never master this skill using the traditional subtraction algorithm. It should be noted that the standard algorithm is based on shortcut notation where *individual digits* stand for tens, hundreds, thousands, and so on. When it is necessary to rename multiple times in an exercise, the shortcut can be quite confusing to some students.

The alternative subtraction algorithm described on page 66 and practiced on page 67 utilizes expanded notation to help students visualize the actions that occur in each step. You may want to review expanded notation with students before presenting this algorithm, reminding them that expanded notation is used to rename a number as a sum of the values of the digits in the number. **Ask,** "How do you write 289 in expanded notation?" (200 + 80 + 9.) **Ask,** "How do you write 705 in expanded notation?" (700 + 0 + 5.)

Another alternative subtraction algorithm, *using compensation*, is included with Error Pattern 10—and should benefit students who have difficulty with the renaming process.

Alternative Subtraction Algorithm: Using Expanded Notation

Write the minuend and subtrahend in expanded notation as shown. Parentheses are used to show that we are subtracting the entire number $(200 + 80 + 9)$ from the minuend.

$$
\begin{array}{ll}
705 & \rightarrow \\
-\,289 & \rightarrow
\end{array}
\qquad
\begin{array}{l}
(\ 700 \ + \ 0 \ + \ 5\ ) \\
-(\ 200 \ + \ 80 \ + \ 9\ )
\end{array}
$$

Subtract in each place-value position beginning with the ones. **Ask,** "Are there enough ones to subtract 9 ones from 5 ones?" (No.) Explain that to get more ones, you can first rename 700 as $600 + 100$. Record the 600 in the hundreds position and the 100 in the tens position as shown (crossing out the 700 and 0).

$$
\begin{array}{ll}
705 & \rightarrow \\
-\,289 & \rightarrow
\end{array}
\qquad
\begin{array}{l}
\quad\ \ ^{600}\qquad\ \ ^{100} \\
(\ \cancel{700} \ + \ \cancel{0} \ + \ 5\ ) \\
-(\ 200 \ + \ 80 \ + \ 9\ )
\end{array}
$$

Now, rename $100 + 5$ (from the tens and ones positions) as $90 + 15$. (This is akin to renaming 10 tens and 5 ones as 9 tens and 15 ones.) Record the 90 in the tens position and the 15 in the ones position as shown (crossing out the 100 and the 5).

$$
\begin{array}{ll}
705 & \rightarrow \\
-\,289 & \rightarrow
\end{array}
\qquad
\begin{array}{l}
\quad\ \ ^{600}\qquad\ \ ^{\overset{90}{\cancel{100}}}\qquad\ ^{15} \\
(\ \cancel{700} \ + \ \cancel{0} \ + \ \cancel{5}\ ) \\
-(\ 200 \ + \ 80 \ + \ 9\ )
\end{array}
$$

Now, subtract in each position $(15 - 9 = 6; 90 - 80 = 10; 600 - 200 = 400)$. Then, write the answer in *standard notation:* $400 + 10 + 6 = 416$.

$$
\begin{array}{ll}
705 & \rightarrow \\
-\,289 & \rightarrow
\end{array}
\qquad
\begin{array}{l}
\quad\ \ ^{600}\qquad\ \ ^{\overset{90}{\cancel{100}}}\qquad\ ^{15} \\
(\ \cancel{700} \ + \ \cancel{0} \ + \ \cancel{5}\ ) \\
-(\ 200 \ + \ 80 \ + \ 9\ ) \\
\hline
\quad\ 400 \ + \ 10 \ + \ 6 \quad = \quad 416
\end{array}
$$

You may want to photocopy the Guided Problems on page 67 so that students may practice using this alternative algorithm.

Guided Problem 1

Use the alternative algorithm to subtract 485 from 903. First, write each number in expanded notation.

```
  903    →    ( _____  +  ____  +  __ )
- 485    →   -( _____  +  ____  +  __ )
_____        _____
```

Since we do not have enough ones to take 5 ones from 3 ones, we rename 900 as 800 + 100. Record the renaming (800 in the hundreds column; 100 in the tens column).

```
  903    →    (  900  +   0  +  3  )
- 485    →   -(  400  +  80  +  5  )
_____        _____
```

Now rename 100 + 3 as 90 + 13 (in the tens and ones positions).

```
                 800       100
  903    →    (  900  +    0  +  3  )
- 485    →   -(  400  +   80  +  5  )
_____        _____
```

Now subtract in each place-value position. Then write the difference in standard form.

```
                        90
                 800   100       13
  903    →    (  900  +  0  +   3  )
- 485    →   -(  400  + 80  +   5  )
_____        _____

              _____  +  ____  +  __  = _____
```

Guided Problem 2

Use the alternative algorithm to subtract 1,753 from 6,000.

```
                5,000    1,000
  6,000   →   ( 6,000  +   0  +  0  +  0 )
- 1,753   →  -( _____  + ____ + __ + __ )
_____        _____

              _____ + ____ + __ + __ = _____
```

Alternative Intervention: Using Mental Math on an Empty Number Line

Some students will experience success finding differences when the minuend contains 0s by using mental math on an empty number line. (See the Alternative Intervention for Error Pattern 2.) Consider the exercise 2,001 – 3. According to Reeves and Reeves (2003), to find 2,001 – 3, most students will write the 3 below the 2,001, then subtract by renaming across the 0s, eventually obtaining 1,998 (hopefully). Reeves and Reeves found that more than 95% of the students in their study responded in such a way—even though in subsequent discussions they could readily identify easier ways to find the answer.

Use an empty number line to find 2,001 – 3:

To find 2,001 – 3, write 2,001 at the far right below the number line. To subtract 3, simply count down 3 units to obtain 1,998.

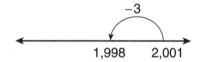

Error Pattern 9

Some students rename when it is not necessary to rename.

	3			14			16			18		
				4̶	18		8̶ 6̶	13		4̶ 8̶	11	
	4̶	8		1̶ 5̶	8		9̶ 7̶	3̶		5̶ 9̶	0̶	
–	1	7	–		5 6	– 4	0	6	– 4	2	2	
	2	1			9 12	4	16	7		16	9	

The student erroneously renames 4 tens as 3 tens.	The student unnecessarily renames 5 tens and 8 ones as 4 tens and 18 ones. Then, 6 is subtracted from 18, with 12 recorded in the ones position. The student then correctly renames the hundreds and tens.	The student renames 7 tens and 3 ones as 6 tens and 13 ones. Then, 9 hundreds and 6 tens are renamed as 8 hundreds and 16 tens.	9 tens and 0 ones are renamed as 8 tens and 11 ones. Then, 5 hundreds and 8 tens are renamed as 4 hundreds and 18 tens.

Intervention

For 158 – 56, display 1 hundred-dollar bill, 5 ten-dollar bills, and 8 one-dollar bills. **Ask,** "Can you take 6 one-dollar bills from 8 one-dollar bills *without* trading?" (Yes.) **Ask,** "Can you take 5 ten-dollar bills from 5 ten-dollar bills *without* trading?" (Yes.) **Ask,** "Can you take 0 hundred-dollar bills from 1 hundred-dollar bill *without* trading?" (Yes.)

Then use the Intervention for Error Pattern 5 to find 590 – 522. **Ask,** "Can you take 2 one-dollar bills from 0 one-dollar bills *without* trading? (No.) **Ask,** "In subtraction, when do you need to trade? When should you *not* trade?" Students should conclude that in a given place-value position, if the digit in the subtrahend *is less than or equal to* the digit in the minuend, no renaming is done. If the digit in the subtrahend *is greater than* the digit in the minuend, then renaming is needed. Have students use the intervention to complete the subtraction.

Error Pattern 10

When renaming is necessary in the ones position, some students rename the digit in the tens position by subtracting the smaller digit in the tens positions from the larger digit (rather than renaming the digit in the minuend as one less ten).

```
        5   13                              16
    6   9̶   3̶                      7    6̶   1̶2̶
                              9,   8̶    7̶    2̶
  −     4   5                  −      1    7    9
  ─────────────                ───────────────────
    6   1   8                  9,   6    9    3
```

Rather than renaming 9 tens and 3 ones as 8 tens and 13 ones, the student renames them as 5 tens and 13 ones. The student obtains the 5 tens by subtracting 4 from 9.

To obtain the renamed tens digit in the minuend, the student subtracts 1 from 7 to obtain 6 tens. Then renaming occurs again, and the student renames 8 hundreds and 6 tens as (8 − 1) or 7 hundreds and 16 tens.

Intervention

Supply a subtraction exercise on a place-value grid and also a place-value mat on tagboard. Also supply each student with a set of digit cards (provided on page 171).

To subtract 45 from 693, guide students in placing 6 hundred-dollar bills, 9 ten-dollar bills, and 3 one-dollar bills on the mat to represent 693. To emphasize the digit to be subtracted in each place-value position, have students place a digit card in each place-value position for each digit of the subtrahend as shown below. So, a 0 card is placed below in the hundreds position (because only a two-digit number is being subtracted), a 4 card is placed below in the tens position, and a 5 card is placed below in the ones position.

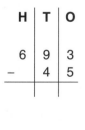

H	T	O
6	9	3
−	4	5

Hundreds	Tens	Ones
100 100	10 10	1 1
100 100	10 10	1
100 100	10 10	
	10 10	
	10	
0	**4**	**5**

Complete the subtraction by using the Intervention for Error Pattern 5. Emphasize that to obtain enough ones to subtract 5 ones, you rename 9 tens and 3 ones as 8 tens and 13 ones. Explain that the 4 tens that are to be subtracted (in the subtrahend) are *not* part of this renaming process. **Ask,** "After you rename, how many tens are left in the minuend? (8 tens.) "How many tens will you have left after you subtract the 4 tens?" (4 tens.)

Alternative Subtraction Algorithm: Using Compensation (Also Known as the "Equal Additions Method" and the "European-Latino Method")

This method is used in most European and Latin countries, among others. According to Ron (1998), "because parents will always try to help their children with mathematics as they know it, it is helpful for teachers to understand the European-Latino algorithm. . . . The phrase 'my family taught me this way' is often heard in the classroom as an explanation for a procedure that students realize was not taught in class" (pp. 115, 117).

Ron suggests that teachers accept such valid alternative algorithms students bring from home rather than disallowing their use. It should be noted, however, that children exposed to both the U.S. traditional and European-Latino algorithms often make errors by mixing the two algorithms. So, asking students to explain their subtraction work is especially important to help teachers sort through any such errors.

By using the concept of *compensation,* this algorithm avoids the "borrowing" process. Thus, students who struggle with the "borrowing" process may especially benefit from using this algorithm. Before presenting the algorithm, develop the concept of compensation by displaying Exercises A, B, C, and D below and then asking the questions that follow.

A	B	C	D
5 7	6 7	7 9 0	8 9 0
− 3 4	− 4 4	− 4 3 0	− 5 3 0

Questions:

Find each subtraction result in A and B. What do you notice about each difference? (Each difference is 23.)

What can you say about the minuends and subtrahends in A and B? (Sample: The minuend and subtrahend in B are each 10 more than the minuend and subtrahend in A.)

Find each subtraction result in C and D. What do you notice about each difference? (Each difference is 360.)

What can you say about the minuends and subtrahends in C and D? (Sample: The minuend and subtrahend in D are each 100 more than the minuend and subtrahend in C.)

Suppose you add the same number to the minuend and subtrahend of a subtraction exercise. How will that affect the difference of the two original numbers? Explain. (Sample: The difference, or spread, will be unchanged. The two new numbers will be just as far apart as before because each one was increased by the same amount.)

Once students understand the concept of compensation as it relates to subtraction, display the exercises below. Write the digits a bit larger than normal with extra horizontal space between the digits.

H	T	O
6	9	3
−	4	5

Th	H	T	O
9,	8	4	2
−	1	7	9

In the first exercise, because there are not enough ones to take 5 ones from 3 ones, you can add 10 in the ones column of the minuend (shown at right as 13, giving 13 ones). **Ask,** "What must we do to the subtrahend to maintain the same original spread between the two original numbers?" (Sample: Add 10 to the subtrahend.) Advise students that in the subtrahend the 1 ten is added in the tens column (giving 5 tens). Cross out the 4 in the tens column as shown. Then, subtract as shown to obtain 648.

In the second exercise, because there are not enough ones to take 9 ones from 2 ones, add 10 in the ones column of the minuend (giving 12 ones), and add 1 ten in the tens column of the subtrahend (giving 8 tens). Cross out the 7 in the tens column.

In the tens column, because you do not have enough tens to subtract 8 tens from 4 tens, add 100 in the tens column of the minuend. This is shown as $^{1}4$, or 14 tens, which is equal to 140. **Ask,** "What must you do to the subtrahend? Why?" (Sample: Add 1 hundred in the hundreds column of the subtrahend, giving 2 hundreds. You need to do this to maintain the original spread between the two numbers.) Then subtract as shown to obtain 9,663.

H	T	O
6	9	$^{1}3$
−	5 4	5
6	4	8

Subtract the ones:
13 − 5 = 8.

Subtract the tens:
9 tens − 5 tens = 4 tens.

Subtract the hundreds:
6 hundreds − 0 hundreds = 6 hundreds.

Th	H	T	O
9,	8	$^{1}4$	$^{1}2$
−	2 1	8 7	9
9,	6	6	3

Subtract the ones: 12 − 9 = 3.

Subtract the tens: 14 tens − 8 tens = 6 tens.

Subtract the hundreds: 8 hundreds − 2 hundreds = 6 hundreds.

Subtract the thousands: 9 thousands − 0 thousands = 9 thousands.

Error Pattern 11

Error Pattern 11a: When one of the digits in a given place-value position is 0, some students record 0 as the difference for that position.

```
   9  0
 - 7  4
 ──────
   2  0
```

The student subtracts 4 from 0 and obtains 0.

```
   8  6  7
 -    5  0
 ─────────
   8  1  0
```

The student subtracts 0 from 7 and obtains 0.

```
       0  12
   8   ̶1̶  ̶2̶
 - 2   6   3
 ───────────
   6   0   9
```

The student renames 1 ten and 12 ones as 0 tens and 12 ones. But then the student subtracts 6 tens from 0 tens and obtains 0.

```
   5,  0  0  4
 -      6  1  0
 ─────────────
   5,  0  0  0
```

The student obtains a difference of 0 in each place-value position where a 0 occurs— regardless of what is being subtracted.

Error Pattern 11b: When a number is subtracted from itself in a place-value position, some students fail to record a difference of 0. (This, of course, is only an issue when that 0 serves as a placeholder in the difference.)

```
        6  10
    8   ̶7̶  ̶0̶
  - 3   6   3
  ───────────
    5       7
```

The difference, 0, in the tens column (from 6 tens − 6 tens) is omitted.

Intervention

For students who obtain 20 when they compute 90 − 74, have them find 90 − 70. They should conclude that 90 − 70 = 20. **Ask,** "Can both 90 − 74 and 90 − 70 have the same answer? Explain." (No. Sample: Because you are subtracting different amounts from 90, the answers have to be different. Because 74 is greater than 70, the answer to 90 − 70 has to be greater than the answer for 90 − 74.)

You may also want students to discuss what procedures they used to obtain an incorrect result. They may explain that they used the following erroneous rules: "0 minus any number is that number" or "any number minus 0 is 0." Some students obtain a 0 difference because they confuse subtracting 0 with multiplying by 0.

Use the Alternative Subtraction Algorithm (Intervention for Error Pattern 8), emphasizing the need for regrouping and renaming when subtracting from 0. Also, bring out that when you subtract 0 from any number, the result is that number.

For students who obtain 57 when they compute 870 − 363, have them use estimation to consider whether or not 57 is a reasonable result. They should conclude that subtracting about 400 from 900 cannot possibly be about 60.

Using Student Journaling: You may also want students to write several word problems that can be solved by using subtraction. Discuss with students some of the actions and problem structures for subtraction (see pages 18–19), and have students explain why the actions written into their problems suggest that subtraction should be used.

Follow-Up Activity: Editor Error Search (+/−)
(See page 158 for the activity. Students work individually or in pairs. Complete answers, including answers for the extension, are on page 196.)

This activity is ideal to use at the end of the unit on subtraction because it reinforces and provides a review of addition and subtraction skills and concepts in a motivating way.

In this activity, students pretend they are mathematics editors for a textbook company. Their job is to correct all the errors they can find in a "manuscript" on addition and subtraction. Because the manuscript includes spelling and grammatical errors (as well as math errors), this activity integrates language arts skills with math.

Students often enjoy playing the role of a teacher, and in particular, correcting errors made by someone else. As such, students may become so engrossed in uncovering the errors that they may not be cognizant of the "disguised drill" nature of the activity.

This activity is designed to provide the following benefits to students:

It reinforces editing and proofreading skills.

It encourages students to *think* about what they read.

It helps students become more discriminating readers of written problems.

It provides a vehicle for students to play the role of teacher.

It provides a source for alternative assessment. Being able to see that something is wrong often only occurs if the basic processes have been understood.

Extension for Editor Error Search

As an extension to the Editor Error Search activity, have students work in small groups to discuss the incorrect answers in the manuscript and try to describe a possible *error pattern* for each error. (Each error in the manuscript is based on an error pattern.) For example, for the first error (35 + 4 = 79), 4 was added to the 5 and to the 3 tens to incorrectly obtain 79.

Instructional Game: Target Math (+/−)
(See pages 159–162 for the game rules, game board, and problems to use. This game is teacher-directed—with the entire class, divided into four or five teams, playing the game together.)

The problems used in this game are based on addition/subtraction computation concepts and problem solving. The problems are organized according to five levels of difficulty—from 5-point problems to 25-point problems. In this game, each student participates by selecting the level of difficulty of a problem according to his or her personal desires. It is also a game where keen concentration can help a team win. *The game may be played at any time during the unit.*

Practice Exercises
Subtraction of Whole Numbers

Part 1

1. $15 - 6 =$ _____

2. $18 - 9 =$ _____

3. $12 -$ _____ $= 4$

4. $16 -$ _____ $= 9$

5. _____ $- 7 = 8$

6. _____ $- 9 = 1$

7. $17 - 8 =$ _____

8. _____ $- 7 = 7$

Part 2

9.
```
    9 9
 -    9
-------
```

10.
```
  7 5 8
-   4 0
-------
```

11.
```
  8 0 6
-     4
-------
```

12.
```
  8 7 0
- 8 6 0
-------
```

13.
```
  9, 8 7 6
- 6, 7 7 6
----------
```

14.
```
  5, 9 0 4
-    9 0 3
----------
```

15. $879 - 27$

16. $9,987 - 80$

Part 3

17.
```
  5 7
- 2 9
-----
```

18.
```
  5 2 9
- 4 6 8
-------
```

19.
```
  9 1 2
- 6 9 7
-------
```

20.
```
  7 7 4
-   6 5
-------
```

21.
```
  6, 8 3 6
- 1, 8 6 6
----------
```

22.
```
  5, 2 9 1
-    8 6 3
----------
```

23. $268 - 9$

24. $6,987 - 188$

Part 4

25.
```
  9 0
- 5 9
-----
```

26.
```
  7 6 0
- 2 6 4
-------
```

27.
```
  7 0 2
-   9 5
-------
```

28.
```
  4 0 4
- 3 4 0
-------
```

29.
```
  5, 0 0 1
- 2, 7 1 3
----------
```

30.
```
  8, 0 0 0
-    8 9 9
----------
```

31. $600 - 8$

32. $2,300 - 222$

QUESTIONS FOR TEACHER REFLECTION

1. When teaching the addition/subtraction facts, why is it important to present the unknown in different positions? Discuss how the instructional game *Balance the +/– Number Sentence!* promotes student fluency with addition and subtraction. How are those two operations related?

2. Discuss how you would teach the traditional algorithm for subtraction of whole numbers in a manner that reduces the chances your students may develop misunderstandings that lead to error patterns. Use specific examples, including one where students must "cross 0s" in the minuend.

3. Compare and contrast the traditional algorithm for subtraction with an alternative algorithm for subtraction. Discuss any advantages or disadvantages of using either algorithm.

4. Choose one of the subtraction error patterns that you believe is practiced by many students. Explain what a student did and what mathematical concept or procedure was likely misunderstood. Provide a specific strategy you would use with students to correct that misunderstanding and error.

5. Explain how you would teach students how to use mental math to find $80 - 27$.

6. Invent your own strategy or algorithm to find the difference $507 - 138$. Compare your method with the traditional subtraction algorithm in terms of efficiency, ease of use for a struggling student, and student understanding of the subtraction process. Is your method valid to be used to solve any problem involving the subtraction of whole numbers? Explain.

Unit 3

Multiplication of Whole Numbers

The 20-question Diagnostic Test for Multiplication of Whole Numbers, in multiple-choice format, consists of four parts: multiplication facts, two-digit by one-digit multiplication, three- or four-digit by one-digit multiplication, and multiplying by a two-digit number. The test allows you to pinpoint specific skills and concepts that require more student work. For information on how to use this test to help identify specific student error patterns, see pages 80 through 82.

Students should be encouraged to use estimation to check to see if their answers are reasonable. Reproducible lessons for estimating products using front-end estimation and for estimating using compatible numbers (for all operations) are on pages 167 and 176, respectively.

Pages 163 through 172 provide instructional games and follow-up activities (reproducible) to support multiplication concepts.

Diagnostic Test
Multiplication of Whole Numbers

Multiple Choice: Circle the correct answer. If your answer is not given, circle *Not here.*

Part 1

1. $8 \times 7 = \square$ **A** 48   **B** 54   **C** 56   **D** 63   **E** Not here

2. $6 \times 9 = \square$ **A** 45   **B** 54   **C** 56   **D** 72   **E** Not here

3. $9 = 1 \times \square$ **A** 1   **B** 8   **C** 9   **D** 10   **E** Not here

4. $7 \times \square = 63$ **A** 6   **B** 7   **C** 8   **D** 9   **E** Not here

5. $\square = 8 \times 0$ **A** 0   **B** 1   **C** 8   **D** 9   **E** Not here

Part 2

6. $\square = 7 \times 10$ **A** 0   **B** 7   **C** 17   **D** 70   **E** Not here

7. $5 \times 60 = \square$ **A** 0   **B** 3   **C** 30   **D** 300   **E** Not here

8. $\begin{array}{r} 16 \\ \times \ 3 \\ \hline \end{array}$ **A** 48   **B** 68   **C** 111   **D** 318   **E** Not here

9. $\begin{array}{r} 27 \\ \times \ 3 \\ \hline \end{array}$ **A** 41   **B** 61   **C** 81   **D** 121   **E** Not here

10. $\begin{array}{r} 47 \\ \times \ 8 \\ \hline \end{array}$ **A** 96   **B** 376   **C** 385   **D** 726   **E** Not here

```
    6  5  8
×        3
```
A 24   **B** 1,854   **C** 1,974   **D** 181,524   **E** Not here

```
    4  9  6
×        2
```
A 502   **B** 821   **C** 992   **D** 1,202   **E** Not here

```
    7  2  5
×        8
```
A 5,660   **B** 5,800   **C** 6,214   **D** 8,880   **E** Not here

```
  7, 0  4  9
×           5
```
A 35,245   **B** 35,005   **C** 45,005   **D** 3,502,045   **E** Not here

```
  8, 0  0  9
×           6
```
A 4,854   **B** 48,004   **C** 48,045   **D** 48,054   **E** Not here

$40 \times 500 = $ _____   **A** 20   **B** 200   **C** 2,000   **D** 20,000   **E** Not here

```
    1  6
×  1  3
```
A 64
B 118
C 208
D 1,918
E Not here

18.
```
    8  4
×  2  7
```
A 756
B 1,628
C 2,268
D 166,428
E Not here

```
    4  1  3
×      8  9
```
A 7,021
B 8,677
C 36,757
D 53,917
E Not here

20.
```
    3  8  7
×        8  0
```
A 3,096
B 24,460
C 24,750
D 30,960
E Not here

79

ITEM ANALYSIS FOR DIAGNOSTIC TEST
Multiplication of Whole Numbers

Using the Item Analysis Table

- The correct answer for each item on the Diagnostic Test is indicated by a ✓ in the Item Analysis Table on page 82.

- Each *incorrect* answer choice is keyed to a specific error pattern and corresponding Intervention Activity found on pages 83 through 108. Because each item on the Diagnostic Test is an item that is analyzed in one of the error patterns, teachers may be able to use the Intervention Activities with identical problems that students may have missed on the test.

- Students should be encouraged to circle *Not here* if their obtained answer is not one of the given answer choices. Although *Not here* is never a correct answer on the Diagnostic Test, the use of this answer choice should aid in the diagnostic process. The intention is that students who do not see their obtained answer among the choices will select *Not here* rather than guess at one of the other choices. This should strengthen the likelihood that students who select an incorrect answer choice actually made the error associated with an error pattern.

- The Item Analysis Table should only be used as a *guide*. Although many errors are procedural in nature, others may be due to an incorrect recall of facts or carelessness. A diagnostic test is just one of many tools that should be considered when assessing student work and making prescriptive decisions. Before being certain that a student has a misconception about a procedure or concept, further analysis may be needed (see below). This is especially true for students who frequently select *Not here* as an answer choice.

- A set of practice exercises, keyed to each of the four parts of the Diagnostic Test, is provided on page 109. Because the four parts of the set of practice exercises match the four parts on the Diagnostic Test, the set of practice exercises could be used as a posttest.

Using Teacher-Directed Questioning and Journaling

Discussions and observations should be used to help distinguish misconceptions about concepts and procedures (which often are discovered by examining error patterns) from student carelessness or lack of fact recall. Any discussion of errors should be done in a *positive* manner—with the clear purpose being to get inside student thinking. The Intervention Activities are replete with teacher-directed questioning, frequently asking students to *explain their reasoning*. Students should also be asked to *write* about their thinking as they work through an algorithm—and, when alternative algorithms are used, explain why they may prefer one algorithm over another. You may also want students to write word problems based on *multiplication*—and then explain why multiplication can be used to solve them. This would be a good time to discuss with students the various actions and problem structures for multiplication (see pages 20–21).

Additional Resources for Multiplication

- A lesson on using *front-end estimation* is provided on page 167; a lesson on using *compatible numbers* for estimation (for all operations) is on page 176. These lessons may be used at any point in the instructional process. When students engage in estimation activities, they should discuss why they believe a computed answer may or may not be reasonable. Students should also compare and contrast estimation strategies.

- Instructional games and follow-up activities designed to promote multiplication concepts are provided on pages 163 through 172. This material may be used at any point in the instructional process. The game *How Close Can You Get?* promotes estimation skills in a motivating way. The follow-up activity *Editor Error Search* provides a rich opportunity for students to play the role of editor to find and correct errors in a manuscript. Students also are asked to discuss the error patterns they observe in the manuscript.

The correct answer for each item on the Diagnostic Test is indicated by a ✓ in this table.

	Item	Answer Choices				Topic	Practice Exercises
		A	B	C	D		
	1	Error 1a	Error 1a	✓	Error 1a or 2	Multiplication facts	Part 1, p.
	2	Error 1a or 2	✓	Error 1a	Error 1a	Multiplication facts	Part 1, p.
	3	Error 1b	Error 1b	✓	Error 1b	Multiplication facts	Part 1, p.
	4	Error 1a or 2	Error 1a	Error 1a or 2	✓	Multiplication facts	Part 1, p.
Part 1	5	✓	Error 1b	Error 1b	Error 1b	Multiplication facts	Part 1, p.
	6	Error 8b	Error 3a	Error 1a	✓	2-digit by 1-digit multiplication	Part 2, p.
	7	Error 8b	Error 3a or b	Error 3a or b	✓	2-digit by 1-digit multiplication	Part 2, p.
	8	✓	Error 5a	Error 6	Error 8a	2-digit by 1-digit multiplication	Part 2, p.
	9	Error 5b	Error 4	✓	Error 5a	2-digit by 1-digit multiplication	Part 2, p.
Part 2	10	Error 5b	✓	Error 6	Error 5a	2-digit by 1-digit multiplication	Part 2, p.
	11	Error 8b	Error 4	✓	Error 8a	3- or 4-digt by 1-digit multiplication	Part 3, p.
	12	Error 5b	Error 6	✓	Error 5a	3- or 4-digt by 1-digit multiplication	Part 3, p.
	13	Error 4	✓	Error 6	Error 5a	3- or 4-digt by 1-digit multiplication	Part 3, p.
	14	✓	Error 4	Error 5a	Error 8a	3- or 4-digt by 1-digit multiplication	Part 3, p.
Part 3	15	Error 3a	Error 4	Error 6	✓	3- or 4-digt by 1-digit multiplication	Part 3, p.
	16	Error 3a	Error 3a	Error 3b or 7	✓	Multiplying by a 2-digit number	Part 4, p.
	17	Error 7	Error 8b	✓	Error 8a	Multiplying by a 2-digit number	Part 4, p.
	18	Error 7	Error 8b	✓	Error 8a	Multiplying by a 2-digit number	Part 4, p.
	19	Error 7	Error 5b	✓	Error 5a	Multiplying by a 2-digit number	Part 4, p.
Part 4	20	Error 7 or 3a	Error 4	Error 6	✓	Multiplying by a 2-digit number	Part 4, p.

ERROR PATTERNS & INTERVENTION ACTIVITIES
Multiplication of Whole Numbers

Error Pattern 1

Error Pattern 1a: Some students have difficulty recalling basic multiplication facts (through 9×9).

Error Pattern 1b: When multiplying a nonzero number and 0, some students write the nonzero number for the product. When one of the factors is 1, some students write 1 for the product. Others "add 1" when they multiply by 1.

$$8 \times 0 = 8 \qquad 0 \times 5 = 5 \qquad 9 \times 1 = 1 \qquad 1 \times 9 = 10$$

Error Pattern 1c: Some students do not understand the concept of "turn-around facts" (based on the *Commutative Property of Multiplication*) when recalling the facts. These students may know that, say, $9 \times 7 = 63$, but they may not realize that 7×9 is also equal to 63.

Intervention

The Intervention Activities for the multiplication facts is divided into two main sections. Section I addresses general strategies to help students learn the facts. These include drawing intersecting line segments, shading a grid, using fingers, and making/using a multiplication table. Section II details strategies to help students learn *specific* categories of facts (beginning with the 2s, moving on to the 5s, then on to the 0s and 1s, and so on). Van de Walle (2001), citing several researchers, states that it has been "recognized that children use different thought processes with different facts" and that "there is a strong interest among mathematics educators in the idea of directly teaching strategies to children" (p. 129).

I. General Strategies for Learning the Facts

- **Drawing Intersecting Line Segments:** To find a product, say, 4×9, have students draw 9 vertical segments and 4 horizontal segments that intersect (cross) the vertical segments as shown below. **Ask,** "Why are we able to find the product by counting the points of intersection? How could you count them quickly?" (Sample: Because there are 9 points of intersection in each row, you can use the points of intersection to help you skip count by 9s: 9, 18, 27, 36. So, $4 \times 9 = 36$.)

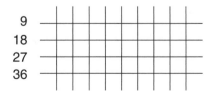

- **Shading a Grid:** Provide students with a set of exercises and a grid as shown at right (for finding the facts from 1×7 through 9×7). For the 7s, use a grid of nine rows with seven columns in each row. (For the 8s, the grid would have nine rows with eight columns in each row.)

$1 \times 7 =$ ___7___

$2 \times 7 =$ _____

$3 \times 7 =$ _____

$4 \times 7 =$ _____

$5 \times 7 =$ _____

$6 \times 7 =$ _____

$7 \times 7 =$ _____

$8 \times 7 =$ _____

$9 \times 7 =$ _____

Have students shade one row at a time to show each group of 7 squares for the fact that is being considered. The first row in the grid is shaded to show 1 group of 7, or $1 \times 7 = 7$. Students record the 7 to complete the multiplication fact. When the second row is shaded, they are showing 2 groups of 7, or $2 \times 7 = 14$. So, they record 14 to complete the fact 2×7. When the entire grid is shaded, students should skip count by 7s and relate what they count to the respective fact.

- **Using Fingers:** Students may enjoy producing the multiplication facts from 5×5 through 9×9 by using their fingers. A method for using fingers to produce those facts, *Touching on the Facts With Your Fingers,* is provided in blackline form on page 165. It is interesting to note that the word *digit* comes from the Latin *digitus,* meaning "finger"—so this may be a natural way to help students master the facts. (For teacher edification, a justification proving *why* the finger multiplication algorithm works is provided on page 166. The proof is based on elementary algebra and is *not* intended for use with students at this level.)

- **Making/Using a Multiplication Table:** Have students use any of the aforementioned strategies to help them complete a multiplication table. (A blank multiplication table is provided on page 190.) Once the table is completed, have students study it for patterns. **Ask,** "How can you use the table to skip count by 8s?" (Sample: Begin with the 8 in the 8 row, and count across; or begin with the 8 in the 8 column, and count down.) Relate the skip counting to the respective facts.

Students may need to refer to the table, as necessary, until they have mastered the facts. Ultimately, rote memorization may be required for some facts—but use of the general strategies described above and the specific ones that follow should lessen the number of facts to be memorized.

To further promote the learning of the facts, have students use the table to help complete multiplication facts prepared as shown below—with the unknowns in *different* positions.

×	0	1	2	3	4	5	6	7	8	9
0	0	0	0	0	0	0	0	0	0	0
1	0	1	2	3	4	5	6	7	8	9
2	0	2	4	6	8	10	12	14	16	18
3	0	3	6	9	12	15	18	21	24	27
4	0	4	8	12	16	20	24	28	32	36
5	0	5	10	15	20	25	30	35	40	45
6	0	6	12	18	24	30	36	42	48	54
7	0	7	14	21	28	35	42	49	56	63
8	0	8	16	24	32	40	48	56	64	72
9	0	9	18	27	36	45	54	63	72	81

$$8 \times 7 = \square$$

$$6 \times \square = 48$$

$$63 = \square \times 7$$

II. Strategies for Learning Specific Categories of Facts

These strategies are organized so that you may progress with students from what may be the easiest facts to those that may be more difficult. All of the facts through 9×9 are covered in this section. The use of models, properties of operations, patterns, and mathematical reasoning (relating new facts to what students already know about other facts) should lessen the need for students to master the facts by using rote memorization. (It should be noted that some students will need additional work—beyond what is provided in this book—in order to attain automaticity.)

Facts Involving the 2s: Doubles (Error Patterns 1a and 1c)

Students who are learning the multiplication facts should already know the addition facts. So, advise them that the facts that have 2 as a factor are equivalent to adding doubles:

$$2 \times 5 \rightarrow \text{Related addition double: } 5 + 5 = 10$$

Point out that not only is 2×5 a double, but so is 5×2. To illustrate that $2 \times 5 = 5 \times 2$, often called "turn-around facts" (based on the *Commutative Property of Multiplication*), provide illustrations like these:

2 groups of 5 each

2 × 5 = 10

5 groups of 2 each

5 × 2 = 10

Have students use a multiplication table to review the facts where 2 is a factor. Shade a multiplication table as shown at the right (or have students make and shade a table).

×	0	1	2	3	4	5	6	7	8	9
0			0							
1			2							
2	0	2	4	6	8	10	12	14	16	18
3			6							
4			8							
5			10							
6			12							
7			14							
8			16							
9			18							

Ask, "How many facts in the table involve doubles (those shown by the shaded products)?" (19 facts.) Have students recite specific facts (such as $2 \times 6 = 12$) for specific products shaded in the table.

Ask, "When the table is completed to show all of the products, how many facts will there be in all? How did you obtain your answer?" (100 facts. Sample: There are 10 rows of 10 facts each in the table. Counting by 10s, you go 10, 20, 30, all the way to 100.)

Facts With 5 as a Factor:
Counting by 5s on a Clock (Error Pattern 1a)

To reinforce the facts for the 5s (any fact where 5 is the first or second factor), have students count by 5s to 45. Then connect the multiples of 5 to the facts for 5. Point out that 5 is 1×5 (or 5×1), 10 is 2×5 (or 5×2), 15 is 3×5 (or 5×3), and so on.

To help students count by 5s, have them use the minute hand on a clock. For the clock at the right, students begin at the 12. Then they move their finger to the 1 and say, "5." Then they point to the 2 and say, "10," then they move forward on the clock and say "15," "20," "25," "30," "35," and "40" (ending at the 8).

Then, have students complete the following sentence: The clock shows __?__ minutes past the hour. (40.)

Emphasize that we have counted 8 groups of 5. **Ask,** "What multiplication fact have we shown?" ($8 \times 5 = 40$.)

Have students use a multiplication table to review the facts where 5 is a factor. Shade a multiplication table as shown below to highlight the facts that involve 5s. **Ask,** "How many of the 100 basic facts involve 5s?" (19 facts.)

×	0	1	2	3	4	5	6	7	8	9
0						0				
1						5				
2						10				
3						15				
4						20				
5	0	5	10	15	20	25	30	35	40	45
6						30				
7						35				
8						40				
9						45				

You may want students to record the facts for the 5s in the table they previously made for the doubles. Point out that two of the facts for the 5s—namely, 2×5 and 5×2—have already been learned as doubles. Have students examine the "combined" table. **Ask,** "How many of the 100 basic facts are either doubles or 5s?" (Sample: $19 + 17$, or 36, of the facts are either doubles or 5s.) Conclude by pointing out that *more than a third* of the facts should thus be relatively easy for students to learn.

Facts With 0 or 1 as a Factor: Counting Down; Wallets (Error Pattern 1b)

Some students confuse multiplication facts involving 0 or 1 with addition facts involving 0 or 1. Some examples follow.

- For $8 + 0$, students have learned that the 8 "stays the same." But although $8 \times 0 = 0$, some students think $8 \times 0 = 8$.

- For $6 + 1$, students have learned the "1 more idea." But although $6 \times 1 = 6$ (with the 6 "staying the same"), some students think that $6 \times 1 = 7$. Others write 1 as the product.

To help students understand the concept that 1 times any number is equal to that number (as described by the *Identity Property of Multiplication*), and that 0 times any number is equal to 0, provide them with small objects (such as beans) and a set of exercises as shown below.

a. Make 3 rows of 4. $3 \times 4 = $ _____

b. Remove one row of 4. Now, you have 2 rows of 4. $2 \times 4 = $ _____

c. Remove one more row of 4. Now, you have 1 row of 4. $1 \times 4 = $ _____

d. Remove the last row of 4. Now, you have 0 rows of 4. $0 \times 4 = $ _____

While students are doing the exercises and removing successive rows of objects, develop the pattern of answers to bring out the idea that the product of 1 and any number is that number, and the product of 0 and any number is 0.

$$
\begin{aligned}
3 \times 4 &= \underline{12} \\
2 \times 4 &= \underline{8} \quad -4 \\
1 \times 4 &= \underline{4} \quad -4 \\
0 \times 4 &= \underline{0} \quad -4
\end{aligned}
$$

To further amplify the concepts of multiplying by 0 or 1, have students think of wallets and dollars.

- **Ask,** "How many dollars would you have if you had 1 wallet containing 0 dollars?" (0 dollars.) Relate that to $1 \times 0 = 0$. Repeat for 2 wallets each containing 0 dollars, and so on. For each question, provide a drawing and the related fact as shown below at the left. **Ask,** "Suppose you had 50 wallets each containing 0 dollars. How much money would you have?" (0 dollars.)

- **Ask,** "How many dollars would you have if you had 1 wallet containing 1 dollar? (1 dollar.) Relate that to $1 \times 1 = 1$. Repeat for 2 wallets each containing 1 dollar, and so on. For each question, provide a drawing and the related fact as shown below at the right. **Ask,** "Suppose you had 50 wallets each containing 1 dollar. How much money would you have?" (50 dollars.)

$$3 \times 0 = 0 \qquad\qquad 5 \times 1 = 5$$

Have students use a multiplication table to review the facts where a 0 or a 1 is a factor. Shade a multiplication table as shown to highlight those facts. Ask, "How many of the 100 basic facts involve a 0 or a 1?" (36 facts.)

×	0	1	2	3	4	5	6	7	8	9
0	0	0	0	0	0	0	0	0	0	0
1	0	1	2	3	4	5	6	7	8	9
2	0	2								
3	0	3								
4	0	4								
5	0	5								
6	0	6								
7	0	7								
8	0	8								
9	0	9								

You may want students to record the facts involving 0 or 1 in the table they previously made for the doubles and 5s. Have students examine the "combined" table. **Ask,** "How many of the 100 basic facts are doubles, 5s, 0s, or 1s?" (64 facts.) Point out to students that about two thirds of the basic facts should thus be relatively easy for them to learn.

×	0	1	2	3	4	5	6	7	8	9
0	0	0	0	0	0	0	0	0	0	0
1	0	1	2	3	4	5	6	7	8	9
2	0	2	4	6	8	10	12	14	16	18
3	0	3	6			15				
4	0	4	8			20				
5	0	5	10	15	20	25	30	35	40	45
6	0	6	12			30				
7	0	7	14			35				
8	0	8	16			40				
9	0	9	18			45				

Facts With 3 as a Factor: Using Doubles to Find 3 Times a Number (Error Pattern 1a)

This strategy is based on *mathematical reasoning*. To develop the facts where 3 is a factor, students should first think of multiplying by 2. Then, they add one more group. For 3×7, students should think of 2×7, and then one more group of 7. So, $3 \times 7 = 14 + 7$, or 21.

To promote the reasoning of "using doubles and one more group" to find 3×7, ask students to outline a three-by-seven rectangle on grid paper. Then ask them to shade the first two rows of the rectangle in red. **Ask,** "How many red squares are there?" (14 red squares.) **Ask,** "How do you know?" (Sample: Because there are 2 rows of 7 squares each, you can find $2 \times 7 = 14$.) Then, ask students to shade the third row in yellow. Ask, "How many groups of 7 are shaded in all in the rectangle?" (3 groups.) **Ask,** "How can you use the 2 groups of red squares and the 1 group of yellow squares to show that $3 \times 7 = 21$?" (Sample: There are 2 groups of 7, and 1 more group of 7. So, $14 + 7 = 21$.)

Think:

$$3 \times 7 = (2 \times 7) + (1 \times 7) =$$
$$14 \quad + \quad 7 \quad = 21.$$

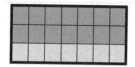

Repeat the activity to show how to find 3×9 on a grid by considering 2 groups of 9 and then 1 more group of 9. After students shade two rows of 9 in red and one row of 9 in yellow, they should think: $3 \times 9 = (2 \times 9) + (1 \times 9) = 18 + 9 = 27$.

Use additional examples as needed to lead students to conclude that they can use what they already know about the 2s to find products where 3 is a factor. Then, have students complete a multiplication table to show the products where 3 is a factor. Have them skip count by 3s, relating each multiple of 3 to its corresponding multiplication fact.

Facts With 4 as a Factor: Doubling the Doubles (Error Pattern 1a)

This strategy is based on *mathematical reasoning.* To develop the facts where 4 is a factor, students first think of multiplying by 2. Then, they double that result. For 4×8, students should think of 2×8—and then double the answer. So, $4 \times 8 =$ "double 16," or 32.

To promote the reasoning of "doubling the doubles" to find 4×8, ask students to outline a four-by-eight rectangle on grid paper. Then, ask them to shade the first two rows of the rectangle in red. **Ask,** "How many red squares are there?" (16 red squares.) **Ask,** "How do you know?" (Sample: Because there are 2 rows of 8 squares each, you can find $2 \times 8 = 16$.) Then ask students to shade the third and fourth rows in yellow. **Ask,** "How many groups of 8 are shaded in the entire rectangle?" (4 groups.) **Ask,** "How can you use the number of red squares to find the total number of shaded squares in the rectangle?" (Sample: Because the total number of squares is twice the number of red squares, you can double the number of red squares. When you double 16, you get a total of 32 squares.)

Think:

$$4 \times 8 = \text{"double } 2 \times 8\text{"} =$$
$$\text{"double 16"} \quad = 32$$

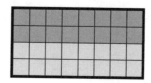

Use additional examples as needed to lead students to conclude that they can use what they already know about the 2s to find products where 4 is a factor. Then, have students complete a multiplication table to show the products for the 4s. Have them use the table to skip count by 4s, relating each multiple of 4 to its corresponding multiplication fact.

Facts With 9 as a Factor: Using Groups of (10 – 1); Using Patterns (Error Pattern 1a)

Distribute small objects or strips of paper showing 10 squares each. With this strategy, students relate the facts involving 9s to facts involving 10s. For 3×9, have students display three rows of 10 objects each (or 3 strips of 10 squares each). **Ask,** "What multiplication fact is represented by your rows of objects (or strips)?" (3×10.) Have students recite out loud as they point to each row: "10, 20, 30." **Ask,** "To represent 3×9, what could we do with the objects (or strips)?" (Sample: Remove one object from each row—or cut off one square from each strip.) Have students remove 1 object (or square) from each row.

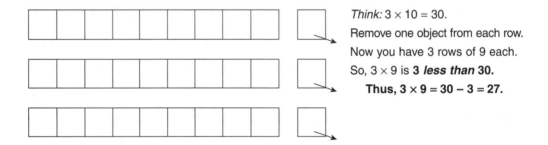

Think: $3 \times 10 = 30$.
Remove one object from each row.
Now you have 3 rows of 9 each.
So, 3×9 is **3 *less than* 30**.
   Thus, $3 \times 9 = 30 - 3 = 27$.

Have students use objects or strips to find 4×9. Then **ask,** "How did you use your objects (or strips) to find 4×9?" (Sample: First, I made 4 rows of 10 each to show $4 \times 10 = 40$. Then, I removed 1 object from each row to show 4×9. Because I removed a total of 4 objects, I knew that 4×9 is 4 less than 4×10. So, $4 \times 9 = 40 - 4 = 36$.) Have students explain how they would find other facts where 9 is one of the factors.

Now, have students complete a multiplication table to show the products where 9 is a factor. Have them skip count by 9s, relating each multiple of 9 to its corresponding fact. Then have students search for *patterns* in the multiplication table. For the following questions, have them consider the products looking down the 9 column at the far right:

Ask, "Beginning with 2×9, how is the tens digit of the product related to the first factor?" (Sample: The tens digit of the product is always 1 less than the first factor.)

Ask, "Beginning with 2×9, what can you say about the sum of the two digits of each product?" (Sample: The sum of the two digits in each product is 9.)

Repeat the above questioning by having students consider the products for 3×9, 4×9, and so on, looking across the 9 row at the bottom of the table.

Now **ask,** "How could you use patterns to find 9×6?" (Sample: I know that the tens digit in the product must be 5. Because the sum of the two digits in the product must equal 9, the ones digit must be 4. So, $9 \times 6 = 54$.) Repeat with other facts for the 9s.

×	0	1	2	3	4	5	6	7	8	9
0										0
1										9
2										18
3										27
4										36
5										45
6										54
7										63
8										72
9	0	9	18	27	36	45	54	63	72	81

The Rest of the Facts: Using Mathematical Reasoning (Error Pattern 1a)

So far, these "Strategies for Learning Specific Categories of Facts" have addressed all of the facts for the 2s, 5s, 0s, 1s, 3s, 4s, and 9s. The only facts that have not yet been addressed are the nine facts shown in the multiplication table at right. Advise students that thanks to the "turn-around facts" (based on the *Commutative Property of Multiplication*), there are only six "different" facts left to address.

Ask, "Which pairs of the remaining facts in the table have the same products?" (6×7 and 7×6, 6×8 and 8×6, and 8×7 and 7×8.)

×	0	1	2	3	4	5	6	7	8	9
0										
1										
2										
3										
4										
5										
6							36	42	48	
7							42	49	56	
8							48	56	64	
9										

Explain that each remaining fact in the table can be learned by relating it to a fact that has already been learned.

- For those facts where 6 is a factor (6×7, 6×8, their corresponding turn-around facts, and 6×6), have students think of multiplying by 5—and then adding one more group of the other number (to make 6 groups). For 6×8, have them draw a six-by-eight rectangle on grid paper. Ask them to shade five rows red and one row yellow. Lead them to conclude that 6×8 is equivalent to 5 groups of 8, plus one more group of 8. So, $6 \times 8 = (5 \times 8) + (1 \times 8)$. Thus, $6 \times 8 = 40 + 8 = 48$. Repeat for the other facts where 6 is a factor.

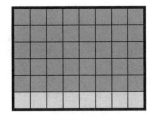

- For 7×7, have students use a strategy similar to what is described above for the 6s. Have students draw a rectangle with 7 rows and the number of columns to match the second factor (in this case, 7). For 7×7, have them shade five rows red and two rows yellow. **Ask,** "How could you use the shaded grid to find 7×7?" (Sample: There are 5 groups of 7, plus two more groups of 7. So, $7 \times 7 = (5 \times 7) + (2 \times 7)$. Thus, $7 \times 7 = 35 + 14 = 49$.)

- The fact 7×8 is developed in a fashion similar to that for 7×7. Of course, once 7×8 is established, students should then also know 8×7.

Error Pattern 2

Some students are unaware of the following rule:

If two numbers are odd, their product is odd.
Otherwise, the product of two numbers is even.

Awareness of this rule, in and of itself, will not necessarily produce correct products. However, such knowledge should enable students to recognize and discard incorrect products such as those below.

$$
\begin{array}{r} 9 \\ \times\,7 \\ \hline 7\ \ 2 \end{array}
\qquad\qquad
\begin{array}{r} 6 \\ \times\,9 \\ \hline 5\ \ 3 \end{array}
\qquad\qquad
\begin{array}{r} 4\ \ 8 \\ \times\quad 8 \\ \hline 3\ \ 8\ \ 3 \end{array}
$$

Intervention

To help students learn the rule about even and odd products, ask them to complete a multiplication table for all products of *two odd numbers*. (See the table below.) Then, ask them to examine the products to search for a pattern. **Ask,** "What pattern do you notice?" (Sample: *The product of two odd numbers is an odd number.*)

×	0	1	2	3	4	5	6	7	8	9
0										
1		1		3		5		7		9
2										
3		3		9		15		21		27
4										
5		5		15		25		35		45
6										
7		7		21		35		49		63
8										
9		9		27		45		63		81

Then ask students to complete a second table for all products of an *odd number and an even number*. (See below.) **Ask,** "What pattern do you notice?" (Sample: *The product of an odd number and an even number is an even number.*)

Finally, ask students to complete a third table for all products of *two even numbers*. (See below.) **Ask,** "What pattern do you notice?" (Sample: *The product of two even numbers is an even number.*)

×	0	1	2	3	4	5	6	7	8	9
0		0		0		0		0		0
1	0		2		4		6		8	
2		2		6		10		14		18
3	0		6		12		18		24	
4		4		12		20		28		36
5	0		10		20		30		40	
6		6		18		30		42		54
7	0		14		28		42		56	
8		8		24		40		56		72
9	0		18		36		54		72	

×	0	1	2	3	4	5	6	7	8	9
0	0		0		0		0		0	
1										
2	0		4		8		12		16	
3										
4	0		8		16		24		32	
5										
6	0		12		24		36		48	
7										
8	0		16		32		48		64	
9										

Error Pattern 3

Error Pattern 3a: Some students fail to record partial products of 0.

10	70	500	8,000	8,000	8,009
× 7	× 9	× 6	× 6	× 60	× 6
7	63	30	48	48 or 480	4,854

Error Pattern 3b: When the product of two nonzero digits contains a 0 (such as $5 \times 6 = 30$), some students ignore that 0 and only include in the product any 0s that appear in the factors.

6 0	5 0 0	6, 0 0 0	5 0 0
× 5	× 6	× 5	× 4 0
3 0	3 0 0	3, 0 0 0	2, 0 0 0

Intervention

To reinforce the multiplication facts where 10 is a factor, ask students to observe a hundred chart. Have them begin with 10 in the chart and skip count by 10s to 100. **Ask,** "Why does the number sentence $4 \times 10 = 40$ show how many numbers are in 4 rows of the chart?" (Sample: Each of the 4 rows has 10 numbers.) **Ask,** "What multiplication fact containing a 10 has 70 for its product?" ($7 \times 10 = 70$.)

1	2	3	4	5	6	7	8	9	10
11	12	13	14	15	16	17	18	19	20
21	22	23	24	25	26	27	28	29	30
31	32	33	34	35	36	37	38	39	40
41	42	43	44	45	46	47	48	49	50
51	52	53	54	55	56	57	58	59	60
61	62	63	64	65	66	67	68	69	70
71	72	73	74	75	76	77	78	79	80
81	82	83	84	85	86	87	88	89	90
91	92	93	94	95	96	97	98	99	100

Have students write multiplication facts where 10 is a factor for other products shown in the chart. **Ask,** "What is always true about the product when one factor is 10?" (Samples: The product always ends in 0. The digit or digits to the left of the 0 in the product always match the digit or digits in the other factor.) **Ask,** "How can you use your pattern to find 10×10?" (Sample: Use one of the 10s as "the other factor." Insert a 0 after that 10 to produce 100.)

Now **ask,** "How do you know that 7 is an incorrect product for 7×10?" (Samples: 7 groups of 10 cannot possibly be equal to just 7. When you multiply by 10, the product always ends in 0. If you have 7 ten-dollar bills, you have $70, not $7.)

To reinforce the importance of each digit in a whole number—namely, that each digit (including 0) is a placeholder with a value—begin by writing the following numbers on the board:

$$\$7 \quad \$77 \quad \$777 \quad \$7,777$$

Ask, "Do you think each of these names the same amount of money? Explain." (No. Sample: $7 is less than $10, but $77 is almost $100. The amount $777 is close to $1,000, but $7,777 is almost $10,000.)

Now, have a similar discussion with students for these amounts of money:

$$\$7 \quad \$70 \quad \$700 \quad \$7,000$$

Students should conclude that the 0s in a numeral are as important as any other digit.

Write the following exercises on the board:

```
    7          7 0         7 0 0          7, 0 0 0
  × 1        ×     1      ×       1      ×           1
 ─────       ───────     ─────────      ─────────────
```

Ask, "Do you think each of these products is the same? Explain." (No. Sample: One group of 7 is equal to 7, one group of 70 is equal to 70, and so on. Because

7 does not equal 70, the products are not the same.) **Ask,** "So, when you multiply a number that contains 0s, why must you record each of those 0s in the product?" (Sample: The 0s serve as placeholders.)

Now provide exercises like the following. For students who might think that $5 \times 600 = 30$ or 300, **ask,** "Does it make sense that 5 groups of 600 would be equal to just 30 or 300? Use play money to explain your reasoning." (No. Sample: When you make 5 piles of $600 each, you could count as follows: $600, $1,200, $1,800, $2,400, $3,000.)

```
    0          6  0  0        7  0  0       7,  0  0  5       8  0  0
  × 9      ×         5     ×         6     ×           6    ×      4  0
  ———      —————————————   ——————————————  ———————————————   ———————————
```

Error Pattern 4

Some students fail to add a digit that is "carried." They may or may not record the "carried" digit or digits in the algorithm.

```
    2              1  2
    2  7           6  5  8          7  0  4  9              1  7
  ×    3        ×        3       ×           5           × 2  6
  ——————        ————————————     ——————————————          ————————
    6  1        18  5  4          35  0  0  5               6  2
                                                          2  4  0
                                                          ————————
                                                          3  0  2
```

Intervention

Note: Base-ten blocks may be used instead of play money.

Supply a multiplication exercise on a place-value grid, a place-value mat on tagboard, and play money. (See pages 184–186 for play money, mat, and grids.) To multiply 27 by 3, guide students in placing play money on the mat to represent 3 groups of $27 each.

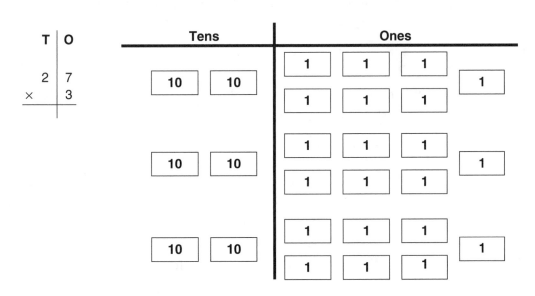

To find the total amount of money, mention that we begin with the one-dollar bills. **Ask,** "How would you find how many one-dollar bills there are in all?" (Sample: There are 3 groups of 7 each, so there are 3×7, or 21 one-dollar bills in all.) **Ask,** "How many digits are you allowed to write in any given place-value position?" (One digit.) **Ask,** "So, what should we do with the one-dollar bills?" (Sample: Combine them. Then, trade each group of 10 one-dollar bills for 1 ten-dollar bill. You end up with 2 ten-dollar bills and 1 one-dollar bill.)

Relate the above to "multiplying the ones" and recording the ones digit (1) in the exercise. **Ask,** "What should we do with the 2 ten-dollar bills?" (Sample: Put them in the tens column of the mat.) Have students put the 2 ten-dollar bills in the tens column of the mat. Relate that to writing a "carried" 2 in the exercise in the tens column.

To find how many ten-dollar bills there are in all, guide students to realize that there are 3 groups of 2 ten-dollar bills each (from the original problem)—plus 2 more ten-dollar bills. Relate that to $(3 \times 2) + 2$, or 8 ten-dollar bills. Have students record the 8 in the tens column in the product of the exercise. Students should conclude that $3 \times 27 = 81$. Review by stressing the importance of recording each "carried" digit in the exercise.

Error Pattern 5

Error Pattern 5a: Some students add a digit that is "carried" before multiplying rather than after multiplying.

Error Pattern 5b: Some students add in a place-value position where a digit is "carried"—but do not multiply in that position.

```
    5
  4 7
×   8
  9 6
```

```
  1   1
  4 9 6
×     2
  5 0 2
```

```
      2
    4 1 3
×   8 9
  3 6 3 7
  5 0 4 0
  8, 6 7 7
```

Intervention

Estimation: Determining If an Answer Is Reasonable

All students, especially those who obtain unreasonable answers, should be encouraged to use estimation either before or after computing. Have students practice performing mental computations for such products as 7×90, 20×50, and 40×800. Then, review rounding and have students estimate products by first rounding the factors. When students round 89 to the nearest ten and 413 to the nearest hundred, they should see that the answer to 89×413 should be about 90×400, or about 36,000. **Ask,** "Are answers such as 53,917 or 8,677 *reasonable? Explain.*" (No. Sample: Even if the problem were 100×413, the product 53,917 would be too great. And 8,677 is unreasonable because that would be about the same as just 20×413.) Being able to find products such as 40×800 is an important skill needed for the alternative algorithm for Error Patterns 6 and 7 (using grids and partial products).

Some students may benefit from using *front-end estimation* as a way to determine if a product is reasonable. The lesson "Using Front-End Estimation to Check for Reasonableness: Multiplication" (page 167) teaches students how to use this strategy. A lesson on using *compatible numbers* to make estimates (for all operations) is on page 176.

Intervention: Using Play Money or Base-Ten Blocks

Supply a multiplication exercise on a place-value grid, a place-value mat on tagboard, and play money. (See pages 184–186 for play money, mat, and grids.) To multiply 496 by 2, guide students in placing play money on the mat to represent 2 groups of $496 each.

H	T	O
4	9	6
×		2

Hundreds	Tens	Ones
100 100 100 100	10 10 10 10 10 10 10 10 10	1 1 1 1 1 1
100 100 100 100	10 10 10 10 10 10 10 10 10	1 1 1 1 1 1

To find the total amount of money, remind students that we begin with the one-dollar bills. **Ask,** "How would you find how many one-dollar bills there are in all?" (Sample: There are 2 groups of 6 each, so there are 2 × 6, or 12 one-dollar bills in all.) **Ask,** "How can we show $12 with the fewest possible bills?" (Sample: Trade so that you end up with 1 ten-dollar bill and 2 one-dollar bills.)

Relate the above to "multiplying the ones" and recording the ones digit (2) in the product of the exercise. **Ask,** "What should we do with the 1 ten-dollar bill?" (Sample: Put it in the tens column on the mat.) Have students put the 1 ten-dollar bill in the tens column of the mat. Relate that to writing a "carried" 1 in the exercise in the tens column.

To find how many ten-dollar bills there are in all, guide students to realize that there are 2 groups of 9 ten-dollar bills each (from the original problem)—plus 1 more ten-dollar bill. **Ask,** "What math expression could we write to show how many ten-dollar bills there are in all?" (Sample: (2 × 9) + 1, or 19 ten-dollar bills.) Relate that to first multiplying in the tens position and then adding the "carried" digit. **Ask,** "How much money is 19 ten-dollar bills?" ($190.) **Ask,** "How could we show $190 with the fewest possible bills?" (Sample: Trade so that you end up with 1 hundred-dollar bill and 9 ten-dollar bills.)

Relate the above to "multiplying the tens" and recording the tens digit in the product of the exercise. **Ask,** "What should we do with the 1 hundred-dollar bill?" (Sample: Put it in the hundreds column of the mat.) Have students put the 1 hundred-dollar bill in the hundreds column. Relate that to writing a "carried" 1 in the hundreds column of the exercise.

H	T	O
1	1	
4	9	6
×		2
	9	2

Hundreds	Tens	Ones
100	10 10 10	1 1
100 100	10 10 10	
100 100	10 10 10	
100 100		
100 100		

To find how many hundred-dollar bills there are in all, guide students to realize that there are 2 groups of 4 hundred-dollar bills each—plus 1 more hundred-dollar bill. Relate that to (2 × 4) + 1, or 9 hundred-dollar bills. Have students record the 9 in the hundreds column in the product of the exercise. Students should conclude that 2 × 496 = 992.

H	T	O
1	1	
4	9	6
×		2
9	9	2

Review the algorithm with students, emphasizing that you *first* multiply in a place-value position—*then* you add any "carried" digit.

Error Pattern 6

Some students "carry" the wrong digit.

```
  8                        6  0                         4  6
     5  6                     7  2  5                3  0  6  6
  ×     3                  ×        8             ×           6
  ─────────                ───────────           ──────────────
    11  1                    62  1  4               18  4  2  3
```

Intervention

Use the Intervention for Error Pattern 5 to bring out that when you multiply the ones, the ones digit of the partial product is recorded in the ones position of the exercise—and the tens digit of that product is "carried" to the tens place. That pattern continues as you multiply in each place-value position.

Alternate Algorithm: Multiplying Using Grids and Partial Products

Students who have difficulty with the renaming process using the traditional algorithm may find more success with the following alternative algorithm that avoids "carrying" digits during the multiplication process. Rather, the algorithm focuses on finding partial products based on the *place value* of the numbers being multiplied. As such, students need to be fluent in finding products such as 8×20 and 8×500. Grids are used to help students determine those partial products. When students use this alternative algorithm for two-digit multiplication (Error Pattern 7), they will need to be fluent with products such as 80×700.

Distribute grid paper to each student or group of students. Advise students that you can model multiplication by outlining a rectangle on grid paper—where the length of the rectangle is one factor and the width is the other factor. The number of squares in the grid outlined by the rectangle is the product.

To find 3×16, outline a rectangle on grid paper that is three-by-sixteen. Draw a heavy vertical rule, as shown below, to mark off the first 10 squares in each row. Write the labels, as shown, to indicate that there are 3 rows of $10 + 6$ squares each. Also, write the exercise to the right of the grid as shown. Note that the model illustrates the *Distributive Property of Multiplication Over Addition*. Here, we will see that $3 \times (10 + 6) = 3 \times 10 + 3 \times 6$.

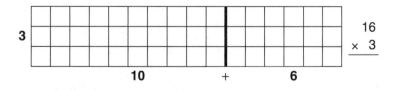

First, multiply the ones. In the grid, there are three rows of 6 ones each. These are denoted by the 18 shaded squares in the grid on the following page. Relate that to $3 \times 6 = 18$ in the exercise.

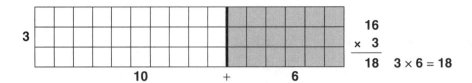

16
× 3
18    $3 \times 6 = 18$

Next, multiply the tens. There are three rows of 1 group of 10 each. These are denoted by the 30 shaded squares in the grid below. Relate that to 3×1 ten in the exercise. Emphasize that 3×1 ten = 3 tens, or 30.

Finally, add the partial products. So, $3 \times 16 = 48$.

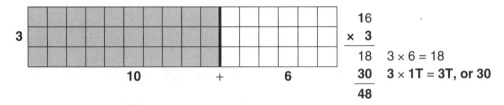

16
× 3
18    $3 \times 6 = 18$
30   **$3 \times 1T = 3T$, or 30**
48

Repeat the process with grids for other exercises where a one-digit number is multiplied by a number between, say, 10 and 20 (such as 6×17). Then, have students use the alternative algorithm without grids for exercises where larger numbers are multiplied by a one-digit number, such as 8×725 (shown at right).

725
×   8
40      $8 \times 5 = 40$
160     $8 \times 2T = 16T$, or 160
5600 $8 \times 7H = 56H$, or 5,600
5,800

Error Pattern 7

When multiplying by a two-digit number, some students record the digits for the second partial product in incorrect place-value positions. These students may not realize that when they multiply by the tens digits of the multiplier, they are multiplying by *tens*. As such, they omit the 0 in the ones position of the partial product.

```
    1  6              5  0                  3  8  7
×  1  3           × 9  5              ×        8  0
    4  8              2  5  0                  0  0  0
    1  6              4  5  0            3  0  9  6
    6  4              7  0  0            3, 0  9  6
```

Intervention

Have students record the exercise on grid paper. This should aid students in keeping the digits in each place-value position aligned. When students multiply by the ones, they should think $3 \times 16 = 48$. But when they multiply by the tens, they should think $1T \times 16 = 16T$, or 160

H	T	O
	1	6
×	1	3
	4	8
1	6	0
2	0	8

Think:

← $3 \times 16 = 48$

← $1T \times 16 = 16T$, or 160

because the 1 in the 13 is in the *tens* place. Advise students that when we multiply by the tens, we automatically write a 0 in the ones place of the partial product as a "shortcut"—and then multiply as we do when we multiply by the ones. Stress, however, that the reason we write the 0 is because we are multiplying by tens.

Alternate Algorithm: Multiplying Using Grids and Partial Products

Students who have difficulty recording digits in the correct place-value positions in the partial products using the traditional algorithm may find more success with the alternative algorithm described for Error Pattern 6. Distribute grid paper to each student or group of students. Shown below is how the alternative algorithm works with two-digit multiplication.

To find 13 × 16, outline a rectangle on grid paper that is thirteen-by-sixteen. Draw a heavy vertical rule, as shown below, to mark off the first 10 squares in each row. Draw a heavy horizontal rule to mark off the first 10 squares in each column. Write the labels, as shown, to indicate that there are thirteen rows of 16 squares each. Also, write the exercise to the right of the grid as shown. Advise students that the grid suggests that we can find the product 13 × 16 by finding (10 + 3) × (10 + 6). Point out that this will involve finding four partial products.

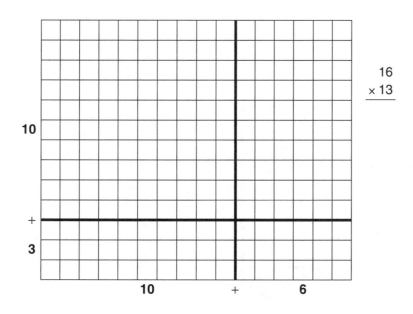

First, multiply the ones. In the grid, there are three rows of 6 each. These are denoted by the 18 shaded squares in the bottom right-hand corner of the grid. Relate that to $3 \times 6 = 18$ in the exercise.

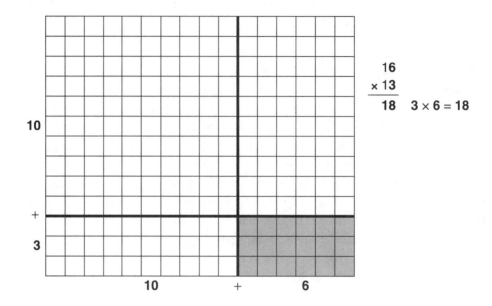

$$\begin{array}{r} 16 \\ \times\, 13 \\ \hline 18 \end{array} \quad 3 \times 6 = 18$$

Next, multiply the tens by the ones. There are three rows of 1 ten each. These are denoted by the 30 shaded squares at the bottom left-hand corner in the grid below. Relate that to 3×1 ten in the exercise. Emphasize that 3×1 ten = 3 tens, or 30.

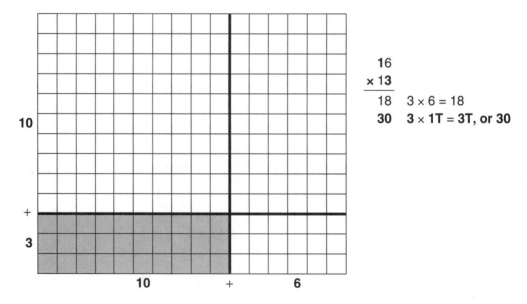

$$\begin{array}{r} 16 \\ \times\, 13 \\ \hline 18 \\ 30 \end{array} \quad \begin{array}{l} 3 \times 6 = 18 \\ 3 \times 1T = 3T, \text{ or } 30 \end{array}$$

Now, multiply the ones by the tens. There is 1 ten row of 6 each (denoted by the 60 shaded squares at the upper right-hand corner of the grid on the following page). Relate that to 1 ten $\times$ 6 in the exercise. Emphasize that 1 ten $\times$ 6 = 6 tens, or 60.

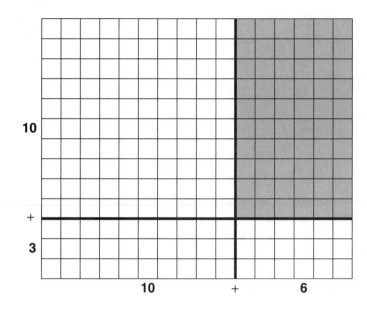

16	
× 13	
18	3 × 6 = 18
30	3 × 1T = 3T, or 30
60	**1T × 6 = 6T, or 60**

To find the fourth partial product, multiply the tens by the tens. There is 1 ten row of 10 (denoted by the 100 shaded squares at the upper left-hand corner). Relate that to 1 ten × 1 ten in the exercise. Emphasize that 1 ten × 1 ten = 1 hundred, or 100.

Finally, add the partial products. So, 13 × 16 = 208.

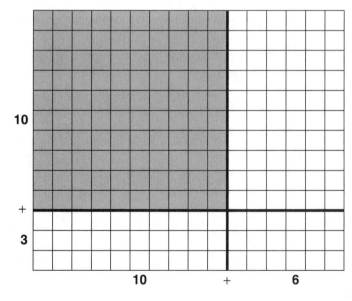

16	
× 13	
18	3 × 6 = 18
30	3 × 1T = 3T, or 30
60	1T × 6 = 6T, or 60
100	**1T × 1T = 1H, or 100**
208	

Note: If you use centimeter grid paper, you can then use base-ten blocks to emphasize the groups of ones, tens, and hundreds in the partial products. For the above example, you can place 18 cubes in the lower right-hand corner to show 18; three rods in the lower left-hand corner to show 3T, or 30; six rods in the upper right-hand corner to show 6T, or 60; and one flat in the upper left-hand corner to show 1H, or 100.

Have students do another example or two using grids to find the product of two numbers each in the teens. For larger numbers, show them how to segment an "empty" rectangle (by tens and ones) to model the algorithm as shown below for 63×25.

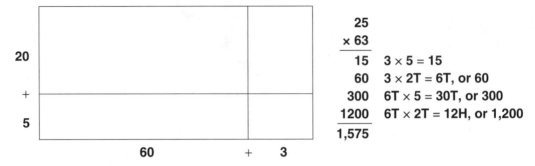

For purposes of teacher edification, it should be noted that the alternative algorithm provides preparation for later work in algebra when students multiply a *binomial* (an expression with two terms) by another binomial. Based on the algorithm, 63×25 is renamed as $(60 + 3) \times (20 + 5)$. The four partial products, 60×20, 60×5, 3×20, and 3×5, are akin to the four partial products produced by the FOIL method used in algebra.

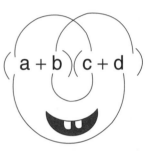

FOIL Method

According to the FOIL method, when $(a + b)(c + d)$ is expanded (multiplied), there are four partial products, as shown below. Spangler (2008) recommends algebra teachers should relate the FOIL method back to the above multiplication algorithm to make a strong connection between algebra and arithmetic. This connection to algebra (a subject often referred to as *generalized arithmetic*) illustrates the belief of Steckroth (2009/2010) that "elementary school mathematics is not elementary at all; it is the cornerstone for all the mathematics that students study in the middle grades and high school" (p. 299).

First terms	Outer terms	Inner terms	Last terms
ac	*ad*	*bc*	*bd*

Finally, the draft *Common Core State Standards* (CCSSO and NGA Center for Best Practices, 2010) states: "There is a world of difference between the student who can summon a mnemonic device such as 'FOIL' to expand a product such as $(a + b)(x + y)$ and a student who can explain where that mnemonic comes from. . . . The student who can explain the rule understands the mathematics, and may have a better chance to succeed at a less familiar task such as expanding $(a + b + c)(x + y)$" (p. 3).

Error Pattern 8

Error Pattern 8a: Some students do not rename, but simply write the partial products in each place-value position.

```
  7  8  6                    8  4                    5  0  9
×        7                 × 2  7                 ×     7  8
 49 56 42                    56 28                   40  0 72
                          16  8  0                   35 63  0
                          16 64 28                   75 63 72
```

Error Pattern 8b: Some students do not multiply the ones, the tens, and the hundreds by each digit of the other factor. Instead, they only multiply digits that have the same place value (erroneously transferring to multiplication what is done in addition).

```
  7  8  6                    8  4                    5  0  9
×        7                 × 2  7                 ×     7  8
        42                 16 28                      0 72
```

Intervention

Have students record the multiplication exercise on grid paper, placing a single digit in each square. This should aid students in keeping the digits in each place-value position aligned. For 7×786, when students multiply by the ones, remind them that only one digit can be recorded in a given place-value position. So the 4 tens in 42 need to be "carried" to the next position—and then added to the partial product obtained from 7×8 tens. For students prone to Error Pattern 8b, advise students that 7×786 means that there are 7 groups of 786 each; hence, the *entire* number (786) needs to be multiplied by 7.

Alternate Algorithm: Lattice Multiplication

Students who experience difficulties with the traditional algorithm for multidigit multiplication may experience success using *lattice multiplication.* For this algorithm, a sieve-like grid (lattice) is used to record the digits of the partial products. Lattice multiplication dates back to tenth-century India (Nelson, Joseph, & Williams, 1993). Fibonacci introduced it to Europe in 1202 in his *Liber abaci (Book of Calculation).* Some teachers, however, believe lattice multiplication "ignores place value," is "just an arrangement of numbers," and has "little value beyond being an alternative multiplication algorithm" (Nugent, 2007, p. 111). Nugent suggests that by integrating place-value concepts into lattice multiplication, student understanding of the overall multiplication process will be promoted. The lattice method described in this book embeds place value.

Provide students with blank lattice multiplication grids. (Blank grids for lattice multiplication are provided on page 108.) To multiply 27×84, follow these three steps:

1. Use large numerals to write 27 along the side of the grid and 84 across the top (above the grid), as shown on the next page.

2. Multiply each digit of one factor by each digit of the other factor. The product goes in the cell that is aligned (vertically and horizontally) with the two factors. When a partial product is a two-digit number (such as in

$7 \times 4 = 28$), record the left-most digit above the diagonal in the cell and the right-most digit below the diagonal. When a partial product is less than 10 (such as in $2T \times 4 = 8T$), record a 0 above the diagonal and the single digit below the diagonal (in this case, 08 is written). The order of computing the partial products does not matter. The key is placing the partial products in the correct cells.

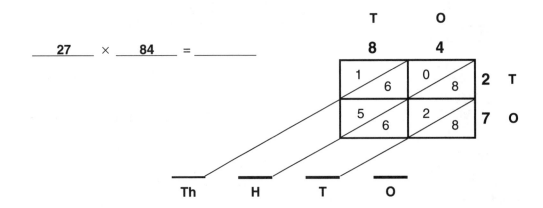

3. Add the partial products (the numbers *inside* the grid) along the diagonals beginning with the bottom right digit. Record the sums in the place-value positions below the grid. When the sum of the digits along a diagonal is 10 or greater, "carry" the tens digit to the next place-value position. In the example, record 8 as the ones digit of the product. Then, find $8 + 2 + 6 = 16$. Record 6 as the tens digit, and "carry" the 1. As shown below, the product is 2,268.

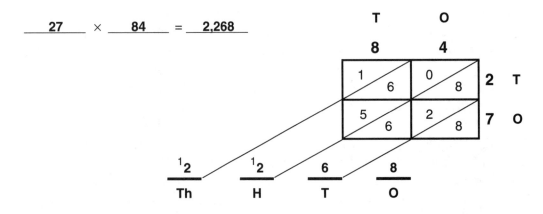

When students add the partial products along the diagonals, be sure to discuss the role of place value in the algorithm—and that ones are added to ones, tens to tens, and so on.

- When students find $7 \times 4 = 28$, point out that the 8 will be added along the diagonal for the ones; the 2 will be added with the tens.

- When students find $2 \times 4 = 08$, emphasize that they are finding 2 tens $\times$ 4. So the answer is 80—and the 8 will be added with the tens.

- When students find $7 \times 8 = 56$, emphasize that they are finding 7×8 tens. So, the answer is 56 tens, or 560. **Ask,** "In what place-value position will the 6 be added?" (Tens position.) **Ask,** "Where will the 5 be added?" (Hundreds position.)

- When students find $2 \times 8 = 16$, emphasize that they are finding 2 tens $\times$ 8 tens. So, the answer is 16 hundreds. **Ask,** "What is the standard form for 16 hundreds?" (1,600.) **Ask,** "In what place-value position will the 6 be added?" (Hundreds position.) **Ask,** "Where will the 1 be added?" (Thousands position.)

Using Student Journaling: Have students select a multiplication algorithm and write about the steps they use to find various products. Also, have students explain which multiplication algorithm they prefer to use and compare and contrast it with other multiplication algorithms.

You may also want students to write several word problems that can be solved by using multiplication. Discuss with students the various actions and problem structures for multiplication (see pages 20–21), and have students explain why the *actions* written into their problems suggest that multiplication can be used.

Follow-Up Activity: Editor Error Search ($\times$)
(See page 172 for the activity. Students work individually or in pairs. Complete answers, including answers for the extension, are on pages 197–198.)

This activity is ideal to use at the end of the unit on multiplication because it reinforces and provides a review of multiplication skills and concepts in a motivating way. Students pretend they are mathematics editors for a textbook company. Their job is to correct all the errors they can find in a "manuscript" on multiplication. Because the worksheet includes spelling and grammatical errors (in addition to math errors), this activity integrates language arts skills with math. This activity is similar to the one for addition/subtraction (on page 158). The student benefits for participating in this activity are detailed on page 73.

Extension for Editor Error Search

As an extension to the Editor Error Search activity, have students work in small groups to discuss the incorrect answers in the manuscript and try to describe a possible *error pattern* for each mathematics error. (Each mathematics error in the manuscript is based on an error pattern—except for Exercises 1 and 3, which are based on a lack of fact recall.) For example, for Exercise 7 ($32 \times 7 = 2,114$), renaming was not done in each place-value position. The partial products (14 and 21) were written directly in the final product.

Grids for Lattice Multiplication

three-digit by one-digit multiplication

_____ × _____ = _____

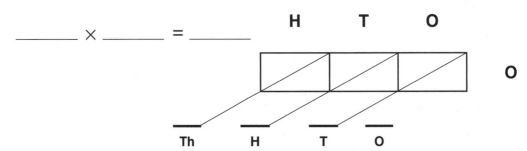

two-digit by two-digit multiplication

_____ × _____ = _____

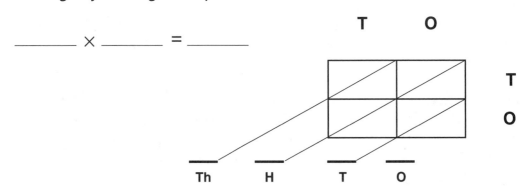

three-digit by two-digit multiplication

_____ × _____ = _____

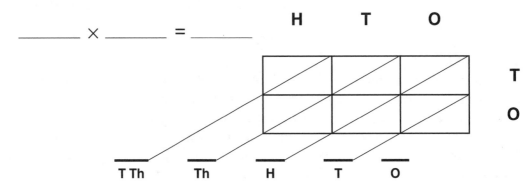

Practice Exercises
Multiplication of Whole Numbers

rt 1

1. $4 \times 8 =$ _____ **2.** $9 \times 3 =$ _____ **3.** _____ $= 8 \times 6$ **4.** $7 \times 1 =$ _____

5. _____ $= 0 \times 6$ **6.** $9 \times$ _____ $= 81$ **7.** $42 = 7 \times$ _____ **8.** _____ $\times 9 = 72$

rt 2

9.
```
   1 0
×    7
```

10.
```
   5 0
×    8
```

11.
```
   1 7
×    4
```

12.
```
   2 5
×    6
```

3.
```
   3 9
×    5
```

14.
```
   7 8
×    8
```

15.
```
   9 1
×    9
```

16.
```
   6 7
×    7
```

rt 3

7.
```
   7 0 0
×      9
```

18.
```
   8, 0 0 0
×        5
```

19.
```
   3 0 8
×      7
```

20.
```
   5 1 6
×      6
```

1.
```
   1, 2 3 4
×        5
```

22.
```
   6, 0 9 8
×        7
```

23.
```
   8, 0 4 0
×        6
```

24.
```
   3, 7 2 8
×        8
```

rt 4

5.
```
   8 0
× 5 0
```

26.
```
   1 9
× 1 9
```

27.
```
   3 9
× 2 7
```

28.
```
   5 6
× 8 3
```

9.
```
   7 0 0
×   6 0
```

30.
```
   9 0 8
×   4 7
```

31.
```
   6 5 4
×   3 0
```

32.
```
   8 9 7
×   8 9
```

QUESTIONS FOR TEACHER REFLECTION

1. Suppose a number of students in your classroom need additional work in mastering the multiplication facts. Discuss some strategies that you would use with those students to build automaticity. Explain what you would tell your students as to why they need to master the multiplication facts.

2. Discuss how you would teach the traditional algorithm for multiplication of whole numbers in a manner that reduces the chances your students may develop misunderstandings that lead to error patterns. Use specific examples.

3. Choose one of the multiplication error patterns that you believe is practiced by many students. Explain what the students did and what mathematical concept or procedure was likely misunderstood. Provide a specific strategy you would use with students to correct that misunderstanding and error.

4. When using the traditional algorithm to multiply two-digit numbers with renaming, why do you multiply the next digit in the multiplicand *before* you add, rather than after? Why do you move the second partial product one space to the left?

5. Compare and contrast the traditional algorithm for multiplication with an alternative algorithm for multiplication. Discuss any advantages or disadvantages of using either algorithm.

6. Suppose your school district asks you to design an intervention program for whole number computation. Describe the components and resources that would be needed to create a successful program. Draw a graphic organizer, such as a flowchart, to show how students might progress and be monitored through the program.

Unit 4

Division of Whole Numbers

Diagnostic Test

The 20-question Diagnostic Test for Division of Whole Numbers, in multiple-choice format, consists of four parts: multiplication facts, two-digit by one-digit division, three- or four-digit by one-digit division, and dividing by a two-digit number. The test allows you to pinpoint specific skills and concepts that require more student work. For information on how to use this test to help identify specific student error patterns, see pages 114 through 116.

Students should be encouraged to use estimation to check to see if their answers are reasonable. Reproducible lessons for estimating quotients using front-end estimation and for estimating using compatible numbers (for all operations) are on pages 175 and 176.

Pages 173 through 181 provide instructional games and follow-up activities (reproducible) to support division and multiplication concepts.

Name _____ Date _____ Class _____

Diagnostic Test
Division of Whole Numbers

Multiple Choice: Circle the correct answer. If your answer is not given, circle *Not here.*

Part 1

1. $48 \div 6 = \square$	**A** 6	**B** 7	**C** 8	**D** 9	**E** Not he
2. $72 \div 9 = \square$	**A** 6	**B** 7	**C** 8	**D** 9	**E** Not he
3. $0 \div 6 = \square$	**A** 0	**B** 1	**C** 6	**D** 60	**E** Not he
4. $3 \div \square = 1$	**A** 1	**B** 2	**C** 3	**D** 4	**E** Not he
5. $6 = \square \div 9$	**A** 3	**B** 6	**C** 36	**D** 54	**E** Not he

Part 2

6. $7\overline{)59}$	**A** 7 R7	**B** 7 R10	**C** 8	**D** 8 R3	**E** Not he
7. $3\overline{)16}$	**A** 5	**B** 5 R1	**C** 32	**D** 50 R1	**E** Not he
8. $2\overline{)37}$	**A** 13	**B** 18 R1	**C** 81 R1	**D** 153 R1	**E** Not he
9. $9\overline{)79}$	**A** 8	**B** 8 R7	**C** 9 R2	**D** 9 R9	**E** Not he
10. $4\overline{)84}$	**A** 2	**B** 12	**C** 20	**D** 21	**E** Not he

Part 3

11. 2$\overline{)7\ 1\ 2}$

    A 301
    B 311
    C 356
    D 3,501 R1
    E Not here

12. 4$\overline{)8\ 0\ 7}$

    A 21 R3
    B 102 R3
    C 201
    D 201 R3
    E Not here

13. 6$\overline{)5\ 1\ 2}$

    A 80 R5
    B 85 R2
    C 163
    D 850 R2
    E Not here

14. 7$\overline{)5,\ 7\ 4\ 2}$

    A 82 R2
    B 806
    C 820 R2
    D 8,200 R2
    E Not here

15. 8$\overline{)3,\ 9\ 0\ 4}$ **A** 488   **B** 884   **C** 2,102   **D** 4,880   **E** Not here

Part 4

16. 8,000 ÷ 20 = ☐   **A** 4   **B** 40   **C** 400   **D** 4,000   **E** Not here

17. 12$\overline{)4\ 0\ 8}$

    A 30
    B 31
    C 34
    D 43
    E Not here

18. 15$\overline{)6,\ 1\ 2\ 9}$

    A 48 R9
    B 408 R9
    C 612 R9
    D 4,080 R9
    E Not here

19. 24$\overline{)1,\ 3\ 8\ 0}$

    A 50
    B 57 R12
    C 69
    D 690
    E Not here

20. 45$\overline{)4,\ 8\ 0\ 9}$

    A 16 R39
    B 106 R39
    C 120 R9
    D 1,202 R1
    E Not here

ITEM ANALYSIS FOR DIAGNOSTIC TEST
Division of Whole Numbers

Using the Item Analysis Table

- The correct answer for each item on the Diagnostic Test is indicated by a ✓ in the Item Analysis Table on page 116.

- Each *incorrect* answer choice is keyed to a specific error pattern and corresponding Intervention Activity found on pages 117 through 134. Because each item on the Diagnostic Test is an item that is analyzed in one of the error patterns, teachers may be able to use the Intervention Activities with identical problems that students may have missed on the test.

- Students should be encouraged to circle *Not here* if their obtained answer is not one of the given answer choices. Although *Not here* is never a correct answer on the Diagnostic Test, the use of this answer choice should aid in the diagnostic process. The intention is that students who do not see their obtained answer among the choices will select *Not here* rather than guess at one of the other choices. This should strengthen the likelihood that students who select an incorrect answer choice actually made the error associated with an error pattern.

- The Item Analysis Table should only be used as a *guide*. Although many errors are procedural in nature, others may be due to an incorrect recall of facts or carelessness. A diagnostic test is just one of many tools that should be considered when assessing student work and making prescriptive decisions. Before being certain that a student has a misconception about a procedure or concept, further analysis may be needed (see below). This is especially true for students who frequently select *Not here* as an answer choice.

- A set of practice exercises, keyed to each of the four parts of the Diagnostic Test, is provided on page 135. Because the four parts of the set of practice exercises match the four parts on the Diagnostic Test, the set of practice exercises could be used as a posttest.

Using Teacher-Directed Questioning and Journaling

Discussions and observations should be used to help distinguish misconceptions about concepts and procedures (which often are discovered by examining error patterns) from student carelessness or lack of fact recall. Any discussion of errors should be done in a *positive* manner—with the clear purpose being to get inside student thinking. The Intervention Activities are replete with teacher-directed questioning, frequently asking students to *explain their reasoning*. Students should also be asked to *write* about their thinking as they work through an algorithm—and, when alternative algorithms are used, explain why they may prefer one algorithm over another. You may also want students to write word problems based on *division*—and then explain why division can be used to solve them. This would be a good time to discuss with students the various actions and problem structures for division (see pages 21–23).

Additional Resources for Division

- A lesson on using front-end estimation is provided on page 175; a lesson on using compatible numbers for estimation (for all operations) is on page 176. These lessons may be used at any point in the instructional process. When students engage in estimation activities, they should discuss why they believe a computed answer may or may not be reasonable. Students should also compare and contrast estimation strategies.

- Instructional games and follow-up activities designed to promote division concepts are provided on pages 173 through 181. This material may be used at any point in the instructional process. The games *Balance the Number Sentence!* and *Target Math* may be used as vehicles for observing student behavior in trial-and-error thinking, computation, and problem solving. The follow-up activity *Abbott and Costello's Number* Non*sense* provides a fun way to examine the meaning of division while uncovering some humorous errors.

The correct answer for each item on the Diagnostic Test is indicated by a ✓ in this table.

	Item	Answer Choices				Topic	Practice Exercises
		A	B	C	D		
	1	Error 1a	Error 1a	✓	Error 1a	Division facts	Part 1, p. 1
	2	Error 1a	Error 1a	✓	Error 1a	Division facts	Part 1, p. 1
	3	✓	Error 1d	Error 1d	Error 1d	Division facts	Part 1, p. 1
	4	Error 1c	Error 1c	✓	Error 1c	Division facts	Part 1, p. 1
Part 1	5	Error 1a	Error 1a	Error 1a	✓	Division facts	Part 1, p. 1
	6	Error 2	Error 2	Error 2 or 5	✓	2-digit by 1-digit division	Part 2, p. 1
	7	Error 2 or 5	✓	Error 3	Error 8	2-digit by 1-digit division	Part 2, p. 1
	8	Error 3	✓	Error 4a	Error 4b	2-digit by 1-digit division	Part 2, p. 1
	9	Error 2 or 5	✓	Error 2	Error 2	2-digit by 1-digit division	Part 2, p. 1
Part 2	10	Errors 1c & 4a	Error 4a	Error 1c	✓	2-digit by 1-digit division	Part 2, p. 1
	11	Error 3 or 5	Error 6	✓	Error 4b	3- or 4-digit by 1-digit division	Part 3, p. 1
	12	Error 7	Error 4a	Error 3 or 5	✓	3- or 4-digit by 1-digit division	Part 3, p. 1
	13	Error 6	✓	Error 3	Error 8	3- or 4-digit by 1-digit division	Part 3, p. 1
	14	Error 7	Error 5	✓	Error 8	3- or 4-digit by 1-digit division	Part 3, p. 1
Part 3	15	✓	Error 4a	Error 3	Error 8	3- or 4-digit by 1-digit division	Part 3, p. 1
	16	Error 7	Error 7	✓	Error 8	Dividing by a 2-digit number	Part 4, p. 1
	17	Error 5	Error 6	✓	Error 4a	Dividing by a 2-digit number	Part 4, p. 1
	18	Error 7	✓	Error 9a	Error 8	Dividing by a 2-digit number	Part 4, p. 1
	19	Error 5	✓	Error 9a	Error 9b	Dividing by a 2-digit number	Part 4, p. 1
Part 4	20	Error 7	✓	Error 9a	Error 9b	Dividing by a 2-digit number	Part 4, p. 1

ERROR PATTERNS & INTERVENTION ACTIVITIES
Division of Whole Numbers

Error Pattern 1

Error Pattern 1a: Some students have difficulty recalling basic division facts (through $81 \div 9$). A lack of understanding of the *do/undo* (inverse) relationship between multiplication and division is often a contributing factor to making these errors.

Error Pattern 1b: When dividing by 1, some students record 1 for the quotient. (For $3 \div 1$, they record 1 for the quotient.)

Error Pattern 1c: Some students are unaware that any *nonzero* number divided by itself is 1. (For $3 \div 3$, they may record 0 or some other value for the quotient.)

Error Pattern 1d: Some students are unaware that 0 divided by any *nonzero* number is 0. (For $0 \div 3$, they may record 3 or some other value for the quotient.) It should be noted that some students are unaware that *0 cannot be a divisor*—and that is why "nonzero" is included in the statements of Error Patterns 1c and 1d.

Intervention

Have students "think multiplication" when they do division by finding the missing part of a division sentence. For example, for $48 \div 6 = \square$, have students think (from right to left), "*What* times 6 makes 48?" If students cannot recall that $8 \times 6 = 48$, have them make or use a multiplication table to help them recall the facts. (A blank table and a completed table are provided on pages 190–191.)

Students could find 6 in the shaded column on the left in the table, then slide across (along dashed arrow) to 48, and finally slide up to see that 8 (circled in the top row) answers "*What* times 6 makes 48?" Repeat the above for $48 \div 8 = \square$. The solid arrows in the table show that 6 answers "*What* times 8 makes 48?"

×	0	1	2	3	4	5	⑥	7	⑧	9
0	0	0	0	0	0	0	0	0	0	0
1	0	1	2	3	4	5	6	7	8	9
2	0	2	4	6	8	10	12	14	16	18
3	0	3	6	9	12	15	18	21	24	27
4	0	4	8	12	16	20	24	28	32	36
5	0	5	10	15	20	25	30	35	40	45
6	0	6	12	18	24	30	36	42	48	54
7	0	7	14	21	28	35	42	49	56	63
8	0	8	16	24	32	40	48	56	64	72
9	0	9	18	27	36	45	54	63	72	81

Repeat with division sentences where the missing part is *not* on the right-hand side of the equal sign, such as $56 \div \square = 8$ or $\square \div 9 = 7$. Such sentences encourage students to think of the equal sign in terms of *equality* and *balance* (rather than of "find the answer").

As you relate division facts to the multiplication facts students already know, bring out the idea of fact families. Provide a multiplication sentence and then have students write the three corresponding related sentences. For $8 \times 9 = 72$, students should write all four facts in the family as shown below.

$8 \times 9 = 72$	$9 \times 8 = 72$
$72 \div 9 = 8$	$72 \div 8 = 9$

Error Patterns 1b through 1d: Give each student or group of students three small objects and three paper cups. **Ask,** "How could you use your objects and cups to model $3 \div 3$? What quotient do you get?" (Sample: Equally place the three objects into the three cups. You end up with one object in each cup. So, $3 \div 3 = 1$.) **Ask,** "How could you use your objects and cups to model $3 \div 1$? What quotient do you get?" (Sample: Place all three objects into one cup. Because you end up with three objects in the cup, $3 \div 1 = 3$.) Now **ask,** "Suppose you have zero objects and three cups. How many objects can you put in each cup?" (0 objects.) **Ask,** "What is the quotient $0 \div 3$?" (0.) Finally, write $3 \div 0$ on the board. **Ask,** "Can you divide three objects into zero cups? Explain." (No. Sample: There are no cups in which to put the objects, so this cannot be done.)

Ask students to perform each of the division exercises discussed above ($3 \div 3$, $3 \div 1$, $0 \div 3$, and $3 \div 0$) on a calculator. **Ask,** "What does your calculator show when you try to divide by 0?" (Sample: You get an error message.) Emphasize that division by 0 is impossible.

Using "Do/Undo" Operations
to Show That Division by 0 Is Impossible

To provide further amplification that you cannot divide by 0, you may want to use this mathematical reasoning argument based on "do/undo" (inverse) operations. Remind students that because $15 \div 5 = 3$, we know that $3 \times 5 = 15$. Advise students that we will use do/undo operations to address the following two cases: Case 1, dividing a nonzero number by 0, and Case 2, dividing 0 by 0.

Case 1: Use do/undo operations to find $\square$ in $15 \div 0 = \square$.
   Because $15 \div 0 = \square$, we know that $\square \times 0 = 15$. But we know that *no number* times 0 is equal to 15. So there is *no solution*.
   You cannot divide a nonzero number by 0.

Case 2: Use do/undo operations to find □ in 0 ÷ 0 = □. (Note: It is important to address this case because some students who understand the results in Case 1 may view 0 ÷ 0 differently. They may believe that 0 ÷ 0 = 1 or 0.)

Because 0 ÷ 0 = □, we know that □ × 0 = 0. But because *any number* will satisfy □ × 0 = 0, *any number* would be a solution to 0 ÷ 0 = □. So, you could say that 0 ÷ 0 = 3, because 3 × 0 = 0. But you could also say that 0 ÷ 0 = 4, because 4 × 0 = 0. According to the *Transitive Property of Equality,* if $a = b$ and $b = c$, then $a = c$. So, if the above division results were allowed, then because

$$3 = (0 \div 0) \text{ and } (0 \div 0) = 4,$$

we would have to conclude that 3 = 4 (because both 3 and 4 would be equal to 0 ÷ 0). But we know that 3 ≠ 4! So, we say that 0 ÷ 0 is meaningless.

You cannot divide 0 by 0.

Reviewing Division of 0 by a Nonzero Number: After a discussion on division by 0, some students may become confused about dividing 0 by a nonzero number. So, it is instructive to remind students that 0 divided by a nonzero number is equal to 0. Have students find □ in 0 ÷ 5 = □. **Ask,** "Because □ × 5 = 0, what do we know about the value of □? Explain." (□ = 0. When the product of two numbers is 0, at least one of the numbers must be 0.)

A nonzero number divided by 0 is equal to 0.

Instructional Game: Balance the ×/÷ Number Sentence!
(See pages 154–155 for game instructions. See pages 177–178 for game pieces. Students work in groups of 2 or 3.)

This domino-type game promotes memorization of the facts while having students use trial-and-error thinking to balance multiplication and division number sentences. Students use playing cards as "dominoes" to match either a number sentence with its solution or a solution with its number sentence. (Shown below, the card with the white 8 was placed next to the card with 32 ÷ □ = 4 because 8 makes that sentence true.)

□ ÷ 9 = 5	8	32 ÷ □ = 4	5

Most of the game cards involve the use of basic facts. However, advise students that those cards that show two-digit computation can be solved using mathematical reasoning rather than by performing actual computations. For example, to solve 11 × 46 = □ × 11, students can simply use the *Commutative Property of Multiplication* to determine that □ = 46.

Error Pattern 2

Some students do not recognize "near facts" and are unable to do them mentally. Near facts are close to the basic facts, but have a nonzero remainder (as in 59 ÷ 7). Students may make any of the errors shown below. Some errors are made due to a lack of understanding of the possible values of a remainder in division.

$$\overset{7 \text{ R7 or R10}}{7\overline{)5\,9}}$$

The student selects 49, the multiple of 7 right before the desired multiple (56). The student then counts up to determine the remainder to either 56 (to obtain R7) or to 59 (to obtain R10). The student may not be aware that the possible remainders when you divide by 7 are *less than* 7.

$$\overset{8}{7\overline{)5\,9}}$$

The student determines the correct quotient, but omits the remainder.

$$\overset{9 \text{ R4 or R7}}{7\overline{)5\,9}}$$

The student selects 63, the multiple of 7 right after 56, and determines the remainder by counting back. The student may count back to 59 (to obtain R4), or back to 56 (to obtain R7).

Intervention

For 7$\overline{)59}$, display 59 small objects. **Ask,** "You would like to form as many groups of 7 objects each as possible. How many groups of 7 can you make?" (8 groups.) **Ask,** "What multiplication fact shows how many objects are in the 8 groups?" (7 × 8 = 56.)

Now, have students look at a multiplication table. **Ask,** "What times 7 gets you an answer that is *as close to 59 as possible—without going over 59*? What product in the table are you using?" (8; 56.) **Ask,** "How much is left over?" (3.) Explain that the amount left over is called the *remainder,* and the answer is written *8 R3.*

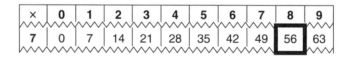

×	0	1	2	3	4	5	6	7	8	9
7	0	7	14	21	28	35	42	49	56	63

Now display 56 objects. **Ask,** "When you divide the 56 objects into 7 equal groups, how many are left over?" (0 objects.) **Ask,** "Suppose we have 57 objects to equally divide into 7 groups. How many will be left over?" (1 object.) **Ask,** "Why is there a (nonzero) remainder when you divide 57 by 7?" (Sample: 57 is not divisible by 7.) Repeat for 58 objects, 59 objects, all the way through 62 objects. **Ask,** "What happens when you divide 63 objects into 7 equal groups?" (Sample: There will be 9 in each group with a remainder of 0.) **Ask,** "What is the greatest possible remainder when you divide by 7?" (6.) **Ask,** "How does a remainder in any division exercise compare with the divisor in the exercise? Explain." (Sample: The remainder is always less than the divisor. If the remainder were equal to or greater than the divisor, there would be enough left over to increase the quotient.)

For purposes of teacher edification, it should be noted that many educators avoid the use of the "R" notation for remainders in equations (as in $59 \div 7 = 8$ R3). They believe the R notation is essentially intended for use only with the division algorithm (as in $7\overline{)59}$). One reason why the R notation with equations is avoided is because multiple unequal division problems have the same answer when the answers are given with the R notation. Note that another division problem that has 8 R3 as its answer is $35 \div 4$. However, according to the *Transitive Property of Equality*,

if **$59 \div 7 = 8$ R3** and **8 R3 $= 35 \div 4$**, then **$59 \div 7 = 35 \div 4$**.

But $59 \div 7 = 8.43$ (to the nearest hundredth) and $35 \div 4 = 8.75$. So, $59 \div 7$ and $35 \div 4$ are *not* equal. To avoid using an equal sign with the R notation, some educators use an arrow and record the problem as $59 \div 7 \rightarrow 8$ R3. Use your discretion as to how you prefer your students to show such division results.

Error Pattern 3

Some students compare a one-digit divisor with each digit of the dividend— and divide the larger number by the smaller number. They ignore any remainders and record no numerals below the dividend. Essentially, the student views each digit of the dividend separately—and performs a division with that digit and the divisor.

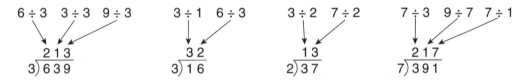

Note: In the first example, although the correct answer is given, the fact that no work is shown is a clue that perhaps the student has a misconception about the algorithm. A discussion with the student would be helpful in determining the student's thinking.

Intervention

Estimation: Determining If an Answer Is Reasonable

All students, especially those who obtain unreasonable answers, should be encouraged to use estimation either before or after computing. For $16 \div 3 = 32$, **ask,** "Is it reasonable that 16 objects divided into 3 equal groups would give you 32 objects per group? Explain." (No. Sample: $32 \times 3 = 96$. This is far greater than the number of objects with which we started.) For $391 \div 7 = 217$, **ask,** "Why is the quotient 217 not reasonable?" (Sample: If you round 217 to the nearest 100, you get 200. The product of 7 and 200 is 1,400. This is far greater than the dividend.) **Ask,** "How would you estimate $391 \div 7$?" (Sample: Think of 391 as being about 350. Because $35 \div 7 = 5$, $350 \div 7 = 50$. So the answer should be close to 50.)

Some students may benefit from using *front-end estimation* to determine if a quotient is reasonable. The lesson "Using Front-End Estimation to Check for Reasonableness: Division" (page 175) teaches students how to use this strategy. A lesson on using *compatible numbers* to make estimates (for all operations) is on page 176. This strategy is especially effective for division—and is used in the estimate explained earlier for 391 ÷ 7.

Although estimation provides a good vehicle to determine whether or not an answer is reasonable, often a division result may be "reasonable" but incorrect. As such, students should be encouraged to check their answers by multiplying the quotient by the divisor and adding any remainder. If that result is equal to the dividend, the answer is correct.

Intervention: Using Play Money or Base-Ten Blocks

Supply play money (or base-ten blocks) and a division exercise on a place-value grid. (See page 184 for play money and page 187 for grids.) To divide 37 by 2, have students display $37 and draw 2 large rings to represent 2 groups as shown.

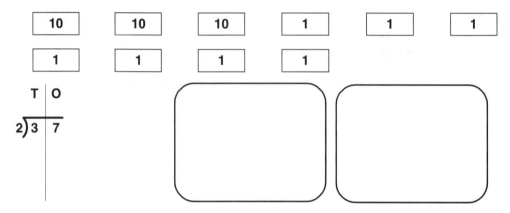

Guide students in interpreting 2)37 as putting $37 into 2 equal groups. **Ask,** "Are there enough ten-dollar bills to put 1 in each group?" (Yes.) **Ask,** "So, how many digits will be in the quotient?" (2 digits.) **Ask,** "Are there enough ten-dollar bills left to put another ten-dollar bill in each group?" (No.) **Ask,** "What is an estimate for the quotient?" (Sample: The quotient will be between 10 and 20.) It should be noted that such questions help focus students' attention on an estimate for the entire quotient—and not just on the first digit.

Have students put 1 ten-dollar bill in each group and record 1 in the tens position of the exercise. To show how much money was placed in the rings, instruct them to multiply the 1 ten in each ring by 2 (the number of rings) as shown. Then have them subtract the tens to show that there is 1 ten left—along with the 7 ones.

Guide students in trading the 1 ten-dollar bill that is left over for 10 one-dollar bills. Have students join those bills with the original 7 one-dollar bills, giving 17 to put in the 2 groups. Relate that to "bring down the 7" in the algorithm. Advise students that we must now put *as many one-dollar bills in each group as possible.*

Ask, "What is the greatest number of one-dollar bills you can put in each ring?" (8 one-dollar bills.) Have students place the 8 one-dollar bills in each ring and have them record 8 in the ones column of the exercise. **Ask,** "How much money is left over?" ($1.) Advise students to record R1 in the exercise.

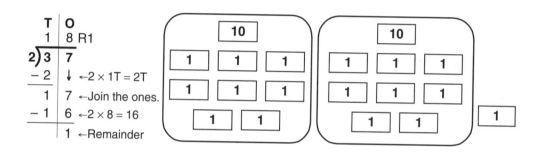

Follow-Up Activity: Abbott and Costello's Number *Non*sense
(See pages 179–180 for the activity. Students work as an entire class, in pairs, or in small groups.)

This activity is based on an Abbott and Costello comedy routine where they attempt to perform a division computation (from their movie *In the Navy,* Gottlieb, Lubin, Horman, & Grant, 1941). In this routine, Lou Costello attempts to divide 28 by 7 but makes a series of errors. Bud Abbott tries to correct the errors by showing how to check the division—first using multiplication, then using addition. But each of Bud's attempts is countered by Lou's continued errors. In the activity, students are asked to explain the errors that were made and explain the rationale behind using multiplication and addition to check the work.

Error Pattern 4

Error Pattern 4a: Some students record the tens digit of the quotient in the ones place and the ones digit of the quotient in the tens place. The student perhaps erroneously transfers to division what is done in addition, subtraction, and multiplication—namely, recording the answer from right to left.

```
    1 2              8 1 R1            0 5 R1              4 3
4)8 4            2)3 7             7)3 5 1           12)4 0 8
 -8               -2                -3 5               -3 6
 ___              ___               ____               ____
  4                1 7                  1               4 8
 -4               -1 6                 -0              -4 8
 ___              ____               ____              ____
  0                  1                  1                 0
```

Error Pattern 4b: Some students first divide the ones digit of the dividend, then the tens digit, and finally the hundreds digit—rather than beginning with the leftmost digit.

```
    2 1            1 5 3 R1          4 7 0 R4            4 0 0
4)8 4            2)3 7             7)3 5 1           12)4 0 8
 -4               -6                 -0                 -0
 ___              ___               ____               ____
  8                3 1               5 1               0 8
 -8               -3 0               -4 9               -0
 ___              ____               ____               ____
  0                  1               3 2                4 8
                                     -2 8              -4 8
                                     ____              ____
                                       4                 0
```

Note: In the first example, the correct answer is given. However, observation of the work reveals that the student first divided the ones digit by 4 and then the tens digit by 4. A discussion with the student would be helpful in determining the student's thinking.

In the other examples, this misconception leads to incorrect answers. For example, in the second example, the student first divides 7 by 2, and records 3 in the ones position. The 3 from the dividend is then "brought down" and combined with the 1 that was left over to form 31. Then 31 is divided by 2, yielding 15 in the quotient.

Intervention

Use the Intervention Activity for Error Pattern 3, emphasizing that we record the digits in the quotient from *left to right* as you divide in each place-value position from *left to right*. Encourage students to use estimation to determine if their answers are reasonable. To help students focus on dividing from left to right, have them use an index card to cover the digits in the columns that are *not* under consideration in a given step as shown at the right for 351 ÷ 7.

```
    H  T
       5
7)3  5
 -3  5
```

Error Pattern 5

Some students fail to subtract before "bringing down" the next digit. Any remainders are omitted.

```
      5          8        3 0 1        3 1 0          2 0
   3)1 6      9)7 9      2)7 1 2     8)3,1 9 7     25)5 5 8
     1 5        7 2        6           2 4            5 0
                          ───          ───           ───
                            1            9              8
                            0            8              0
                           ───          ───
                            2            7
                            2            0
```

Intervention

Provide the *mnemonic device* on the right to help students remember the steps of the traditional division algorithm. Emphasize that after you subtract, you check to make sure the difference is less than the divisor—and that the next step is to "bring down."

Divide	→	**D**ad
Multiply	→	**M**other
Subtract	→	**S**ister
Check	→	**C**ousin
(**Ask,** "Is the difference less than the divisor?")		
Bring Down	→	**B**rother

Modified Algorithm: Subtracting Entire Partial Products

This algorithm is a modification of the traditional algorithm. It has the advantage of avoiding the "bring down" process. Each partial product is subtracted from the entire dividend—not just from the "front-end digits." (When you only subtract from the front-end digits, you must then bring down the next digit of the dividend.) By focusing on the *entire dividend* rather than on digits, an understanding is provided of what goes on in the traditional algorithm. (Each time you divide, you divide out the largest possible multiple of a power of 10 of the divisor. You then subtract that value to determine what remains to be divided out—and then repeat the process.)

As shown on the next page, this algorithm and the traditional algorithm may be displayed side by side—with the modified algorithm being used to "justify" what goes on in the traditional algorithm. (This algorithm is also used with the Intervention for Error Pattern 7.)

Supply play money and an exercise on a place-value grid to each student or group of students. (Play money is on page 184; place-value grids for division are on page 187.) To find 712 ÷ 2, have students display $712. Mention that we can think of 712 ÷ 2 as finding how much money each person will get when $712 is equally shared between 2 people.

Play Money for $712:

100	100	100	100	100
100	100	10	1	1

Advise students that they should first estimate the result. **Ask,** "Is there enough money so that each person will get at least $100? Explain." (Yes. Sample: Because $2 \times 100 = 200$, there is enough money to give each person at least 1 hundred-dollar bill.) **Ask,** "So, how many digits will the quotient have? Where will the first digit go?" (Three digits. The first digit will go in the hundreds place.)

Have students follow the steps described below to find $712 \div 2$. The computation on the left side shows the alternative algorithm. The traditional algorithm is modeled at the right. Bold type is used to highlight what is being done in each step.

- Equally distribute the hundred-dollar bills so that each person gets as many as possible. Record the results in the exercise and then multiply to show how much money was used.

Modified Algorithm

Traditional Algorithm

```
   H  T  O                                        H  T  O
   3                                              3
 2)7  1  2                                      2)7  1  2
  -6  0  0    2 × 300                            -6  ↓       2 × 3H = 6H
   1  1  2    Subtract.                           1  1
```

- Each person gets **3** $100 bills.
- ← $600 is used.
- ←$112 is left over.

```
   H  T  O                                        H  T  O
   3  5                                           3  5
 2)7  1  2                                      2)7  1  2
  -6  0  0                                       -6  ↓
   1  1  2                                        1  1
  -1  0  0    2 × 50                             -1  0  ↓    2 × 5T = 10T
      1  2    Subtract.                              1  2
```

- Trade the remaining $100 bill for 10 $10 bills.
- There are now 11 $10 bills.
- Each person gets **5** $10 bills.
- ← $100 is used.
- ← $12 is left over.

```
   H  T  O                                        H  T  O
   3  5  6                                        3  5  6
 2)7  1  2                                      2)7  1  2
  -6  0  0                                       -6  ↓
   1  1  2                                        1  1
  -1  0  0                                       -1  0  ↓
      1  2                                           1  2
     -1  2    2 × 6                                 -1  2    2 × 6 = 12
         0    Subtract.                                 0
```

- Trade the remaining $10 bill for 10 $1 bills.
- There are now 12 $1 bills.
- Each person gets **6** $1 bills.
- ← $12 is used.
- ←$0 is left over.

The quotient is 356. So, each person gets $356.

Error Pattern 6

After subtracting the partial product, some students add the difference to the next digit of the dividend (rather than use it as the lead digit of the number formed when the next digit is brought down).

After subtracting 48 from 51, the student adds the difference, 3, to the 2 that is to be brought down, obtaining 5. The 5 is then brought down.

Because 6 goes into 5 zero times, 0 is written in the quotient in the tens position. The number left over, 5, is then added to the 7 that is to be brought down, obtaining 12. The 12 is then brought down.

Because 12 ÷ 6 = 2, a 2 is recorded in the ones position of the quotient

$$
\begin{array}{r}
8\,0\,2 \\
6)\overline{5,1\,2\,7} \\
4\ 8 \\
5 \\
1\,2
\end{array}
$$

Intervention

Use the modified algorithm for Error Pattern 5 with appropriate exercises to avoid the bring down process. When students record 8 in the hundreds position of the quotient for $6)\overline{5{,}127}$, they obtain a partial product of 4,800. When they subtract 4,800 from the dividend, they obtain 327. Emphasize that with the alternative algorithm they should see that the 3 in 327 stands for 3 hundreds—and cannot be added to the 2 to obtain 5 tens.

Error Pattern 7

Some students do not record necessary 0s in the quotient. They may leave out ending 0s, or they may leave out 0s that need to appear in the quotient between nonzero digits.

$$
\begin{array}{r}
1 \\
6)\overline{6\,0} \\
-6 \\
\end{array}
\qquad
\begin{array}{r}
2\quad 1\ \text{R3} \\
4)\overline{8\,0\,7} \\
-8 \\
\hline
7 \\
-4 \\
\hline
3
\end{array}
\qquad
\begin{array}{r}
8\,2\quad \text{R2} \\
7)\overline{5,7\,4\,2} \\
-5\ 6 \\
\hline
1\,4 \\
-1\,4 \\
\hline
2
\end{array}
\qquad
\begin{array}{r}
4\quad 8\ \text{R9} \\
15)\overline{6,1\,2\,9} \\
-6\ 0 \\
\hline
1\,2\,9 \\
-1\,2\,0 \\
\hline
9
\end{array}
\qquad
\begin{array}{r}
4\ \text{or}\ 40 \\
20)\overline{8,0\,0\,0} \\
-8\ 0 \\
\hline
0
\end{array}
$$

Intervention

Modified Algorithm: Subtracting Entire Partial Products

This modification of the traditional algorithm is also used with the Intervention Activity for Error Pattern 5. The beauty of this algorithm is that it can be shown side by side with the traditional algorithm to help reinforce what actually goes on in the traditional algorithm. With an emphasis on distributing play money into equal groups based on the entire partial product—and recording a digit in the quotient to show how much of each denomination goes into each group—this algorithm minimizes the chance of omitting digits in the quotient, such as 0s.

Supply play money and an exercise on a place-value grid to each student or group of students. (Play money is on page 184; place-value grids are on page 187.) To find 5,742 ÷ 7, have students display $5,742. Mention that we can think of $5,742 ÷ 7 as finding how much money each person will get when $5,742 is equally shared among 7 people.

1000	1000	1000	1000	1000	100
100	100	100	100	100	100
10	10	10	10	1	1

Advise students that they should first estimate 5,742 ÷ 7. **Ask,** "Will each person get at least $1,000? Explain." (No. Sample: 1,000 × 7 = 7,000. This is too big!) **Ask,** "So, will there be a digit in the thousands place?" (No.) **Ask,** "Will each person get at least $100? Explain. (Yes. Sample: 100 × 7 = 700. So, only $700 of the $5,742 would be used up.) **Ask,** "How many digits will the quotient have, and where will the first digit go?" (There will be three digits. The first digit will be in the hundreds place.)

Have students follow the steps described below and on page 129 to find 5,742 ÷ 7. The computation on the left side shows the alternative algorithm. The traditional algorithm is modeled at the right. Bold type is used to highlight what is being done in each step.

- Because there are not enough thousand-dollar bills to distribute at least 1 to each person, think of trading the 5 thousand-dollar bills for 50 hundred-dollar bills. (Because the numbers are large, it may be sufficient for students to just think of these trades rather than physically making the trades.)

Ask, "How many hundred-dollar bills are there in all?" (57 hundred-dollar bills.)

- Think of equally distributing the hundred-dollar bills so that each person *gets as many as possible.*

Ask, "How many hundred-dollar bills will each person get?" (8 hundred-dollar bills.)

- Record the results in the exercise and then multiply to show how much money was used.

Modified Algorithm

Th	H	T	O
	8		

```
  Th   H   T   O
      8
7) 5,  7   4   2
 - 5   6   0   0     7 x 800
       1   4   2     Subtract.
```
• Each person gets 8 $100 bills.
←$5,600 is used. $142 is left over.

```
  Th   H   T   O
      8   2
7) 5,  7   4   2
 - 5   6   0   0
       1   4   2
     - 1   4   0     7 x 20
               2     Subtract.
```
• Trade the remaining $100 bill for 10 $10 bills.
There are now 14 $10 bills.
• Each person gets 2 $10 bills.
←$140 is used. $2 is left over.

```
  Th   H   T   O
      8   2   0  R2
7) 5,  7   4   2
 - 5   6   0   0
       1   4   2
     - 1   4   0
               2
             - 0     7 x 0
               2     Subtract.
```
• There are only 2 $1 bills. So there are not enough $1 bills to distribute.
• Each person gets 0 $1 bills. Record 0 in the quotient.
←$0 is used. $2 is left over. Record this as R2 in the quotient.

Traditional Algorithm

```
  Th   H   T   O
      8
7) 5,  7   4   2
 - 5   6   ↓          7 x 8H = 56H
       1   4
```

```
  Th   H   T   O
      8   2
7) 5,  7   4   2
 - 5,  6   ↓
       1   4
     - 1   4   ↓      7 x 2T = 14T
           0   2
```

```
  Th   H   T   O
      8   2   0  R2
7) 5,  7   4   2
 - 5,  6   ↓
       1   4
     - 1   4   ↓
           0   2
         - 0          7 x 0 = 0
           2
```

The quotient is 820 with a remainder of 2. So each person gets $820, with $2 left over.

Error Pattern 8

When the divisor is greater than the first digit of the dividend, some students estimate incorrectly and automatically begin recording quotient digits in the first position on the left. Because the quotient digits are thus shifted one place to the left, students may or may not erroneously continue dividing when they should be done—and record an extraneous digit (usually 0) in the ones place.

```
   8 5  R2            8 5 0 R2           4 8 8 0              2 5 0
6) 5 1 2           6) 5 1 2           8) 3,9 0 4          20) 5 0 0
 - 4 8              - 4 8              - 3 2                - 4 0
   ─────              ─────              ─────                ─────
     3 2                3 2                7 0                1 0 0
   - 3 0              - 3 0              - 6 4              - 1 0 0
   ─────              ─────              ─────                ─────
       2                  2                6 4                    0
```

Note: In the first example, although the student obtained the correct quotient, the digits are in the wrong place-value positions. This suggests that the student may have a misconception that could lead to errors as shown in the other three examples.

Intervention

Use the modified algorithm for Error Pattern 7 for a division exercise such as 6$\overline{)512}$. Emphasize that since you are unable to put a hundred-dollar bill in each of 6 groups, you trade the 5 hundred-dollar bills for 50 ten-dollar bills. Point out that although you do not record a leading 0 in the quotient, the number of ten-dollar bills put in each group should be recorded above the tens digit of the dividend.

			8	5	R2
6$)$	5	1	2		
−	4	8			
		3	2		
	−	3	0		
			2		

For some students, it may be sufficient to do division exercises on grid paper as shown at right. This should help students keep digits with the same place value aligned.

Error Patterns 3 Through 8

Many students experience difficulty with the traditional division algorithm. They may make any combination of the errors described in Error Patterns 3 through 8. They may even make errors that are not identified in this book. Carroll and Porter (1998) describe two important reasons why so many students find the traditional division algorithm to be difficult: "First, the standard algorithm requires students to get an exact answer in the quotient at each step. . . . Second, the standard algorithm requires students to ignore place value. In dividing 847 by 9, the student asks, 'How many times does 9 go into 84?' rather than 'How many 9s can I get out of 847?'" (p. 112).

The alternative division algorithm that follows allows students to gradually subtract out "easy" *multiples of the divisor*. The algorithm utilizes place-value concepts, and students use number sense as they continue to subtract out partial quotients from each new dividend. This method dates back to a book written by Isaac Greenwood (*Arithmetick*; 1729)—generally believed to be the first arithmetic book written by an American author.

Intervention

Alternative Algorithm: Partial Quotients (Also Known as "Repeated Subtraction")

Pose a division exercise for students, and have them draw a vertical line to the right of the exercise as shown. The partial quotients are recorded to the right of this line; the partial products (total amounts to be subtracted off) are written below the exercise.

8$\overline{)739}$

Advise students that they will perform a series of estimations to see how many times they can subtract off multiples of the divisor from the dividend. Point out that each time they subtract off a multiple of the divisor, the amount left to divide becomes smaller. The process continues until no more multiples of the divisor can be subtracted off. This, of course, occurs when the number left to divide is less than the divisor.

Advise students that $8\overline{)739}$ may be thought of as asking, "How many groups of 8 objects each can you make from 739 objects?" Because the dividend, 739, is in *hundreds,* you first see how many *hundreds* of groups of 8 can be made. Then you see how many *tens* of groups of 8 can be made, and so on.

Ask, "Are there enough hundreds in 739 so that you can make at least 100 groups of 8 objects each?" (No.) **Ask,** "How many tens are there in all when the 7 hundreds are combined with the 3 tens? What is the standard name for that number?" (73 tens; 730.) **Ask,** "Are there enough tens in 739 so that you can make at least 10 groups of 8 each? Explain." (Yes. Sample: There are 73 tens to divide up, so you can easily subtract off 10 groups of 8, or 80.)

Advise students that with the partial-quotients algorithm you do *not* have to find the greatest number of tens to subtract off right away. Rather, you can subtract off the tens gradually. So, if you subtract off 10 groups of 8, you use up 8×10, or 80, of the 739 objects. Have students record the 80 objects used up below the 739, subtract 80 from 739, and then record the difference, 659. *Then have them record the partial quotient, 10, to the right of the line as shown.* Mention that 659 remains to be divided.

$$
\begin{array}{r|r}
8\overline{)739} & \\
-\;8\,0 & 10 \\
\hline
6\,5\,9 & \\
\end{array}
$$

Ask, "Are there enough tens in 659 to make 10 more groups of 8 objects each?" (Yes.) **Ask,** "How about 20 more groups of 8 objects each?" (Yes.) **Ask,** "If we subtract off 20 groups of 8 objects each, how much will we be subtracting off in all?" (160.) Have students record the 160 objects used up below the 659 and find the difference, 499. *Then have them record the partial quotient, 20, to the right of the vertical line.* Mention that so far they have divided out 30 groups of 8 objects each and that 499 now remains to be divided.

$$
\begin{array}{r|r}
8\overline{)739} & \\
-\;8\,0 & 10 \\
\hline
6\,5\,9 & \\
-\;1\,6\,0 & 20 \\
\hline
4\,9\,9 & \\
\end{array}
$$

Ask, "Do you think we can speed up the division process? If yes, explain how you would do it." (Sample: Yes, we can certainly divide out more than 10 or 20 at a time. Because 499 contains 49 tens, and because there are six 8s in 49, we can divide by 6 tens, or 60.) **Ask,** "How many objects are in 60 groups of 8 objects each?" (480 objects.) Have students record 480 below the 499 and find the difference, 19. *Then, have them record the partial quotient, 60, to the right of the vertical line.* **Ask,** "How much is left to divide? Can you subtract off 10 more groups of 8 objects each from that number?" (19; so, no.)

$$
\begin{array}{r|r}
8\overline{)739} & \\
-\;8\,0 & 10 \\
\hline
6\,5\,9 & \\
-\;1\,6\,0 & 20 \\
\hline
4\,9\,9 & \\
-\;4\,8\,0 & 60 \\
\hline
1\,9 & \\
\end{array}
$$

Ask, "How many groups of 8 objects each have been divided out so far? Explain how you found your answer." (90 groups. Sample: I found the sum of the partial quotients: 10 + 20 + 60 = 90.)

Ask, "With just 19 objects left over, how many groups of 8 each can be made? How many objects will be left over?" (2 groups can be made; 3 objects will be left over.) Have students record the number of objects used, 16, the partial quotient, 2, and the number of objects left over, 3, as shown. Ask, "What should we do to find the quotient for 739 ÷ 8? What is the remainder?" (The quotient is the sum of the partial products, 92. The remainder is 3.)

Advise students that they can draw a line under the partial quotients and write their sum as shown at the right. They should then record the sum and the remainder at the top of the division exercise as shown.

```
          9 2  R3
      8)7 3 9  │
      - 8 0    │  10
      -----    │
        6 5 9  │
      - 1 6 0  │  20
      -------  │
        4 9 9  │
      - 4 8 0  │  60
      -------  │
          1 9  │
      -  1 6   │   2
      -------  └──────
            3     92
```

Another Way to Use the Algorithm: It is important to emphasize with students that there are *many ways* to apply this algorithm to obtain the correct quotient because the particular multiples to subtract off at each step are *selected by the student* based on how many steps the student chooses to use to solve the problem. So, for 739 ÷ 8, a student could first subtract off 50 groups of 8 each (400), as shown at the right. Then 40 groups of 8 each (320) could be subtracted off. Finally, 2 groups of 8 each (16) are subtracted off. So, the student found the same result, 92 R3, in three steps instead of four. Both procedures should be viewed as being equally acceptable.

```
          9 2  R3
      8)7 3 9  │
      - 4 0 0  │  50
      -------  │
        3 3 9  │
      - 3 2 0  │  40
      -------  │
          1 9  │
      -  1 6   │   2
      -------  └──────
            3     92
```

Using Student Journaling: Because this algorithm permits students to find quotients in an individualized way—with students essentially making their own judgments to determine what steps to use—the algorithm lends itself nicely to *student journaling*. Ask students to describe the steps they use. Also have them compare and contrast this algorithm with other algorithms for division.

You may also want students to write several word problems that can be solved by using division. Discuss with students the various actions and problem structures for division (see pages 21–23) and have them explain why the *actions* written into their problems suggest that division can be used.

Error Pattern 9

Error Pattern 9a: When dividing by a two-digit number, some students do not multiply by the ones digits of the divisor when determining the partial products.

```
       6 9
24) 1,3 8 0
   - 1 2 0
   ─────────
     1 8 0
   - 1 8 0
   ─────────
         0
```

The divisor, 24, is treated as if it were just 20. So, the digits in the quotient are determined by 138 ÷ 20 and 180 ÷ 20, respectively.

```
       1 2 0 R9
45) 4,8 0 9
   - 4 0
   ─────────
       8 0
   - 8 0
   ─────────
       0 9
```

The divisor, 45, is treated as if it were just 40. So, the digits in the quotient are determined by 48 ÷ 40, and 80 ÷ 40, and 9 ÷ 40, respectively.

Error Pattern 9b: When dividing by a two-digit number, some students ignore the ones digit of the divisor and divide (and then multiply) by only the tens digit.

```
       6 9 0
24) 1,3 8 0
   - 1 2
   ─────────
     1 8
   - 1 8
   ─────────
       0
```

The digits in the quotient are determined by 13 ÷ 2, 18 ÷ 2, and 0 ÷ 2, respectively. The partial products are determined by 2 × 6 and 2 × 9, respectively.

```
       1 2 0 2 R1
45) 4,8 0 9
   - 4
   ─────────
     0 8
   - 0 8
   ─────────
       0 0
           9
         - 8
       ─────────
           1
```

The digits in the quotient are determined by 4 ÷ 4, 8 ÷ 4, 0 ÷ 4, and 9 ÷ 4, respectively. The partial products are determined by 4 × 1, 4 × 2, 4 × 0, and 4 × 2, respectively.

Intervention

Alternative Algorithm: Partial Quotients (Also Known as "Repeated Subtraction")

This algorithm, fully described in the section "Error Patterns 3 Through 8," works nicely to help students focus on the *full divisor* at all times (rather than just on the front-end digits). As shown at the right for 1,380 ÷ 24, students subtract off various *multiples of 24* during a series of steps. The particular multiples of 24 to use are *selected by the student* based on how "quickly" the student wants to find the quotient. In the example, first 50 groups of 24 each, or 1,200, are subtracted off. Then 5 groups of 24 each, or 120, are subtracted off. Finally 2 groups of 24 each, or 48, are subtracted off. In all, 57 groups of 24 each are subtracted off, with a remainder of 12.

$$
\begin{array}{r|r}
 \text{5 7 R12} & \\
 24)\overline{1,380} & \\
 -1,200 & 50 \\ \hline
 180 & \\
 -120 & 5 \\ \hline
 60 & \\
 -48 & 2 \\ \hline
 12 & 57 \\
\end{array}
$$

Remind students that to *check a division problem*, they should multiply the divisor by the quotient and then add any remainder. Because $57 \times 24 + 12 = 1,368 + 12 = 1,380$, we know that the problem was done correctly.

Instructional Game: Target Math (×/÷)

(The game rules and game board are provided in the Resources for Subtraction on pages 159–160. The problems for the multiplication and division versions of the game are on pages 181–182. This game is teacher-directed—with the entire class, divided into four or five teams, playing the game together.)

The problems used in this game are based on multiplication/division computation concepts and problem solving. The problems are organized according to five levels of difficulty—from 5-point problems to 25-point problems. In this game, each student participates by selecting the level of difficulty of a problem according to his or her personal desires. It is also a game where keen concentration can help a team win. The game may be played at any time during the unit.

Practice Exercises
Division of Whole Numbers

rt 1
_____

1. $36 \div 4 =$ _____

2. $49 \div 7 =$ _____

3. _____ $= 63 \div 7$

4. $0 =$ _____ $\div 3$

5. $8 \div 8 =$ _____

6. $81 \div$ _____ $= 9$

7. $9 = 54 \div$ _____

8. _____ $\div 8 = 6$

rt 2
_____

9. $5\overline{)1\,8}$

10. $4\overline{)2\,7}$

11. $9\overline{)5\,0}$

12. $8\overline{)7\,7}$

13. $3\overline{)9\,6}$

14. $3\overline{)8\,6}$

15. $6\overline{)7\,8}$

16. $7\overline{)9\,3}$

rt 3
_____

17. $2\overline{)7\,4\,9}$

18. $6\overline{)3\,0\,0}$

19. $4\overline{)8\,2\,0}$

20. $7\overline{)6\,2\,0}$

21. $2\overline{)8,4\,9\,5}$

22. $5\overline{)2,9\,9\,0}$

23. $9\overline{)9,8\,1\,8}$

24. $8\overline{)6,0\,1\,6}$

rt 4
_____

25. $30\overline{)2,1\,0\,0}$

26. $16\overline{)5\,1\,9}$

27. $85\overline{)8,8\,1\,6}$

28. $39\overline{)3,6\,0\,9}$

QUESTIONS FOR TEACHER REFLECTION

1. When teaching the multiplication/division facts, why is it important to present the unknown in different positions? Discuss how the instructional game *Balance the ×/÷ Number Sentence!* promotes student fluency with multiplication and division. How are those two operations related?

2. Discuss how you would teach the traditional algorithm for division of whole numbers in a manner that reduces the chances your students may develop misunderstandings that lead to error patterns. Use specific examples, including one where there is at least one 0 in the quotient.

3. Choose one of the division error patterns that you believe is practiced by many students. Explain what the students did and what mathematical concept or procedure was likely misunderstood. Provide a specific strategy you would use with students to correct that misunderstanding and error.

4. When using the traditional algorithm for long division, why do you multiply and subtract as part of the process? What is the reason for the use of the phrase *bring down?*

5. Compare and contrast the traditional algorithm for division with an alternative algorithm for division. Discuss any advantages or disadvantages of using either algorithm. Be sure to discuss why the traditional algorithm for division is so difficult for many students.

6. Suppose you sit down with a struggling student who cannot get started with a division problem, say, 6,809 ÷ 9. What questions would you ask the student? How would you get the student started?

7. The quote below is used on page 8 of this book.

   "A promising approach that has emerged from research in mathematics education and cognitive psychology emphasizes the role of comparison—comparing and contrasting multiple solution methods—in helping students learn to estimate." (Star, Kenyon, Jointer, & Rittle-Johnson, 2010)

   Estimate 5,296 ÷ 17 three different ways. Use rounding, front-end estimation, and compatible numbers. Compare and contrast the methods, discussing any advantages or disadvantages using the various methods. Then explain why you believe students may become better estimators when engaged in such an activity, as suggested by the quote above.

Resources
for Estimation,
Instructional Games,
and Follow-Up
Activities (Blacklines)

Resources for Addition

(Estimation, Instructional Games, and Follow-Up Activities)

Follow-Up Activity: Next Number, Please

In this activity, students *mentally* decide what multiple of 10, 100, or 1,000 must be added or subtracted to obtain the next End Number. Then they use a *calculator* to check their results. In addition to promoting mental math skills, the activity relies heavily on students' ability to apply place-value concepts. Answers are provided on pages 193–194. *The activity provides an ideal follow-up to work with adding and subtracting multiples of 10, 100, and 1,000* (Error Pattern 5 for addition).

Roller Coaster Rounding

This activity provides a model to help students *visualize* the rounding process. By examining a roller coaster that will slide down one of two sides of a hill to a value at the base, students are able to focus on just two possible answer choices when they round a number. Essentially, the "laws of gravity" help students decide which of two possible multiples (of 10, 100, or 1,000) is the correct answer. Answers are provided on page 194. *The activity may be used whenever rounding is used to estimate results for any operation.*

Using Front-End Estimation to Check for Reasonableness: Addition

This lesson provides a practical way for students to determine if an addition result is *reasonable*. The process involves adding the front-end digits (the most important digits in determining an approximate answer). The process also involves "making an adjustment" to that sum by taking the remaining digits into account. For some students, the adjustment process may be difficult—and for those students it may be omitted. Answers are provided on pages 194–195. (For exercises 16–23, you may want students to also *explain* their reasoning for determining their Yes/No answers.) *The lesson may be used at any time during the instructional process.*

Instructional Game: Keeping Score in Bowling   146

In this game, students learn how to keep score in bowling. Then, they play and score a bowling game by using number cubes to simulate each roll. The game promotes mental math skills related to two-digit addition. *The game can be used any time after students have learned how to add two-digit numbers with renaming.*

Think before you punch!

In this activity, you mentally decide what multiple of 10, 100, or 1,000 must be added or subtracted to obtain the next *End Number.* You then use a calculator to check your results.

Work with a partner and a calculator. One person decides what computation to make to obtain the End Number; the other person performs the calculation on the calculator.

To begin a round, enter the first *Start Number* into a calculator. To obtain the first End Number, use the calculator to make *one* computation (add or subtract a number). You may not press the "Clear" key as part of your computation.

The End Number becomes the next Start Number. Continue by making *one* computation on the Start Number to obtain the next End Number.

If a mistake is made, clear the mistake and enter the previous End Number. Then, try another computation. Continue until you obtain the final end number in the list. Then, switch roles and play another round!

Round 1

Start Number	To obtain the End Number, what must you *add* or *subtract*?	End Number
Enter 20		60
60		360
360		330
330		300
300		900
900		990
990		1,000
1,000		1,020

Round 2

Start Number	To obtain the End Number, what must you *add* or *subtract*?	End Number
Enter 30		80
80		980
980		1,000
1,000		1,500
1,500		1,550
1,550		1,750
1,750		750
750		0

Next Number, Please (page 2)

Round 3

Start Number	To obtain the End Number, what must you *add* or *subtract*?	End Number
Enter 200		800
800		880
880		950
950		50
50		500
500		5,000
5,000		4,900
4,900		5,000

Round 4

Start Number	To obtain the End Number, what must you *add* or *subtract*?	End Number
Enter 9,000		5,000
5,000		5,050
5,050		5,200
5,200		7,000
7,000		700
700		70
70		7,000
7,000		5,990

Round 5

Start Number	To obtain the End Number, what must you *add* or *subtract*?	End Number
Enter two thousand five		3,000
3,000		Twenty-nine hundred
2,900		Ten thousand
10,000		1,000

Roller Coaster Rounding

round a whole number to a given place value, you can follow these steps:

. Underline the digit in the place value to which you are rounding.

. Look at the digit to the right of the underlined digit and compare it to 5.
   - If it is greater than or equal to 5, increase the underlined digit by 1.
   - If it is less than 5, leave the underlined digit as it is.

. Change every digit to the right of the underlined digit to 0.

e *roller coaster model* described below should help you round whole numbers.

round "Car 34" and "Car 37" to the nearest ten, k of a roller coaster with 35 at the top, 30 at left-hand base, and 40 at the right-hand base. For each number, the two possible tens to nd to are 30 and 40. As you can see, 34 rounds des down) to 30, and 37 rounds (slides vn) to 40.

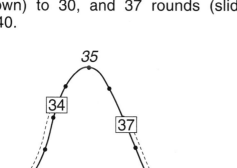

1. Draw cars on the tracks to show how to round 628 and 682 to the nearest hundred. The two possible hundreds to round to are

   _____ and _____.

   628 rounds to _____.

   682 rounds to _____.

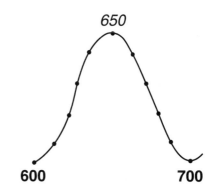

Complete the model to round 83 and 86 to the nearest ten. Be sure to show where the numbers go on the tracks.

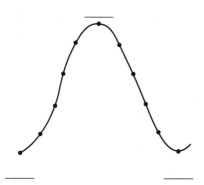

rounds to _____.

rounds to _____.

3. Complete the model to round 555 and 529 to the nearest hundred. Show where the numbers go on the tracks.

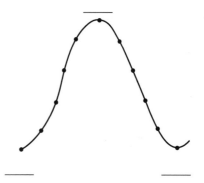

555 rounds to _____.

529 rounds to _____.

Roller Coaster Rounding (page 2)

In Exercises 4 through 6, first complete the model. Then, use the model to help you round the given numbers to the given place value.

4. Round 82, 89, 94, 96, and 109 to the nearest **ten**.

82: _____ 89: _____ 94: _____ 96: _____ 109: _____

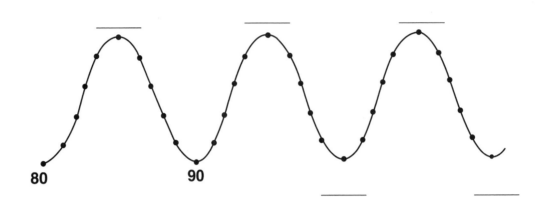

5. Round 740, 771, 805, 949, and 959 to the nearest **hundred**.

740: _____ 771: _____ 805: _____ 949: _____ 959: _____

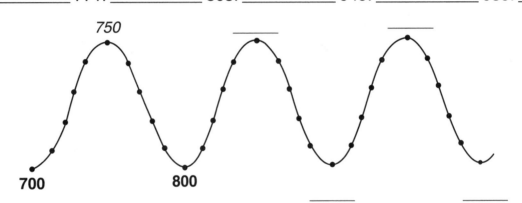

6. Round 300, 930, 1,500, 2,050, and 2,633 to the nearest **thousand**.

300: _____ 930: _____ 1,500: _____ 2,050: _____ 2,633: _____

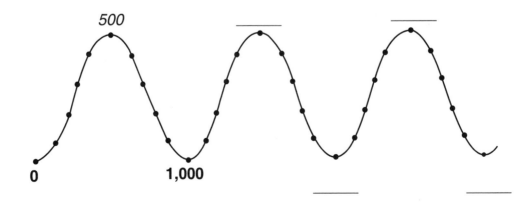

me _____ Date _____ Class _____

Using Front-End Estimation
to Check for Reasonableness: Addition

Front-end estimation involves two steps. First, add the digits in the front end.
Then, look at the other digits to see if you should *adjust* your estimate up.

Estimate the sum.	Add the digits in the front end.	Look at the other digits. Adjust your estimate, if necessary.	
459 + 344	4 + 3 ‾‾‾ 7	459 + 344 ‾‾‾ 7	Because 59 + 44 is about another 100, adjust the estimate up. Estimate: ***about 800***

1 and 2, circle the best estimate.

219
+ 378
‾‾‾‾

a. about 500
b. about 600
c. about 700

2. 867
+ 131
‾‾‾‾

a. about 800
b. about 900
c. about 1,000

3 and 4, use front-end estimation to ·timate each sum.

352
+ 251
‾‾‾‾

4. 3,449
+ 3,448
‾‾‾‾‾

In 5 and 6, estimate each sum by first rounding each addend to the greatest place-value position.

5. 352
+ 251
‾‾‾‾

6. 3,449
+ 3,448
‾‾‾‾‾

In 3 through 6 above, does one method of estimation seem to give better results? Explain.

·e *front-end estimation* to estimate each sum.

188 + 211 _____

369 + 533 _____

228 + 909 _____

3,217 + 1,188 _____

9. 423 + 681 _____

11. 924 + 679 _____

13. 2,445 + 4,493 _____

15. 6,555 + 2,501 _____

·timate to see if the answer given could *possibly* be right. Write *Yes* or *No*.

571 + 431 = 902 _____

607 + 788 = 1,495 _____

6,278 + 1,725 = 9,003 _____

4,657 + 2,348 = 7,005 _____

17. 383 + 114 = 497 _____

19. 744 + 368 = 1,012 _____

21. 5,493 + 3,504 = 8,997 _____

23. 3,912 + 3,079 = 8,991 _____

Keeping Score in Bowling

You can be on a roll bowling—in your sp. time!

How to Keep Score

A game of bowling consists of 10 frames. You roll two balls in each frame, except when you get a *strike*. A strike occurs when you knock down all 10 pins on the first roll.

In Frame 1 of the game below, you knocked down 3 pins on the first roll and 5 pins on the second roll. So, your score for Frame 1 is 8. In Frame 2, you knocked down 8 pins on the first roll and 0 pins (shown by the —) on the second roll. So, your score in Frame 2 is 8 + 8 = 16.

In Frame 3, you knocked down 5 pins on the first roll and the rest the pins on the second roll. Knocking down all of the pins in two rolls is called a *spare* (shown by the /).

A *spare* counts for 10 pins, plus the number of pins knocked down with the *first* ball in the next frame. Note: Until you make your first roll in Frame 4, you cannot write a score in Frame 3.

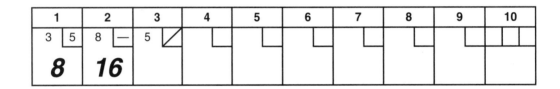

In Frame 4 (below), you knocked down 7 pins on the first throw. So, your score for Frame 3 is computed as follows.

16	+	10	+	7	=	33
score in Frame 2		for the spare in Frame 3		pins on your first roll in Frame 4		

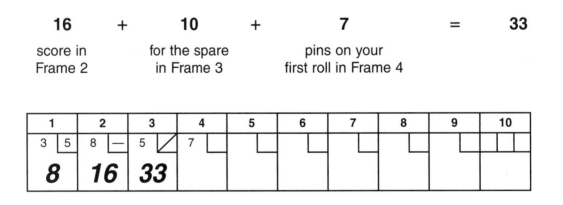

On your second roll in Frame 4, you knocked down 2 pins. So, in Frame 4, you knocked down 7 + 2, or 9, pins in all. Your score in Frame 4 is 33 + 9 = 42. (See score sheet at the top of the next page.)

A *strike* (shown by an X) counts for 10 pins, plus the number of pins you knock down the next *two* rolls. In Frame 5 below, you rolled a strike. Note that until you make your next two rolls, you cannot write a score in Frame 5.

1	2	3	4	5	6	7	8	9	10
3 | 5	8 | —	5 | ⟋	7 | 2	X					
8	**16**	**33**	**42**						

In Frame 6, you knocked down 3 pins in your first roll and 5 pins on your second roll. So, your score in Frame 5 is computed as follows.

$$\underset{\substack{\text{score in}\\ \text{Frame 4}}}{42} \quad + \quad \underset{\text{for the strike}}{10} \quad + \quad \underset{\substack{\text{pins on your}\\ \text{next two rolls}}}{(3+5)} \quad = \quad 60$$

Because you have now completed both rolls in Frame 6, you are able to compute your score for Frame 6: $60 + 8 = 68$.

1	2	3	4	5	6	7	8	9	10
3 | 5	8 | —	5 | ⟋	7 | 2	X	3 | 5				
8	**16**	**33**	**42**	**60**	**68**				

In Frame 7 below, you rolled a spare. Then, you rolled a strike in Frame 8. Your score in Frame 7 is 10 plus the number of pins on your next roll (10). So, your score in Frame 7 is $68 + 10 + 10 = 88$. You are not ready to record a score in Frame 8 because you have not yet made your next two rolls.

1	2	3	4	5	6	7	8	9	10
3 | 5	8 | —	5 | ⟋	7 | 2	X	3 | 5	6 | ⟋	X		
8	**16**	**33**	**42**	**60**	**68**	**88**			

Keeping Score in Bowling (page 3)

In Frame 9 below, you rolled a strike. Then, you rolled another strike in Frame 10. Your score in Frame 8 is computed as follows.

88	+	**10**	+	**(10 + 10)**	=	**118**
score in Frame 7		for the strike in Frame 8		pins on your next two rolls (the strikes in Frames 9 and 10)		

1	2	3	4	5	6	7	8	9	10
3 5	8 —	5 /	7 2	X	3 5	6 /	X	X	X
8	***16***	***33***	***42***	***60***	***68***	***88***	***118***		

- When you roll a strike in Frame 10, you get *two* extra rolls.
- When you roll a spare in Frame 10, you get *one* extra roll.

Because you rolled a strike in Frame 10, you get two more rolls. On the first extra roll (shown below), you rolled a 5. Then you rolled a 2. So, your score in Frame 9 is computed as follows.

118	+	**10**	+	**(10 + 5)**	=	**143**
score in Frame 8		for the strike in Frame 9		pins on your next two rolls		

Your score in Frame 10 is computed as follows.

143	+	**10**	+	**(5 + 2)**	=	**160**
score in Frame 9		for the strike in Frame 10		pins on your next two rolls		

So, your final score is 160.

1	2	3	4	5	6	7	8	9	10
3 5	8 —	5 /	7 2	X	3 5	6 /	X	X	X 5 2
8	***16***	***33***	***42***	***60***	***68***	***88***	***118***	***143***	***160***

aying Keeping Score in Bowling:

You are now ready to play and score a game of bowling. Play the game in groups of three or four. Help each other keep track of your bowling scores.

- Roll a *pair of number cubes* (marked 1–6) for the *first* roll of a frame. The number of pins you knock down is the sum of the numbers shown on the number cubes. If you roll a 10, 11, or 12 on the first roll of a frame, you have a *strike*.

- If you do *not* get a strike, roll *one number cube* for your second roll of the frame. Add the numbers from the two rolls to determine the total number of pins knocked down for the frame. If the number for this second roll of the frame is *greater than or equal to* the number of pins still up (from your first roll), you have a *spare*.

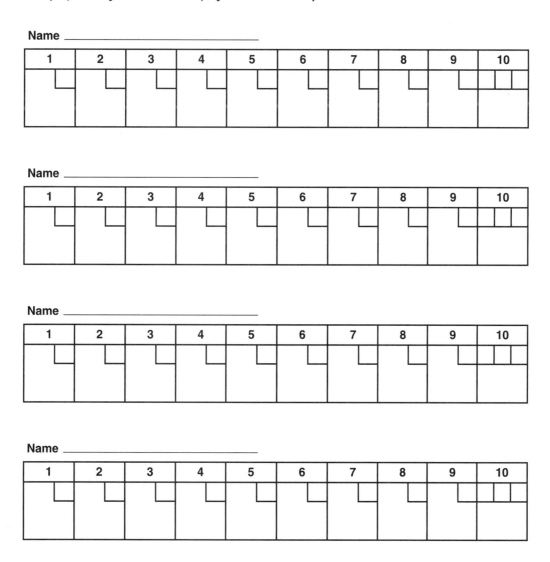

Resources for Subtraction

(Estimation, Instructional Games, and Follow-Up Activities)

Using Front-End Estimation to Check for Reasonableness: Subtraction   153

This lesson provides a practical way for students to determine if a subtraction result is reasonable. The process involves subtracting the front-end digits (the most important digits in determining an approximate answer). The process also involves making an adjustment by taking the remaining digits into account. For some students, the adjustment process may be difficult—and for those students it may be omitted. Answers are provided on page 195. (For exercises 16–21, you may want students to also explain their reasoning for determining their Yes/No answers.) *The lesson may be used at any time during the instructional process.*

Instructional Game: Balance the +/− Number Sentence!   154

This domino-type game promotes the memorization and linkage of the addition/subtraction facts, the use of mental math, and trial-and-error thinking to balance addition and subtraction number sentences. *The game may be played when students are mastering the subtraction facts or at any point during the unit.*

As an alternative to having students actually play the game, the game cards may be used in an activity setting. Have students work in small groups. Have each group display all 32 game cards face up. As a group, have them match all 32 number sentences with their respective solutions. Because each solution (on a card) matches exactly one number sentence (on a card), and because there is exactly one solution (on a card) for each number sentence (on a card), this activity is akin to completing a puzzle.

Follow-Up Activity: Editor Error Search (+/−)   158

In this activity, students pretend they are mathematics editors for a textbook company. Their job is to correct all the errors they can find in a manuscript on addition and subtraction. Because the manuscript includes spelling and grammatical errors (as well as math errors), this activity integrates language arts and math. Answers are provided on page 196. *The activity is ideal to use at the end of the subtraction unit* because it reinforces and reviews addition and subtraction skills and concepts in a motivating way.

As an *extension* to this activity, you may want students to work in small groups to discuss the incorrect answers in the manuscript and try to describe a possible *error pattern* for each error. (Each mathematics error in the manuscript is based on an error pattern.)

Instructional Game: Target Math (+/−)   159

In this game, each student participates by selecting the level of difficulty of a problem according to his or her personal needs and desires. It is a game where keen concentration can help a team win. The problems—based on addition and subtraction concepts and problem solving—are organized according to five levels of difficulty. *The game may be played at any point during the unit.*

Using Front-End Estimation
to Check for Reasonableness: Subtraction

Front-end estimation involves two steps. First, subtract the digits in the front end. Then, look at the other digits to see if you should *adjust* your estimate up or down.

timate the difference.	Subtract the digits in the front end.	Look at the other digits. Adjust your estimate, if necessary.
894 − 245	8 − 2 ――― 6	**894** − **245** 6 ――――――― Because 94 > 45, adjust the estimate *up*. Estimate: ***more than 600***
7,421 − 3,846	7 − 3 ――― 4	7,**421** − 3,**846** ――――――― Because 421 < 846, adjust the 4 estimate *down*. Estimate: ***less than 4,000***

and 2, circle the better estimate.

836 − 572	**a.** less than 300 **b.** more than 300	**2.** 3,963 − 1,258	**a.** less than 2,000 **b.** more than 2,000

and 4, use *front-end estimation* to imate each difference.

In 5 and 6, estimate each difference by first *rounding* each number.

708 − 249	**4.** 8,526 − 5,448	**5.** 708 − 249	**6.** 8,526 − 5,448

In Exercises 3–6, does one method of estimation seem to give better results? Explain.

e *front-end estimation* to estimate each difference.

523 − 446 _____ **9.** 955 − 338 _____

768 − 599 _____ **11.** 873 − 149 _____

940 − 426 _____ **13.** 5,148 − 3,679 _____

8,497 − 4,466 _____ **15.** 7,286 − 3,912 _____

imate to see if the answer given could *possibly* be right. Write *Yes* or *No*.

629 − 485 = 144 _____ **17.** 974 − 258 = 616 _____

346 − 289 = 157 _____ **19.** 526 − 319 = 107 _____

8,624 − 3,897 = 4,727 _____ **21.** 9,168 − 6,432 = 3,736 _____

Balance the +/– Number Sentence!

Rules

1. **Getting Started:** Students work in groups of two or three. Each group is given one copy of the 32 game cards on pages 156 through 157. Ask students to cut out the game cards and thoroughly shuffle them. *Have them deal 5 cards to each player.* The remaining cards are placed facedown in a stack in front of them. *Allow time for the players to study the cards in their hand.* Explain that each card contains a number sentence on the left and a solution to a different number sentence on the right (shown by the white number).

2. **Playing the Cards:** The first player (Player A) begins by placing one card from his or her hand face up on the table. Player B must try to match either end of that card as follows.

   • Player B may place a card to the left of Player A's card so that the white number on Player B's card provides the value of □ on Player A's card.

   Or

   • Player B may place a card to the right of Player A's card so that the number sentence on Player A's card is solved by the white number on Player B's card.

3. **Sample Rounds:** Suppose there are two players and they have the cards shown below. If Player A plays the card on the far left, Player B should play the card on the far right because 14 solves □ − 8 = 6. Then, Player A should play the second card from the left because 15 − □ = 8 is a number sentence for which 7 is the solution.

| □ − 8 = 6 | 7 | 15 − □ = 8 | 6 |

Cards in Player A's Hand

| □ − 9 = 2 | 6 | 17 − □ = 9 | 14 |

Cards in Player B's Hand

The correct placement of the cards on the table for the sample rounds is shown below. Note that when a card is placed on the table, the matching sides of the cards should touch.

| 17 − □ = 9 | 14 | □ − 8 = 6 | 7 | 15 − □ = 8 | 6 |

Balance the +/– Number Sentence! (page 2)

4. **When You Cannot Match a Card on the Table:** If a player is unable to match either end of any card on the table, he or she must draw a new card from the stack. During that turn, the player should then try to use the drawn card to match either end of any card on the table. If that player is unable to play the card, the player must then place any card from his or her hand on the table to begin a new row.

5. **Placement of an Incorrect Card:** If a player places an incorrect card on the table, the card must be returned to the player's hand, and play resumes with the next player.

6. **Scoring Points:** A player earns one point for each card he or she *correctly* places on the table to *solve a problem*. No points are scored if a card is placed incorrectly or if a player has no cards that match and must place a card on the table to begin a new row. Note: During a round, a player may place a card to solve a problem in any of the rows.

7. **When You Have No Cards in Your Hand:** If a player begins a round with no cards in his or her hand, the player draws a card from the stack and attempts to play it. If he or she is unable to play it, the player begins a new row as per Rule 4. If no cards are left in the stack for the player to take, the player loses that turn.

8. **How the Game Ends:** The game ends when no player is able to play a card and there are no more cards left in the stack. The player with the most points wins.

Note that some sentences on the game cards contain more than one □. Advise students that each □ in a given sentence stands for the *same number*.

Game Cards for
Balance the +/− Number Sentence!

When more than one □ appears in a sentence, each □ stands for the same number.

□ − 8 = 6	**7**
15 − 9 = □	**8**
5 + □ = 14	**11**
21 = □ + 0	**5**
23 + □ = 23	**19**
□ + 19 = 23	**30**
□ + □ = 14	**60**
24 + 25 = □ + 24	**100**

17 − □ = 9	**14**
□ − 9 = 2	**6**
14 = 9 + □	**9**
19 − □ = 0	**21**
19 = 22 − □	**0**
100 = □ + 40	**4**
2 + □ + □ = 22	**25**
□ − 15 = 15	**3**

$199 - \square = 100$	**10**
$13 + \square = 12 + 13$	**16**
$\square - \square = 13 - \square$	**18**
$49 + 49 = 100 - \square$	**15**
$9 + 8 + 7 = \square + 7$	**23**
$49 = \square + 99 - 99$	**2**
$31 - 24 = 31 - \square$	**22**
$18 + \square = 40$	**1**

$\square - 50 = 50$	**20**
$\square - 4 = 5 + 6$	**12**
$23 + \square = 47 - 1$	**13**
$16 + 0 = 0 + \square$	**99**
$36 - \square - \square = 0$	**17**
$60 = \square + \square + \square$	**49**
$\square - 22 = 18$	**24**
$51 - 9 = 50 - 9 + \square$	**40**

Name _____ Date _____ Class _____

Editor Error Search (+/−)

This page will be part of a math book. Suppose you are the editor of the book. Your job is to correct all errors that you can find on this page. There are answer error, spellin errors, and more. Have you all ready found some errors

Add or subtract.

1. $\begin{array}{r} 35 \\ + 4 \\ \hline \mathbf{79} \end{array}$

2. $\begin{array}{r} 573 \\ + 335 \\ \hline \mathbf{808} \end{array}$

3. $\begin{array}{r} 96 \\ - 27 \\ \hline \mathbf{79} \end{array}$

4. $\begin{array}{r} 341 \\ - 256 \\ \hline \mathbf{85} \end{array}$

5. $\begin{array}{r} 405 \\ - 368 \\ \hline \mathbf{163} \end{array}$

6. $\begin{array}{r} 582 \\ + 229 \\ \hline \mathbf{7,012} \end{array}$

7. $\begin{array}{r} 870 \\ - 380 \\ \hline \mathbf{490} \end{array}$

8. $\begin{array}{r} 796 \\ + 143 \\ \hline \mathbf{8,139} \end{array}$

9. $\begin{array}{r} 204 \\ - 155 \\ \hline \mathbf{359} \end{array}$

10. $\begin{array}{r} 367 \\ + 429 \\ \hline \mathbf{896} \end{array}$

11. $\begin{array}{r} 900 \\ - 189 \\ \hline \mathbf{721} \end{array}$

12. $\begin{array}{r} 903 \\ - 447 \\ \hline \mathbf{366} \end{array}$

13. $849 + 29 + 504 + 3 = \underline{\mathbf{1,943}}$

Solve each problem

14. Joey was born on July 5, 1990. How old will be on July 5 2020?

    30 years old

15. A candle was 32centimeters long when lit. When the candle was blown out, their were 18 centemeters left. How long was the part that burned away.

    50 cm

16. Nine of Mr Bennys students is absent today cause of a field trip. The other 17 of his students are hear in school. How many students are in his class in all?

    8 students

16. The Willis Tower in chicago has 110 stories and is 1,454 feet tall. It has a 253-foot TV antenna on top of that. What is the total heigt of the building and antena?

    1,817

Target Math (+/–)

This is a game where each student participates by selecting the level of difficulty of a problem according to his or her personal desires. It is a game where keen concentration can help a team win.

Rules:

1. This is a teacher-directed game for the entire class. Begin by dividing the class into four or five teams of approximately equal math ability. (Each team should be seated together, perhaps in a row.) The game is played with a Target Math Game Board (page 160) that is made visible to all students. The board shows "targets" in cells for five categories of problems: 5-point, 10-point, 15-point, 20-point, and 25-point problems. There are five problems (denoted A, B, C, D, and E) for each category. The problems themselves are *not* visible to students until a student selects a cell for a particular problem.

2. The point values reflect the relative difficulty of the problems. The easiest problems are the 5-point problems; the most difficult are the 25-point problems.

3. The game begins when the first student on the first team selects a target from the Target Math Game Board by calling out a cell number, such as 15C. This target corresponds to a particular problem for cell 15C on the Target Math Problems Sheet (pages 161–162). The teacher then writes the problem on the board for the entire class to see. The student who selected the problem has a set amount of time to solve the problem without the use of a calculator. If he or she solves it correctly, his or her team receives the indicated number of points—and the target is crossed out on the Target Math Game Board. If the problem is answered incorrectly, the team receives no points—*and the target (not the problem) remains on the board for a future player to answer in a later turn.* Teammates are not allowed to help a player solve a problem.

4. Upon completion of a problem, whether solved correctly or incorrectly, play always shifts to the next team.

5. Emphasize to students that when they select a target, they may select *any* target on the board that is still available—including any targets for which a problem was previously incorrectly solved. It is also important to point out that the 25 problems used for the game *retain their same cell numbers* (target positions) throughout the entire game. So, when a player selects a target whose problem was previously incorrectly answered, the same problem will appear. This provides an incentive for all students to pay attention—to *concentrate*—when it is not their turn. (Students who are alert may want to select problems of their liking that were previously missed.)

6. The first round is over after the first player on each team has had an opportunity to select a problem. During the second round, the second player on each team selects a problem. For the second round, you may want the team that went last during the first round to go first.

7. After a set number of complete rounds (or when all 25 problems behind the targets have been answered correctly), the team with the most points wins. If all 25 problems are correctly solved before each student has had an opportunity to play, you may want to provide additional problems. (To ensure that all students are actively engaged during the game, you may want all students to work on all problems that are displayed and turn in their work at the end of the game.)

Target Math Game Board

E					
D					
C					
B					
A					
	5	**10**	**15**	**20**	**25**

Target Math Problems Sheet (+/–)

Point Problems		**Answers**
5A	Solve: □ – 9 = 8	□ = 17
5B	Solve: 7 + □ = 15	□ = 8
5C	Solve: 16 – □ = 7	□ = 9
5D	Solve: 15 + 18 = 18 + □	□ = 15
5E	Solve: □ + 19 = 19	□ = 0

Point Problems		**Answers**
10A	295 + 704	999
10B	4,023 + 70	4,093
10C	21 + 4 + 12 + 32	69
10D	999 – 789	210
10E	8,706 – 705	8,001

Point Problems		**Answers**
15A	59 + 34	93
15B	677 + 182	859
15C	786 + 99	885
15D	999 + 123	1,122
15E	6,706 + 794	7,500

Point Problems		**Answers**
20A	647 – 19	628
20B	192 – 97	95
20C	1,500 – 388	1,112
20D	1,000 – 17	983
20E	6,000 – 547	5,453

Target Math Problems Sheet (+/−) (page 2)

25-Point Problems   ***Answers***

25A After spending $199, Mr. Greenback had $400
$201 left. How much money did he have
at the start?

25B You need 1,500 points to win the game.   504 points
So far you have 996 points. How many
more points do you need?

25C There are 200 children in a room.   103 boys
Ninety-seven of them are girls.
How many of them are boys?

25D Ben has saved $57, Jamie has $25
saved $68, and Maria has saved $150.
How much more money has Maria
saved than Ben and Jamie combined?

25E A student subtracted 276 from 734 and
obtained an answer of 368, as shown.
What is the correct answer? Also,
describe the errors the student likely made.

$$\begin{array}{r} \overset{5}{\cancel{7}}\,{}^{1}3\,{}^{1}4 \\ -\ 2\ \ 7\ \ 6 \\ \hline 3\ \ 6\ \ 8 \end{array}$$

Answer: The correct answer is 458.
The student renamed directly from
the 7 hundreds. The student renamed 734
as 5 hundreds, 13 tens, 14 ones.

Resources for Multiplication

(Estimation, Instructional Games, and Follow-Up Activities)

Follow-Up Activity: Editor Error Search (×) 172

In this activity, students pretend they are mathematics editors for a textbook company. Their job is to find and correct all the errors they can find in a manuscript on multiplication. Because the manuscript includes spelling and grammatical errors (as well as math errors), this activity integrates language arts and math. Answers are provided on pages 197–198. *The activity is ideal to use at the end of the multiplication unit* because it reinforces and provides a review of multiplication skills and concepts in a motivating way.

As an extension to the Editor Error Search activity, have students work in small groups to discuss the incorrect answers in the manuscript and try to describe a possible *error pattern* for each mathematics error. (Each mathematics error in the manuscript is based on an error pattern—except for Numbers 1 and 3, which are based on a lack of fact recall.)

Touching on the Facts With Your Fingers

This finger algorithm produces any multiplication fact from 5×5 through 9×9. The fingers on each hand are numbered as shown below.

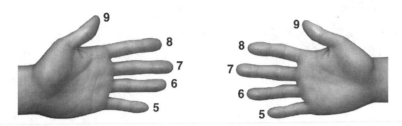

To multiply 8×7, place finger 8 on one hand against finger 7 on the other hand. Then close the fingers below 8 and 7.

You obtain the product by following these steps:

> **a.** Multiply the total number of closed fingers by 10. (Each closed finger is worth 10.)
> **b.** Multiply the number of open fingers on one hand by the number of open fingers on the other hand.
> **c.** Add the results you obtain in **Steps a** and **b**.

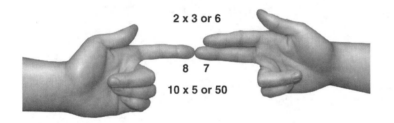

Therefore, $8 \times 7 = 50 + 6$, or 56.

other Example:

find 9×8, have the thumb on the your left
nd touch the finger below your thumb on
ur right hand. Then, close the fingers below
n the left hand and 8 on the right hand.

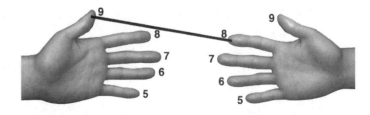

a. Multiply the total number of closed fingers $(4 + 3)$ by 10: $10 \times 7 = 70$.
b. Multiply the number of open fingers on the left hand (1) by the number of open fingers on the right hand (2): $1 \times 2 = 2$.
c. Add the results in **Steps a** and **b**: $70 + 2 = 72$. So, $9 \times 8 = 72$.

Why the Finger Multiplication Algorithm Works

Note: This justification is based on elementary algebra and is intended for teacher edification purposes only.

Finger Multiplication Algorithm

To multiply 6×7, finger 6 on one hand is placed against finger 7 on the other. The fingers below those two fingers are closed. The rest remain open.

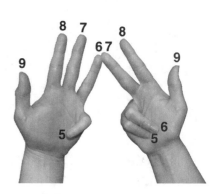

What you do:

a. Multiply the total number of closed fingers by 10.

b. Multiply the number of open fingers on one hand by the number of open fingers on the other hand.

c. Add the results you obtain in Steps **a** and **b**.

What you compute:

$10 \bullet (1 + 2) = 10 \bullet 3 = 30$

$4 \bullet 3 = 12$

$30 + 12 = 42$. So, $6 \times 7 = 42$

Algebra can be used to prove why the algorithm works. Let $x =$ the number to be multiplied on the left hand, and let $y =$ the number to be multiplied on the right hand.

For two numbers x and y, where $5 \leq x \leq 9$ and $5 \leq y \leq 9$, we need to prove that the finger multiplication algorithm yields the product $x \bullet y$.

Proof:

Suppose the finger that represents x is touching the finger that represents y.

Then, $(x - 5) =$ number of *closed* fingers on the left hand.

  Note: If $x = 6$, then the number of closed fingers on the left had is $(6 - 5)$, or 1.

And $(y - 5) =$ number of *closed* fingers on the right hand.

Also, $(10 - x) =$ number of *open* fingers on the left hand.

  Note: If $x = 6$, then the number of open fingers on the left hand is $(10 - 6)$, or 4.

And $(10 - y) =$ number of *open* fingers on the right hand.

Apply the algorithm:

Multiply the total number of *closed* fingers by 10.

Multiply the number of *open* fingers on one hand by the number of *open* fingers on the other hand.

$10 \bullet [(x - 5) + (y - 5)]$ $+$ $(10 - x) \bullet (10 - y)$

Add the results.

$10 \bullet (x + y - 10)$ $+$ $(100 - 10y - 10x + x \bullet y)$

$10x + 10y - 100$ $+$ $100 - 10y - 10x + x \bullet y$

Combine like terms.

$(10x - 10x) + (10y - 10y) + (100 - 100) + x \bullet y = x \bullet y$ ◀—— the desired product

Using Front-End Estimation to Check for Reasonableness: Multiplication

imate 4 × 874:

st, multiply the front-end digits. Think of 4 × 800.	Now, look at the other digits. Think of 4 × 70.	Add the products.	Adjust the estimate, if necessary.
⁷4 → $\begin{array}{r} 800 \\ \times\ 4 \\ \hline 3,200 \end{array}$ 4	$\begin{array}{r} 70 \\ \times\ 4 \\ \hline 280 \end{array}$	$\begin{array}{r} 3,200 \\ +\ 280 \\ \hline 3,480 \end{array}$	Since 74 was rounded down, 3,480 is too small. Adjust the estimate up. Estimate: *more than 3,480.*

imate 7 × 558:

Think of 7 × 500.	Think of 7 × 60.	Add the products.	Adjust, if necessary.
⁵8 → $\begin{array}{r} 500 \\ \times\ 7 \\ \hline 3,500 \end{array}$ 7	$\begin{array}{r} 60 \\ \times\ 7 \\ \hline 420 \end{array}$	$\begin{array}{r} 3,500 \\ +\ 420 \\ \hline 3,920 \end{array}$	Since 58 was rounded up, 3,920 is too large. Adjust the estimate down. Estimate: *less than 3,920.*

imate 77 × 646:

Think of 80 × 600.	Think of 80 × 50.	Add the products.	Adjust, if necessary.
⁴6 → $\begin{array}{r} 600 \\ \times\ 80 \\ \hline 48,000 \end{array}$ ⁷7	$\begin{array}{r} 50 \\ \times\ 80 \\ \hline 4,000 \end{array}$	$\begin{array}{r} 48,000 \\ +\ 4,000 \\ \hline 52,000 \end{array}$	Since both 77 and 46 were rounded up, 52,000 is too large. Adjust down. Estimate: *less than 52,000.*

and 2, circle the better estimate.

$\begin{array}{r} 345 \\ \times\ 5 \\ \hline \end{array}$ **a.** less than 1,750
b. more than 1,750

2. $\begin{array}{r} 274 \\ \times\ 6 \\ \hline \end{array}$ **a.** less than 1,620
b. more than 1,620

front-end estimation to estimate each product.

6 × 591 _____

4. 9 × 663 _____

7 × 365 _____

6. 9 × 589 _____

38 × 597 _____

8. 43 × 609 _____

imate to see if the answer given could *possibly* be right. Write *Yes* or *No*.

5 × 829 = 4,035 _____

10. 9 × 776 = 6,984 _____

6 × 937 = 6,622 _____

12. 7 × 4,927 = 24,489 _____

59 × 707 = 4,543 _____

14. 43 × 389 = 16,727 _____

How Close Can You Get?

Materials

- Leader's Game Sheet (one per group); Player's Game Sheet (one per player)
- Digit Cards (provided on page 171); there are four cards for each digit (0–9)—each team gets [a] full set (you may want to print the cards on tagboard)
- Watch or clock with a second hand
- Calculators

Students play the game in small groups. One person in each group is the leader; the rest are the p[layers]. There are three rounds per game. The winner of a game (based on the three rounds) becomes [the] leader for the next game.

Rules

1. The leader shuffles the cards and secretly turns up one card for each blank listed on the Leader's Ga[me] Sheet for the round. The dealer records the numbers on the blanks without showing the cards or [the] results to the other players. Suppose the Leader's Game Sheet for a round is the one shown belov[w.]

Leader's Game Sheet

Round 1: _____ × _____ _____ _____

Because there are four blanks on the sheet for this round, the dealer turns up four cards. Suppose [the] four cards, in order, are 9, 0, 9, and 4. The dealer would record the following.

Round 1: ___**9**___ × ___**0**___ ___**9**___ ___**4**___

2. After the dealer records all the digits for the round on the blanks, he or she shows the Leader's Ga[me] Sheet to the other players. The players—working independently—have *5 seconds* (or whatever is [rea]sonable for the class) to mentally estimate the result. In the above example, they would estim[ate] 9 × 94. (The "094" is equal to 94.) They may *not* use pencil or paper or a calculator. The leader fi[nds] the *exact answer*—and is allowed to use a calculator.

3. The players record their estimates on their individual Player's Game Sheet for the round. Then, t[hey] record the exact answer as given to them by the leader. Finally, they find the *positive differe*[nce] between their estimate and the exact answer. (The smaller of the two numbers is subtracted from [the] larger.) See the example below.

Player's Game Sheet

	Your Estimate	Exact Answer	Positive Difference
Round 1	810	846	36 (846 − 810)

4. After Round 1 is completed, the procedure is repeated for two more rounds. After all three rounds [are] completed, each player finds the sum of his or her three positive differences. *The player with [the] smallest sum is the winner*—and becomes the leader for the next game (of three rounds).

5. Between games, encourage students to discuss their estimation strategies so that all students par[tici]pating in the game are able to improve their estimation skills.

How Close Can You Get?

Leader's Game Sheet

ne 1 (In Round 3, the first digit cannot be 0.)

Round 1: _____ × _____ _____ _____

Round 2: _____ × _____ _____ _____

Round 3: _____ _____ _____ – _____ _____

ind 1
ct Answer: _____

Round 2
Exact Answer: _____

Round 3
Exact Answer: _____

ne 2 (In Round 3, the first digit cannot be 0.)

Round 1: _____ × _____ _____ _____

Round 2: _____ _____ × _____ _____

Round 3: _____ _____ _____ – _____ _____

ind 1
ct Answer: _____

Round 2
Exact Answer: _____

Round 3
Exact Answer: _____

ne 3 (In Round 3, the first digit cannot be 0.)

Round 1: _____ × _____ _____ _____

Round 2: _____ _____ _____ × _____ _____

Round 3: _____, _____ _____ _____ – _____ _____ _____

ind 1
ct Answer: _____

Round 2
Exact Answer: _____

Round 3
Exact Answer: _____

How Close Can You Get?
Player's Game Sheet

Game 1

	Your Estimate	Exact Answer	Positive Differen
Round 1			
Round 2			
Round 3			
		Sum	

Game 2

	Your Estimate	Exact Answer	Positive Differen
Round 1			
Round 2			
Round 3			
		Sum	

Game 3

	Your Estimate	Exact Answer	Positive Differen
Round 1			
Round 2			
Round 3			
		Sum	

How Close Can You Get?

Digit Cards

0	0	0	0	1	1	1
1	2	2	2	2	3	3
3	3	4	4	4	4	5
5	5	5	6	6	6	6
7	7	7	7	8	8	8
8	9	9	9	9		

Editor Error Search (×)

Let's pretend that you are an editor for a math book. Your job is to correct all errors you can find on this page. They're errors involving answers, spelling grammar, and more Have you already found a error or too?

Multiply.

1. $\begin{array}{r} 6 \\ \times\ 7 \\ \hline 54 \end{array}$

2. $\begin{array}{r} 0 \\ \times\ 6 \\ \hline 6 \end{array}$

3. $\begin{array}{r} 7 \\ \times\ 8 \\ \hline 63 \end{array}$

4. $\begin{array}{r} 8 \\ \times\ 6 \\ \hline 48 \end{array}$

5. $\begin{array}{r} 1 \\ \times\ 7 \\ \hline 8 \end{array}$

6. $\begin{array}{r} 10 \\ \times\ 9 \\ \hline 9 \end{array}$

7. $\begin{array}{r} 32 \\ \times\ 7 \\ \hline 2114 \end{array}$

8. $\begin{array}{r} 109 \\ \times\ 6 \\ \hline 654 \end{array}$

9. $\begin{array}{r} 269 \\ \times\ 9 \\ \hline 1841 \end{array}$

10. $\begin{array}{r} 23 \\ \times\ 47 \\ \hline 253 \end{array}$

Rite the letter for the correct answer.

11. Which of these shows another name for 7×6?

    A $7 \times 7 \times 7 \times 7 \times 7 \times 7$

    B $6 \times 6 \times 6 \times 6 \times 6 \times 6 \times 6$

    C $7 + 7 + 7 + 7 + 7 + 7 + 7$

    D $6 + 6 + 6 + 6 + 6 + 6 + 6$ **B**

12. Which of these can be used to find 9×16?

    A $(10 \times 16) - 1$

    B $9 \times (10 + 6)$

    C $(10 \times 16) - 9$

    D $(9 + 1) \times (16 - 1)$ **C**

Solve each problem.

14. Arsha gave 5 pennys to each of 6 freinds. How many pennies did she give away?

                                    11 pennies

15. Hector made four 1-point baskets, five 2-point baskets, and zero 3-point baskets. How many points did he make in all

                                    17 points

16. Jeens are on sale for $36 purr pair. The regular price if $45. How much does Jamie save if she bys 3 pears?

                                    $108

Resources for Division

(Estimation, Instructional Games, and Follow-Up Activities)

Using Front-End Estimation to Check for Reasonableness: Division

This lesson provides a practical way for students to determine if a division result is reasonable. The process involves dividing the front-end digits (the most important digits in determining an approximate answer). Answers are provided on page 199. (For exercises 13–20, you may want students to also *explain* their reasoning for determining their Yes/No answers.) *The lesson may be used at any time during the instructional process.*

Using Compatible Numbers to Check for Reasonableness (+, −, ×, ÷)

In this lesson, students replace the given numbers in an exercise with compatible numbers ("nice numbers") that are near the given numbers to mentally obtain a result that is near the exact answer. Each of the four operations is addressed in this lesson. Answers are provided on page 199. (For exercises 13–20, you may want students to also *explain* their reasoning for determining their Yes/No answers.) *The lesson may be used at any time during the instructional process for each operation.*

Instructional Game: Balance the ×/÷ Number Sentence!

This domino-type game promotes the memorization and linkage of the multiplication and division facts, the use of mental math, and trial-and-error thinking to balance × and ÷ number sentences. Because this version of the game is played the way the +/− version is played, use the game rules that appear on pages 154–155. *The game may be played when students are mastering the division facts or at any point during the unit.*

As an *alternative* to having students actually play the game, the game cards may be used in an activity setting. Have each group display all 32 game cards face up. As a group, have them match all 32 number sentences with their respective solutions.

Follow-Up Activity:
Abbott and Costello's Number *Nonsense* 179

This activity is based on an Abbott and Costello comedy routine on how to perform a division computation (from their movie *In the Navy* [Gottlieb, Lubin, Horman, & Grant, 1941]). In this routine, Lou Costello makes a series of errors—while Bud Abbott tries to correct the errors. In the activity, students are asked to explain the errors that were made and explain the rationale behind Bud's methods for checking the division. Answers are provided on pages 199–200. *The activity may be used at any point during the unit.*

Instructional Game: Target Math (×/÷) 181

In this game, each student participates by selecting the level of difficulty of a problem according to his or her personal desires. It is a game where keen *concentration* can help a team win. The game rules and board are on pages 159–160. The problems on pages 181–182—based on multiplication and division concepts and problem solving—are organized according to five levels of difficulty. *It is recommended to play the game toward the end of the unit.*

e _____ Date _____ Class _____

Using Front-End Estimation to Check for Reasonableness: Division

To estimate a quotient using front-end estimation, follow these steps:

1. Find out how many digits are in the quotient, and find the first digit.

2. Give the estimate as a range. (For example, suppose the quotient is a three-digit number, and the first digit is 7. Then a range for the quotient would be "between 700 and 800.")

$\dfrac{?\;\text{xxx}}{8\overline{)4{,}289}}$	$\dfrac{5\text{xx}}{8\overline{)4{,}289}}$	$\dfrac{5\text{xx}}{8\overline{)4{,}289}}$
·cause 8 > 4, the first digit is not in ₂ thousands place.	$8\overline{)42}$ is about 5. So, the first digit is 5, and it is in the hundreds place.	The quotient is more than 500. But it is less than 600. So, a reasonable estimate is **between 500 and 600.**

through 4, circle the better estimate.

$9\overline{)496}$
    a. between 50 and 60
    b. between 500 and 600

2. $6\overline{)7{,}206}$
    a. between 100 and 200
    b. between 1,000 and 2,000

$35\overline{)707}$
    a. between 20 and 30
    b. between 200 and 300

4. $41\overline{)2{,}200}$
    a. between 50 and 60
    b. between 200 and 300

front-end estimation to estimate each difference.

$3\overline{)963}$ _____

6. $8\overline{)744}$ _____

$8\overline{)6{,}544}$ _____

8. $4\overline{)9{,}504}$ _____

$39\overline{)399}$ _____

10. $50\overline{)4{,}310}$ _____

$62\overline{)4{,}000}$ _____

12. $26\overline{)5{,}290}$ _____

mate to see if the answer given could *possibly* be right. Write *Yes* or *No*.

$656 \div 8 = 802$ _____

14. $985 \div 5 = 197$ _____

$1{,}587 \div 3 = 59$ _____

16. $5{,}832 \div 9 = 748$ _____

$532 \div 28 = 19$ _____

18. $6{,}633 \div 33 = 102$ _____

$1{,}530 \div 15 = 102$ _____

20. $8{,}000 \div 20 = 4{,}000$ _____

Using Compatible Numbers to Check for Reasonableness (+, −, ×, ÷)

Compatible numbers (also called *nice numbers*) are numbers with which you can compute mentally. To estimate, simply replace one or more numbers in the exercise with numbers that are close to them that you "wish they really were."

To estimate **sums,** use numbers that you can add mentally.

23 + 86 + 149 + 57

Nice numbers: 100 + 200

Estimate: **about 300**

To estimate **differences,** use numbers that you can subtract mentally.

48,321 − 29,469

Nice numbers: 48,000 − 28,000

Estimate: **about 20,000**

To estimate **products,** use numbers that you can multiply mentally.

9 × 845

Nice numbers: 9 × 800

Estimate: **about 7,200**

To estimate **quotients,** use numbers that you can divide mentally.

$6\overline{)4,449}$

Nice numbers: $6\overline{)4,200}$

Estimate: **about 700**

Estimate each result.

1. 26 + 75 + 49 + 59 _____

2. 186 + 39 + 19 + 67 _____

3. 673 + 391 + 488 _____

4. 6,791 − 3,857 _____

5. 17,979 − 8,215 _____

6. 35,308 − 15,765 _____

7. 11 × 56 _____

8. 919 × 46 _____

9. $9\overline{)821}$ _____

10. $5\overline{)2,406}$ _____

11. $19\overline{)4,117}$ _____

12. $52\overline{)5,199}$ _____

Estimate to see if the answer given could possibly be right. Write *Yes* or *No.*

13. 87 + 66 + 17 + 49 = 219 _____

14. 5,249 + 82 + 38 = 6,449 _____

15. 54,381 − 25,677 = 18,704 _____

16. 13,507 − 6,698 = 6,809 _____

17. 58 × 43 = 24,940 _____

18. 84 × 13 = 1,092 _____

19. 8,379 ÷ 9 = 931 _____

20. 19,324 ÷ 4 = 483 _____

Game Cards for
Balance the ×/÷ Number Sentence!

Game instructions are provided on pages 154–155.

□ ÷ 9 = 5	**8**
6 × □ = 42	**45**
17 × □ = 17	**63**
0 ÷ 11 = □	**7**
9 = 54 ÷ □	**17**
□ × 8 = 32	**1**
1 × □ = 11	**4**
24 ÷ □ = 8	**27**

32 ÷ □ = 4	**5**
□ × 9 = 45	**6**
9 = 18 ÷ □	**9**
1 = 17 ÷ □	**2**
□ ÷ 8 = 9	**0**
81 ÷ □ = 9	**72**
□ ÷ 9 = 3	**11**
7 = □ ÷ 9	**3**

Game Cards for Balance the ×/÷ Number Sentence! (page 2)

$\square \div 8 = 6$	**10**	$6 = \square \div 6$	**12**
$\square = 6 \times 9$	**48**	$6 \times \square = 60$	**36**
$\square \times 9 = 9 \times 12$	**54**	$\square \div 18 = 1$	**200**
$8 = \square \div 8$	**28**	$\square \div 10 = 20$	**16**
$\square = 1{,}000 \div 10$	**64**	$8 \times 10 = 4 \times \square$	**60**
$(2 \times 8) \times 9 = \square \times 9$	**100**	$\square \times 5 = 5 \times (8 \times 3)$	**20**
$11 \times 46 = \square \times 11$	**24**	$(\square - 60) \times 6 = 0$	**18**
$14 \div 2 = \square \div 4$	**50**	$50 \div \square = 1$	**46**

Abbott and Costello's Number *Non*sense

It is recommended that the short video clip of Abbott and Costello's routine paraphrased in this activity be played before students begin work on this activity. The routine is from their movie *In the Navy* (Gottlieb et al., 1941). The clip is available on YouTube. It may also be available on TeacherTube at http://teachertube.com/viewVideo.php?video_id=46231&title=abbott_and_costello.

u Costello: There are 28 doughnuts, and I have
even officers to feed. So I have just enough to give
hem 13 doughnuts apiece.

d Abbott: That's ridiculous.

u: It's not ridiculous. I can show that 28 divided by 7 = 13.

u: 7 will not go into 2 no matter how hard you try.
o we can't use the 2 right now. I'll use it later.
We know that 7 goes into 8 at least once. Write the 1.
× 1 = 7. Write the 7, and subtract from 8. This gives 1.

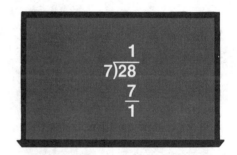

u: A minute ago we didn't use the 2. Now we're
ping to use it. We put it with the 1 to make 21.
e know that 7 goes into 21 three times. Write the 3.
o, 28 divided by 7 = 13.

d: That can't be right!
× 13 does *not* equal 28!

: Oh yes it does. I can show you.

: 7 × 3 = 21. Write the 21.
× 1 = 7. Write the 7.
+ 7 = 28.
, 7 times 13 = 28.

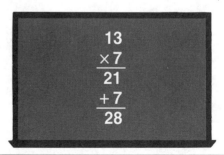

Abbott and Costello's Number *Non*sense (page 2)

Bud: This is ridiculous! I can prove you're wrong.
  Write 13 seven times. We'll add this up.

But Lou does not give Bud a chance to complete his thoughts.

Lou starts at the bottom and counts up.
Lou: 3 + 3 + 3 + 3 + 3 + 3 + 3 = 21.
       Write the 21.

Lou: Now count on by 1 from 21:
   22, 23, 24, 25, 26, 27, 28.
   So, seven 13s make 28.

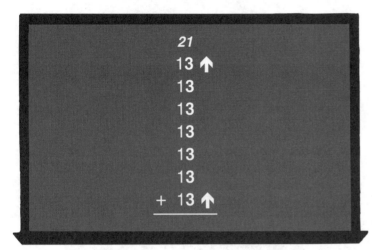

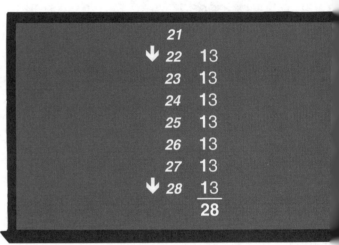

Work in a small group to answer these questions:

1. Give several reasons why 28 ÷ 7 does *not* equal 13.

2. Discuss and explain the errors that were made in each example.

3. How does the discussion of 7 × 13 at the bottom of the first page relate to the division problem about the doughnuts at the top of that page?

4. Why did Bud want Lou to write 13 seven times and then find the sum?

Target Math Problems Sheet (×/÷)

pages 159–160 for game rules and game board.

int Problems	Answers
A Solve: □ × 9 = 54	□ = 6
B Solve: 72 ÷ □ = 9	□ = 8
C Solve: 6 = □ ÷ 8	□ = 48
D Solve: 12 × 6 = 6 × □	□ = 12
E Solve: □ × 23 = 0	□ = 0

Point Problems	Answers
A 15 × 4	60
B 30 ÷ 7	4 R2
C 39 × 7	273
D 89 ÷ 3	29 R2
E 20 × 50	1,000

oint Problems	Answers
A 76 × 42	3,192
B 98 × 67	6,566
C 539 × 68	36,652
D 290 × 90	26,100
E 807 × 49	39,543

oint Problems	Answers
A 800 ÷ 50	16
B 647 ÷ 21	30 R17
C 857 ÷ 94	9 R11
D 7,105 ÷ 35	203
E 4,260 ÷ 59	72 R12

Target Math Problems Sheet (×/÷) (page 2)

25-Point Problems

Answe

25A Brett and his five friends each paid $60 to see a concert. How much money did they pay in all?

$360

25B 57 campers are split into teams of 9 players each. Those campers *not* on teams will be umpires. How many umpires will there be?

3 umpi

25C A theater has 5 rows with 18 seats in each row. The total ticket sales for a show was $540. Suppose a ticket was sold for each seat and each ticket cost the same amount. How much did each ticket cost?

$6

25D A student divided 7,035 by 35 and obtained an answer of 21, as shown. What is the correct answer? Describe the error the student likely made.

$$
\begin{array}{r}
2\ \ \ 1 \\
35\overline{)7,035} \\
-7\ 0 \\
\hline
35 \\
-35 \\
\hline
\end{array}
$$

Answer: The correct answer is 201. The student failed to write a 0 in the tens place of the quotient when 3 tens were divided by 35.

25E When Abraham Lincoln was a teen in the 1820s, he copied math problems and their solutions from a textbook* into an arithmetic copybook. These pages, in Lincoln's handwriting, are the oldest known Lincoln documents. One of the math problems, from a textbook that was first published in London in the 1740s, is shown below:

If 3 ounces of silver cost 17 shillings, what will 48 ounces of silver cost?

Solve Abe Lincoln's "homework" problem.

Answer: 272 shillings

Lincoln actually converted the answer to English (monetary) pounds. There are 20 shillings in a pound, so the price of the silver was 13 pounds, 12 shillings.

*The name of the math book was *The Schoolmaster's Assistant, Being a Compendium of Arithmetic, Both Practical and Theoretical in Five Parts,* by Thomas Dilworth. Until recently, there had been nine known surviving pages from Lincoln's arithmetic copybook. A tenth page, the one housing the above problem, had been torn into two parts, with one part at the University of Chicago and the other part at Brown University in Providence, Rhode Island. In 2010, researchers from the Papers of Abraham Lincoln project (http://www.papersofabrahamlincoln.org) digitally reassembled the page and reported it as a tenth page from Lincoln's arithmetic copybook (Reynolds, 2010).

Multiuse Resources (Blacklines)

Students display play money on the place-value mat as described in the various Intervention Activities. Students also record the exercise in a place-value grid (pages 186–187). As students trade bills and perform operations with the money, they record what they do in the exercise on the grid.

Note: You may want to enlarge the play money and place-value mat (proportionately) to allow for easier student handling. You may want to print the place-value mats on tagboard.

Play Money

1	1	1	1	1	1	1
1	1	1	1	1	1	1
1	1	1	1	1	1	1
1	1	1	1	1	1	1
10	10	10	10	10	10	10
10	10	10	10	10	10	10
10	10	10	10	10	10	10
10	10	10	10	10	10	10
100	100	100	100	100	100	100
100	100	100	100	100	100	100
100	100	100	100	100	100	100
100	100	100	100	100	100	100
1000	1000	1000	1000	1000	1000	1000
1000	1000	1000	1000	1000	1000	1000
1000	1000	1000	1000	1000	1000	1000
1000	1000	1000	1000	1000	1000	1000

Place-Value Mat for Addition/Subtraction

Thousands	Hundreds	Tens	Ones

Place-Value Grids for Addition/Subtraction

H	T	O

H	T	O

H	T	O

H	T	O

Th	H	T	O

Th	H	T	O

Th	H	T	O

Th	H	T	O

Place-Value Grids for Division

T | O

T | O

H | T | O

H | T | O

Th | H | T | O

Blank Addition Table

+	0	1	2	3	4	5	6	7	8	9
0										
1										
2										
3										
4										
5										
6										
7										
8										
9										

Addition/Subtraction Table

+	0	1	2	3	4	5	6	7	8	9
0	0	1	2	3	4	5	6	7	8	9
1	1	2	3	4	5	6	7	8	9	10
2	2	3	4	5	6	7	8	9	10	11
3	3	4	5	6	7	8	9	10	11	12
4	4	5	6	7	8	9	10	11	12	13
5	5	6	7	8	9	10	11	12	13	14
6	6	7	8	9	10	11	12	13	14	15
7	7	8	9	10	11	12	13	14	15	16
8	8	9	10	11	12	13	14	15	16	17
9	9	10	11	12	13	14	15	16	17	18

Blank Multiplication Table

×	0	1	2	3	4	5	6	7	8	9
0										
1										
2										
3										
4										
5										
6										
7										
8										
9										

Multiplication/Division Table

×	0	1	2	3	4	5	6	7	8	9
0	0	0	0	0	0	0	0	0	0	0
1	0	1	2	3	4	5	6	7	8	9
2	0	2	4	6	8	10	12	14	16	18
3	0	3	6	9	12	15	18	21	24	27
4	0	4	8	12	16	20	24	28	32	36
5	0	5	10	15	20	25	30	35	40	45
6	0	6	12	18	24	30	36	42	48	54
7	0	7	14	21	28	35	42	49	56	63
8	0	8	16	24	32	40	48	56	64	72
9	0	9	18	27	36	45	54	63	72	81

Grid Paper (¼ inch)

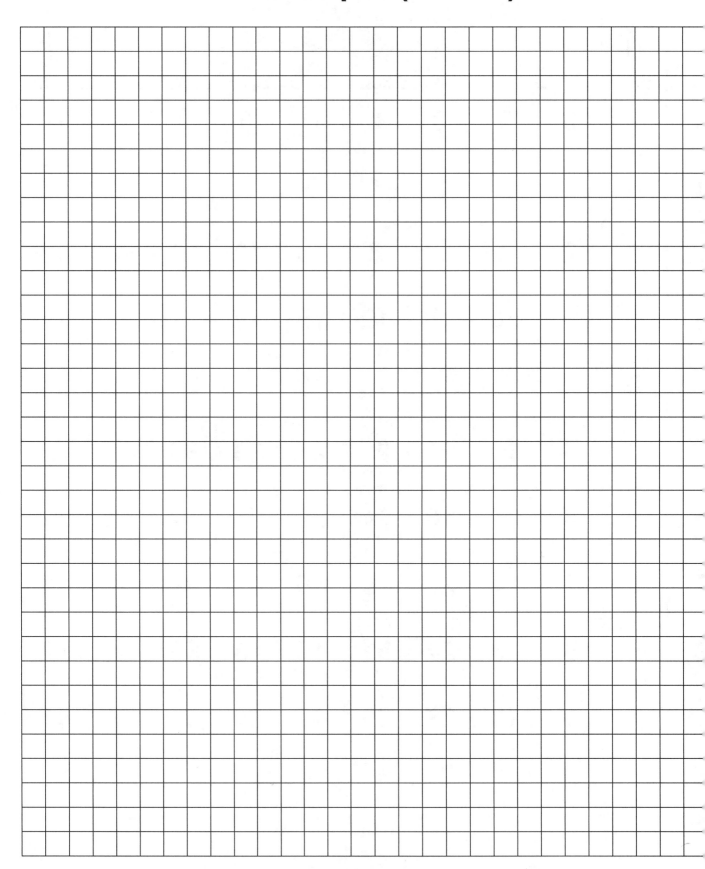

Answers for Student Materials

ANSWERS FOR UNIT 1: ADDITION OF WHOLE NUMBERS

The answers for the Addition Diagnostic Test are included in the Item Analysis Table on page 30.

Practice Exercises: Addition of Whole Numbers (page 47)

1.	9	**9.**	99	**17.**	57	**25.**	18
2.	1	**10.**	909	**18.**	824	**26.**	26
3.	12	**11.**	80	**19.**	908	**27.**	175
4.	7	**12.**	986	**20.**	154	**28.**	1,600
5.	9	**13.**	9,195	**21.**	1,003	**29.**	2,132
6.	17	**14.**	5,555	**22.**	10,061	**30.**	29,969
7.	8	**15.**	8,938	**23.**	356	**31.**	172
8.	9	**16.**	9,999	**24.**	7,175	**32.**	1,671

Next Number, Please (pages 141–142)

Round 1				Round 2			
20	→	Add 40	→ 60	30	→ Add 50	→	80
60	→	Add 300	→ 360	80	→ Add 900	→	980
360	→	Subtract 30	→ 330	880	→ Add 20	→	1,000
330	→	Subtract 30	→ 300	1,000	→ Add 500	→	1,500
300	→	Add 600	→ 900	1,500	→ Add 50	→	1,550
900	→	Add 90	→ 990	1,500	→ Add 200	→	1,750
990	→	Add 10	→ 1,000	1,750	→ Subtract 1,000	→	750
1,000	→	Add 20	→ 1,020	750	→ Subtract 750	→	0

Round 3

200	→	Add 600	→	800
800	→	Add 80	→	880
880	→	Add 70	→	950
950	→	Subtract 900	→	50
50	→	Add 450	→	500
500	→	Add 4,500	→	5,000
5,000	→	Subtract 100	→	4,900
4,900	→	Add 100	→	5,000

Round 4

9,000	→	Subtract 4,000	→	5,000
5,000	→	Add 50	→	5,050
5,050	→	Add 150	→	5,200
5,200	→	Add 1,800	→	7,000
7,000	→	Subtract 6,300	→	700
700	→	Subtract 630	→	70
70	→	Add 6,930	→	7,000
7,000	→	Subtract 1,010	→	5,990

Round 5

2,005	→	Add 995	→	3,000
3,000	→	Subtract 100	→	2,900
2,900	→	Add 7,100	→	10,000
10,000	→	Subtract 9,000	→	1,000

Roller Coaster Rounding (pages 143–144)

1. The two possible hundreds are 600 and 700.
   628 rounds to 600; 682 rounds to 700.

2. Number at top of hill: 85; numbers at bases: 80 and 90.
   83 rounds to 80; 86 rounds to 90.

3. Number at top of hill: 550; numbers at bases: 500 and 600.
   555 rounds to 600; 529 rounds to 500.

4. Numbers at hilltops: 85, 95, and 105; numbers at bases: 100 and 110.
   82 rounds to 80; 89 rounds to 90; 94 rounds to 90; 96 rounds to 100;
   109 rounds to 110.

5. Numbers at hilltops: 850 and 950; numbers at bases: 900 and 1,000.
   740 rounds to 700; 771 rounds to 800; 805 rounds to 800; 949 rounds to 900;
   959 rounds to 1,000.

6. Numbers at hilltops: 1,500 and 2,500; numbers at bases: 2,000 and 3,000.
   300 rounds to 0; 930 rounds to 1,000; 1,500 rounds to 2,000; 2,050 rounds to
   2,000; 2,633 rounds to 3,000.

Using Front-End Estimation to Check for Reasonableness: Addition (page 145)

Estimates may vary.		**6.** about 6,000		**12.** about 1,100		**18.** No	
1. about 600		**7.** See below.		**13.** about 7,000		**19.** No	
2. about 1,000		**8.** about 400		**14.** about 4,000		**20.** No	
3. about 600		**9.** about 1,100		**15.** about 9,000		**21.** Yes	
4. about 7,000		**10.** about 900		**16.** No		**22.** Yes	
5. about 700		**11.** about 1,600		**17.** Yes		**23.** No	

7. Sample: Yes. When you compute the actual results, you find that front-end estimation provides estimates that are closer to the actual sums than what you
   obtain with rounding. This is because both addends in each case "are near the
   middle." In 352 + 251, both 352 and 251 round up. In 3,449 + 3,448, both addends
   round down. With front-end estimation, the 52 and 51 count as 100 (rather than
   as 200), and the 449 and 448 count as 1,000 (rather than as 0).

For exercises 16 through 23, you may want students to also *explain* their reasoning for determining their Yes/No answers. For example, in 16, "571 + 431 = 902" cannot possibly be right because 500 + 400 = 900, and the remaining digits yield about another 100. In 17, "383 + 114 = 497" could possibly be right because 300 + 100 = 400, and the remaining digits yield about another 100.

ANSWERS FOR UNIT 2: SUBTRACTION OF WHOLE NUMBERS

The answers for the Subtraction Diagnostic Test are included in the Item Analysis Table on page 54.

Practice Exercises: Subtraction of Whole Numbers (page 74)

1.	9	9.	90	17.	28	25.	31
2.	9	10.	718	18.	61	26.	496
3.	8	11.	802	19.	215	27.	607
4.	7	12.	10	20.	709	28.	64
5.	15	13.	3,100	21.	4,970	29.	2,288
6.	10	14.	5,001	22.	4,428	30.	7,101
7.	9	15.	852	23.	259	31.	592
8.	14	16.	9,907	24.	6,799	32.	2,078

Using Front-End Estimation to Check for Reasonableness: Subtraction (page 153)

Estimates may vary.	6. 4,000	12. more than 500	18. No
1. less than 300	7. See below.	13. less than 2,000	19. No
2. more than 2,000	8. less than 100	14. more than 4,000	20. Yes
3. less than 500	9. more than 600	15. less than 4,000	21. No
4. more than 3,000	10. less than 200	16. Yes	
5. 500	11. more than 700	17. No	

7. Sample: Yes. When you compute the actual results, you find that front-end estimation provides estimates that are closer to the actual differences than what you obtain with rounding. This is because one or both numbers in each case "are near the middle"—so rounding expands the differences between them. In 708 – 249, rounding 249 down to 200 expands the difference. In 8,526 – 5,448, rounding 8,526 up and 5,448 down also expands the difference.

For exercises 16 through 21, you may want students to also *explain* their reasoning for determining their Yes/No answers. For example, in 16, "629 – 485 = 144," the difference of the hundreds digits is 2. But because 29 < 85, the sum is *less than 200,* so 144 is reasonable. But in 17, "974 – 258 = 616" *cannot* possibly be right because the difference of the hundreds digits is 7, and 74 > 58. So, the difference must be *more than 700.*

Editor Error Search (+/–) (page 158)

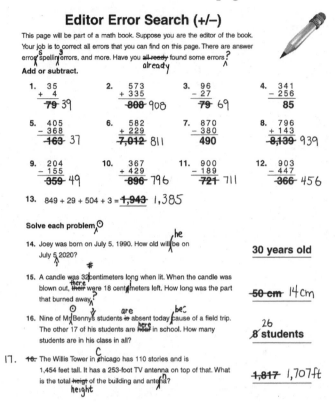

Extension: Sample descriptions of the mathematics errors are provided below.

1. The addend 4 was added to each digit of the first addend.

2. When 7 tens + 3 tens was found, the 1 in the 10 tens was not "carried" to the hundreds place.

3. The 6 was renamed as 16, but the 9 tens were not renamed as 8 tens.

5. The lesser digit was subtracted from the greater digit in the ones and tens positions. Thus, order was ignored.

6. Addition was done from left to right (rather than from right to left). So, the digits in the hundreds position were added first.

8. When 9 + 4 was found in the tens column, 13 was written in the sum rather than just 3, with the 1 being "carried."

9. Addition was performed instead of subtraction.

10. A 1 was "carried" in both the tens and the hundreds positions—even though no renaming should have been done in the tens position.

11. 900 was incorrectly renamed as "7 hundreds, 10 tens, and 10 ones" rather than as "8 hundreds, and 10 tens" and then as "8 hundreds, 9 tens, and 10 ones."

12. 903 was incorrectly renamed as "7 hundreds, 10 tens, and 13 ones" rather than as "8 hundreds, 10 tens, and 3 ones" and then as "8 hundreds, 9 tens, and 13 ones."

13. When the problem was written in vertical form, the digits were aligned flush left with the left-most digit in each number appearing in the hundreds position (rather than flush right according to the ones position).

15. To solve the problem, addition was performed rather than subtraction.

16. To solve the problem, subtraction was performed rather than addition.

17. All three of the numbers given in the problem were added. But just 1,454 and 253 should have been added. Also, the unit of measure, feet, was omitted from the answer.

ANSWERS FOR UNIT 3:
MULTIPLICATION OF WHOLE NUMBERS

The answers for the Multiplication Diagnostic Test are included in the Item Analysis Table on page 82.

Practice Exercises: Multiplication of Whole Numbers (page 109)

1. 32	**9.** 70	**17.** 6,300	**25.** 4,000
2. 27	**10.** 400	**18.** 40,000	**26.** 361
3. 48	**11.** 68	**19.** 2,156	**27.** 1,053
4. 7	**12.** 150	**20.** 3,096	**28.** 4,648
5. 0	**13.** 195	**21.** 6,170	**29.** 42,000
6. 9	**14.** 624	**22.** 42,686	**30.** 42,676
7. 6	**15.** 819	**23.** 48,240	**31.** 19,620
8. 8	**16.** 469	**24.** 29,824	**32.** 79,833

Using Front-End Estimation to Check for Reasonableness: Multiplication (page 167)

Estimates may vary.	**4.** more than 5,940	**8.** more than 24,400	**12.** No
1. less than 1,750	**5.** less than 2,590	**9.** No	**13.** No
2. more than 1,620	**6.** less than 5,310	**10.** Yes	**14.** Yes
3. more than 3,540	**7.** less than 28,000	**11.** No	

For exercises 9 through 14, you may want students to also *explain* their reasoning for determining their Yes/No answers. For example, in 9, "5 × 829 = 4,035" *cannot* possibly be right because 5 × 800 = 4,000 and 5 × 29 is close to 150. The product is close to 4,150, so 4,035 is too small to be correct. In 10, "9 × 776 = 6,984," 9 × 700 = 6,300, and 9 × 76 is about 9 × 80 or about 720. So the product is about 6,300 + 720 or about 7,020. So, the given answer, 6,984, is reasonable.

Editor Error Search (×) (page 172)

Answers for the Editor Error Search activity are shown on page 198.

Extension: Sample descriptions of the mathematics errors are provided below.

1. There is an error in fact recall.

2. The sum of 0 and 6 was found—rather than the product.

3. There is an error in fact recall.

5. The sum of 1 and 7 was found—rather than the product.

6. The partial product, 0 (for 9 × 0), was not recorded.

7. The partial products, 14 and 21, were directly recorded in the final product.

9. The products 9 × 9, 9 × 6, and 9 × 2 were found without "carrying" and adding any digits.

Editor Error Search (x)

Let's pretend that you are an editor for a math book. Your job is to correct all errors
you can find on this page. ~~They're~~ *There are* errors involving answers, spelling, grammar,
and more~~.~~*,* Have you already found ~~a~~ *an* error or ~~too~~ *two*?

Multiply.

1. 6
   × 7
   ~~54~~ 42

2. 0
   × 6
   ~~6~~ 0

3. 7
   × 8
   ~~63~~ 56

4. 8
   × 6
   48

5. 1
   × 7
   ~~8~~ 7

6. 10
   × 9
   ~~9~~ 90

7. 32
   × 7
   ~~2114~~ 224

8. 109
   × 6
   654

9. 269
   × 9
   ~~1841~~
   2,421

10. 23
   × 47
   ~~253~~ 1,081

Write
~~Rite~~ the letter for the correct answer.

11. Which of these shows another name for 7 × 6?

A 7 × 7 × 7 × 7 × 7 × 7
B 6 × 6 × 6 × 6 × 6 × 6
C 7 + 7 + 7 + 7 + 7 + 7 + 7
D 6 + 6 + 6 + 6 + 6 + 6 ~~B~~ D

12. Which of these can be used to find 9 × 16?

A (10 × 16) − 1
B 9 × (10 + 6)
C (10 × 16) − 9
D (9 + 1) × (16 − 1) ~~C~~ B

Solve each problem.

13. ~~14.~~ Arsha gave 5 *pennies* ~~pennys~~ to each of 6 *friends* ~~freinds~~. How many pennies
did she give away?

14. ~~15.~~ Hector made four 1-point baskets, five 2-point baskets, and
zero 3-point baskets. How many points did he make in all*,*?

15. ~~16.~~ Je*a*ns are on sale for $36 *per* ~~purr~~ pair. The regular price *is* ~~if~~ $45.
How much does Jamie save if she *buys* ~~bys~~ 3 *pairs* ~~pears~~?

30
~~11~~ pennies

14
~~17~~ points

~~$108~~ $27

10. The digits for the second partial product were recorded in incorrect place-value positions. The 0 in the ones position of this partial product was omitted.

11. Because 7 × 6 means 7 groups of 6, the correct answer should be D because D shows 6 used as an addend 7 times. The incorrect answer given, B, shows 6 used as a *factor* 7 times.

12. The correct answer, B, applies the *Distributive Property:* 9 × 16 = 9 × (10 + 6). The incorrect answer given, C, is incorrect because in (10 × 16) − 9, only 9 is subtracted from 10 × 16. To be correct, 16 would have to be subtracted (to yield 9 groups of 16).

13. The numbers 5 and 6 were added. But because 5 pennies were given to each of 6 friends, those numbers should have been multiplied.

14. The correct answer is 14, not 17. Although zero 3-point baskets yields 0 points, evidently 3 was added to the 14 to obtain 17.

15. The incorrect answer, $108, represents the total amount spent on the jeans, not the *savings*. Because Jamie saved $9 on each pair, she saved a total of $27.

ANSWERS FOR UNIT 4: DIVISION OF WHOLE NUMBERS

The answers for the Division Diagnostic Test are included in the Item Analysis Table on page 116.

Practice Exercises: Division of Whole Numbers (page 135)

1. 9	6. 9	11. 5 R5	16. 13 R2
2. 7	7. 6	12. 9 R5	17. 374 R1
3. 9	8. 48	13. 32	18. 50
4. 0	9. 3 R3	14. 28 R2	19. 205
5. 1	10. 6 R3	15. 13	20. 88 R4

21. 4,247 R1	**23.** 1,090 R8	**25.** 70	**27.** 103 R61
22. 598	**24.** 752	**26.** 32 R7	**28.** 92 R21

Using Front-End Estimation to Check for Reasonableness: Division (page 175)

Estimates may vary.

1. between 50 and 60	**7.** between 800 and 900	**14.** Yes	
2. between 1,000 and 2,000	**8.** between 2,000 and 3,000	**15.** No	
3. between 20 and 30	**9.** between 10 and 20	**16.** No	
4. between 50 and 60	**10.** between 80 and 90	**17.** Yes	
5. between 300 and 400	**11.** between 60 and 70	**18.** No	
6. between 90 and 100	**12.** between 200 and 300	**19.** Yes	
	13. No	**20.** No	

For exercises 13 through 20, you may want students to also *explain* their reasoning for determining their Yes/No answers. For example, in 13, "656 ÷ 8 = 802," division of the front-end digits (65 ÷ 8) reveals that the quotient has two digits and that the first digit is **8**. Because the correct quotient is between 80 and 90, a quotient of 802 *cannot possibly* be correct. In 14, "985 ÷ 5 = 197," front-end estimation reveals that the quotient has three digits, and the first digit is 1. Because 197 is between 100 and 200, it is possible that it is correct.

Using Compatible Numbers to Check for Reasonableness (+, –, ×, ÷) (page 176)

Estimates may vary.

1. about 200	**6.** about 20,000	**12.** about 100	**18.** Yes
2. about 300	**7.** about 560	**13.** Yes	**19.** Yes
3. about 1,500	**8.** about 45,000	**14.** No	**20.** No
4. about 3,000	**9.** about 90	**15.** No	
5. about 10,000	**10.** about 500	**16.** Yes	
	11. about 200	**17.** No	

For exercises 13 through 20, you may want students to also *explain* their reasoning for determining their Yes/No answers. For example, in 13, "87 + 66 + 17 + 49 = 219," you could form these 2 groups of about 100 each: 87 + 17 and 66 + 49. Because the sum of those numbers is about 200, the given answer of 219 is reasonable. But in 15, "54,381 – 25,677 = 18,704," you could consider the following difference of "nice numbers": 55,000 – 25,000 = 30,000. Because the difference is about 30,000, the given answer of 18,704 *cannot possibly* be correct.

Abbott and Costello's Number *Nonsense* (pages 179–180)

1. Samples: 7 groups of 13 each are equal to 91 (not 28). If you begin with 28 and try to subtract off 13 seven times, you will *not* obtain 0. Rather, if you begin with 28 and subtract off 4 seven times, you will obtain 0. If the quotient were 13, then 26 doughnuts would have been used up with just two of the officers. This would have left just 2 doughnuts for the remaining five officers. You can check the quotient, 13, by multiplying by the divisor, 7. Because 13 × 7 does *not* equal 28, a quotient of 13 is incorrect.

2. Samples:

Division Example: When the divisor is greater than the first digit of the dividend, you then try to divide it into the first two digits of the dividend. So, rather than finding $8 \div 7$, you find $28 \div 7$. Note, you *could* find $8 \div 7$, but the quotient, 1, would have to be recorded in the ones position. However, Lou wrote it in the tens position. The 2 tens that were not initially used *could* be combined with the 1 that was left over from above, giving a quotient of 3. But because the first partial quotient, 1, was written in the tens position, an incorrect quotient of 13 was obtained (rather than 4).

Multiplication Example: When 7 is multiplied by 1 ten, the product is 70, not 7. But because Lou wrote the 7 in the ones position (rather than in the tens position), an incorrect sum of 28 was obtained—thus creating the illusion that the division problem checked.

Addition Example: After the ones were added to obtain 21, the 1 should have been recorded in the ones position of the sum and the 2 should have been "carried" to the tens position. However, Lou "carried" 21 and then added the 1 from each of the seven 13s to the 21 as if each of the 1s were in the tens position (rather than in the ones position). Note, each of the 1s from the 13s *could* be added to the 21, but they have to be treated as tens (not as ones). If that had occurred, 70 would have been added to the 21, and a sum of 91 would have been obtained (verifying that a quotient of 13 was incorrect).

3. Sample: By relating division to multiplication, Bud was suggesting that if 28 doughnuts divided equally among 7 officers yields 13 doughnuts per officer, then (using inverse operations) 7 groups of 13 each would have to equal 28. Multiplication can be used to check division.

4. Sample: Another way to show that 13 groups of 7 each are not equal to 28 is to use repeated addition. Bud hoped that Lou would see that when 13 is used as an addend seven times, the sum of 91 would show that $28 \div 7$ is not equal to 13.

References

Allen, L. E., & Main, D. B. (1976). The effect of instructional gaming on absenteeism: The first step. *Journal for Research in Mathematics Education, 7*(2), 272–274.

Arbaugh, F., Herbel-Eisenmann, B., Ramirez, N., Knuth, E., Kranendonk, H., & Quander, J. R. (2010). *Linking research & practice: The NCTM research agenda conference report.* Reston, VA: National Council of Teachers of Mathematics. Retrieved May 10, 2010, from http://www.nctm.org/news/content.aspx?id=25315

Ashlock, R. B. (2010). *Error patterns in computation: Using error patterns to help each student learn* (10th ed.). Boston: Allyn & Bacon.

Bastche, G., Graden, J. L., Grimes, J., Kovaleski, J. F., Prasse, D., Reschly, D. J., et al. (2005). *Response to intervention: Policy considerations and implementation.* Alexandria, VA: National Association of State Directors of Special Education.

Beattie, J., & Algozzine, B. (1982). Testing for teaching. *Arithmetic Teacher, 30*(1), 47–51.

Behr, M. J., Erlwanger, S., & Nichols, E. (1980). How children view the equals sign. *Mathematics Teaching, 92,* 13–15.

Beishuizen, M. (2001). Different approaches to mastering mental calculation processes. In J. Anghileri (Ed.), *Principles and practices in arithmetic teaching* (pp. 119–130). London: Open University Press.

Bobis, J. (2007, April). The empty number line: A useful tool or just another procedure? *Teaching Children Mathematics, 13*(8), 410–413.

Bright, G. W., Harvey, J. G., & Wheeler, M. M. (1979). Using games to retrain skills with basic multiplication facts. *Journal for Research in Mathematics Education, 10,* 103–110.

Bruner, J. (1966). *Toward a theory of instruction.* Cambridge, MA: Belknap Press.

Campbell, P. (1995). *Project IMPACT: Increasing mathematics power for all children and teachers, phase 1, final report.* College Park, MD: Center for Mathematics Education, University of Maryland.

Carlton, R. A. (1980). *Basic skills in the changing work world* [Monograph]. Ontario: University of Guelph.

Carroll, W. M., & Porter, D. (1998). Alternative algorithms for whole-number operations. In L. Morrow & M. Kenney (Eds.), *The teaching and learning of algorithms in school mathematics, 1998 yearbook of the National Council of Teachers of Mathematics* (pp. 106–114). Reston, VA: National Council of Teachers of Mathematics.

Council of Chief State School Officers (CCSSO) and the National Governors Association (NGA) Center for Best Practices. (2010, March 9). *Common Core State Standards for Mathematics* [draft]. Retrieved March 12, 2010, from http://www.corestandards.org

Cox, L. S. (1975). Using research in teaching: Diagnosing and remediating systematic errors in addition and subtraction computations. *The Arithmetic Teacher, 22*(2), 151–157.

De Corte, E., Greer, B., & Verschaffel, L. (1996). Mathematics teaching and learning. In R. C. Calfee & D. C. Berliner (Eds.), *Handbook of educational psychology* (pp. 491–549). New York: Macmillan.

Dossey, J. A., Mullis, I. V. S., Lindquist, M. M., & Chambers, D. L. (1988). *The mathematics report card—are we measuring up? Trends and achievement based on the 1986 national assessment.* Princeton, NJ: Educational Testing Service.

Ellis, M., & Yeh, C. (2008). Creative arithmetic: Exploring alternative methods. *Teaching Children Mathematics, 14*(6), 367–368.

Englert, G. R., & Sinicrope, R. (1994). Making connections with two-digit multiplication. *Arithmetic Teacher, 41*(8), 446–448.

Fello, S. E., & Paquette, K. R. (2009). Talking and writing in the classroom. *Mathematics Teaching in the Middle School, 14*(7), 410–414.

Ferrucci, B. J., Yeap, B. H., & Carter, J. A. (2003). A modeling approach for enhancing problem solving in the middle grades. *Mathematics Teaching in the Middle School, 8*(9), 470–475.

Fisher, D., & Kopenski, D. (2007/2008). Using item analyses and instructional conversations to improve mathematics achievement. *Teaching Children Mathematics, 14*(5), 278–282.

Fuson, K. C., & Briars, D. J. (1990). Using a base-ten blocks learning/teaching approach for first- and second-grade place-value and multidigit addition and subtraction. *Journal for Research in Mathematics Education, 21*(2), 180–206.

Gardner, H. (1991). *The unschooled mind: How children think and how schools should teach.* New York: Basic Books.

Goldin, G. A. (2003). Representation in school mathematics: A unifying research perspective. In J. Kilpatrick et al. (Eds.), *A research companion to principles and standards for school mathematics* (pp. 275–283). Reston, VA: National Council of Teachers of Mathematics.

Gottlieb, A. (Producer), Lubin, A. (Director), Horman, A. T., & Grant, J. (Writers). (1941). *In the Navy.* Universal City, CA: Universal Pictures.

Gravemeijer, K. (1994). Educational development and developmental research in mathematics education. *Journal for Research in Mathematics Education, 25*(5), 443–471.

Greenwood, I. (1729). *Arithmetick vulgar and decimal: With the application thereof, to a variety of cases in trade and commerce.* Boston: T. Hancock.

Guetzloe, E. (2001). Reflections and perceptions: My third of a century in the field of EBD. *Preventing School Failure, 45,* 65–68.

Hiebert, J. (2003). What research says about the NCTM standards. In J. Kilpatrick et al. (Eds.), *A research companion to principles and standards for school mathematics* (pp. 5–23). Reston, VA: National Council of Teachers of Mathematics.

Hiebert, J., Carpenter, T. P., Fennema, E., Fuson, K. C., Wearne, D., Murray, H., et al. (1997). *Making sense: Teaching and learning mathematics with understanding.* Portsmouth, NH: Heinemann.

Hill, H. C., Ball, D. L., & Schilling, S. G. (2008). Unpacking pedagogical content knowledge: Conceptualizing and measuring teachers' topic-specific knowledge of students. *Journal for Research in Mathematics Education, 39*(4), 372–399.

Hill, H. C., Rowan, B., & Ball, D. L. (2005). Effects of teachers' mathematical knowledge for teaching on student achievement. *American Educational Research Journal, 42*(2), 371–406.

Holton, D., Ahmed, A., Williams, H., & Hill, C. (2001). On the importance of mathematical play. *International Journal of Mathematical Education in Science and Technology, 32*(3), 401–415.

Hutchings, B. (1976). Low-stress algorithms. In D. Nelson & R. E. Reys (Eds.), *Measurement in school mathematics, 1976 yearbook of the National Council of Teachers of Mathematics* (pp. 218–239). Reston, VA: National Council of Teachers of Mathematics.

Individuals with Disabilities Education Improvement Act of 2004 (IDEA). Pub. L. No. 108-446, 108th Congress.

Kilpatrick, J., Swafford, J., & Bradford, F. (Eds.). (2001). *Adding it up: Helping children learn mathematics.* Washington, DC: National Research Council and National Academy Press.

Klein, J. D., & Freitag, E. (1991). Effects of using an instructional game on motivation and performance. *Journal of Educational Research, 84*(5), 303–308.

Knuth, E. R., Stephens, A. C., McNeil, N., & Alibali, M. (2006). Does understanding the equal sign matter? Evidence from solving equations. *Journal for Research in Mathematics Education, 37*(4), 297–312.

Lannin, J. K., Arbaugh, F., Barker, D. D., & Townsend, B. E. (2006, October). Making the most of student errors. *Teaching Children Mathematics, 13*(3), 182–186.

Lin, C. Y. (2007/2008). Teaching multiplication algorithms from other cultures. *Mathematics Teaching in the Middle School, 13*(5), 298–304.

Little, C. A., Hauser, S., & Corbishley, J. (2009). Constructing complexity for differentiated learning. *Mathematics Teaching in the Middle School, 15*(1), 34–42.

Lowenberg Ball, D., Ferrini-Mundy, J., Kilpatrick, J., Milgram, R. J., Schmid, W., & Schaar, R. (2005). Reaching common ground in K–12 mathematics education. *Notices of the American Mathematical Society, 52*(9), 1055–1058.

Martin, H. (2006). *Differentiated instruction for mathematics: Instructions and activities for the diverse classroom.* Portland, ME: J. Weston Walch.

Martin, H. (2007). *Active learning in the mathematics classroom, grades 5–8: Second edition of multiple intelligences in the mathematics classroom.* Thousand Oaks, CA: Corwin.

Maurer, S. B. (1998). What is an algorithm? What is an answer? In L. J. Morrow & M. J. Kenney (Eds.), *The teaching and learning of algorithms in school mathematics, 1998 yearbook of the National Council of Teachers of Mathematics* (pp. 21–31). Reston, VA: National Council of Teachers of Mathematics.

Miller, S., & Hudson, P. J. (2007). Using evidence-based practices to build mathematics competence related to conceptual, procedural, and declarative knowledge. *Learning Disabilities Research and Practice, 22*(1), 47–57.

Mokros, J., Russell, S. J., & Economopoulos, K. (1995). *Beyond arithmetic: Changing mathematics in the elementary classroom.* White Plains, NY: Cuisenaire–Dale Seymour.

National Council of Teachers of Mathematics (NCTM). (2000). *Principles and standards for school mathematics.* Reston, VA: Author.

National Council of Teachers of Mathematics (NCTM). (2006). *Curriculum focal points for prekindergarten through grade 8 mathematics: A quest for coherence.* Reston, VA: Author.

Nelson, D., Joseph, G. G., & Williams, J. (1993). *Multicultural mathematics.* Oxford, UK: Oxford University Press.

Nugent, P. M. (2007). Lattice multiplication in a preservice classroom. *Mathematics Teaching in the Middle School, 13*(2), 110–113.

O'Donnell, B. (2009). Research, reflection, practice: What effective math teachers have in common. *Teaching Children Mathematics, 16*(2), 118–125.

O'Loughlin, T. A. (2007, October). Using research to develop computational fluency in young mathematicians. *Teaching Children Mathematics, 14*(3), 132–138.

Pickreign, J., & Rogers, R. (2006). Do you understand your algorithms? *Mathematics Teaching in the Middle School, 12*(1), 42–47.

Pierce, R., & Adams, C. (2005). Using tiered lessons in mathematics. *Mathematics Teaching in the Middle School, 11*(3), 144–149.

Pincus, M., Coonan, M., Glasser, H., Levy, L., Morgenstern, F., & Shapiro, H. (1975). If you don't know how children think, how can you help them? *The Arithmetic Teacher, 22*(7), 580–585.

Reeves, A., & Reeves, R. (2003). Encouraging students to think about how they think! *Mathematics Teaching in the Middle School, 8*(7), 374–377.

Reynolds, J. (2010, April 15). Reunited set of math problems gives clues to how Lincoln learned. *The State Journal-Register.* Retrieved April 15, 2010, from http://www.sj-r.com/bicentennial/x932336848/Reunited-set-of-math-problems-gives-clues-to-how-Lincoln-learned

Reys, B. J., & Barger, R. H. (1994). Mental computation: Issues from the United States perspective. In R. E. Reys & N. Nohda (Eds.), *Computational alternatives for the twenty-first century: Cross-cultural perspectives from Japan and the United States* (pp. 31–47). Reston, VA: National Council of Teachers of Mathematics.

Reys, B. J., & Reys, R. E. (1990). Estimation—direction from the standards. *Arithmetic Teacher, 37*(7), 22–25.

Ron, P. (1998). My family taught me this way. In L. J. Morrow & M. J. Kenney (Eds.), *The teaching and learning of algorithms in school mathematics, 1998 yearbook of the National Council of Teachers of Mathematics* (pp. 115–119). Reston, VA: National Council of Teachers of Mathematics.

Rossi, R. (2009, July 15). "Outrageous" state race gap in math. *Chicago Sun-Times.*

Rubenstein, R. (2001). Mental mathematics beyond the middle school: Why? What? How? *Mathematics Teacher, 94*(6), 442–446.

Safer, N., & Fleischman, S. (2005). How student progress monitoring improves instruction. *Educational Leadership, 62*(5), 81–83.

Sawyer, W. W. (1943). *Mathematician's delight.* Harmondsworth, England: Penguin Books.

Schulman, L. S. (1987). Knowledge and teaching: Foundations of the new reform. *Harvard Educational Review, 57*(1), 1–22.

Sgroi, L. (1998). An exploration of the Russian peasant method of multiplication. In L. J. Morrow & M. J. Kenney (Eds.), *The teaching and learning of algorithms in school mathematics, 1998 yearbook of the National Council of Teachers of Mathematics* (pp. 81–85). Reston, VA: National Council of Teachers of Mathematics.

Siegler, R. S. (2003). Implications of cognitive science research for mathematics education. In J. Kilpatrick, W. G. Martin, & D. Schifter (Eds.), *A research companion to principles and standards for school mathematics* (pp. 289–303). Reston, VA: National Council of Teachers of Mathematics.

Smith, F. (1982). *Writing and the writer.* New York: Holt, Rinehart & Winston.

Sowell, E. J. (1989). Effects of manipulative materials in mathematics instruction. *Journal for Research in Mathematics Education, 20*(5), 498–505.

Spangler, D. B. (2008). *Mathematics explorations: Detective-style activities for the real world.* Tucson, AZ: Good Year Books.

Star, J. R., Kenyon, M., Joiner, R. M., & Rittle-Johnson, B. (2010). Comparison helps students learn to be better estimators. *Teaching Children Mathematics, 16*(9), 557–563.

Steckroth, J. (2009, December/2010, January). From calculating to calculus. *Teaching Children Mathematics, 16*(5), 292–299.

Steele, M. M. (2002). Strategies for helping students who have learning disabilities in mathematics. *Mathematics Teaching in the Middle School, 8*(3), 140–143.

Stiff, L. V., Johnson, J. L., & Johnson, M. R. (1993). Cognitive issues in mathematics education. In Patricia S. Wilson (Ed.), *Research ideas for the classroom: High school mathematics* (pp. 3–20). New York: Macmillan.

Sutton, J., & Krueger, A. (Eds.). (2002). *EDThoughts: What we know about mathematics teaching and learning.* Aurora, CO: Mid-continent Research for Education and Learning.

Thanheiser, E. (2009). Preservice elementary school teachers' conceptions of multidigit whole numbers. *Journal for Research in Mathematics Education, 40*(3), 251–281.

Thornton, C. A., & Wilson, S. J. (1993). Classroom organization and models of instruction. In Robert J. Jensen (Ed.), *Research ideas for the classroom: Early childhood mathematics* (pp. 269–293). New York: Macmillan Publishing Company.

Tomlinson, C. (1999). *The differentiated classroom: Responding to the needs of all learners.* Alexandria, VA: Association for Supervision and Curriculum Development.

Tomlinson, C., & Allan, S. (2000). *Leadership for differentiating schools and classrooms.* Alexandria, VA: Association for Supervision and Curriculum Development.

Truelove, J. E., Holaway-Johnson, C. A., Leslie, K. M., & Smith, T. E. C. (2007, February). Tips for including elementary students with disabilities in mathematics class. *Teaching Children Mathematics, 13*(6), 336–340.

U.S. Department of Education. (1996). *Pursuing excellence,* NCES 97–198. Washington, DC: National Center for Education Statistics, U.S. Government Printing Office.

Van de Walle, J. (2001). *Elementary and middle school mathematics: Teaching developmentally* (4th ed.). New York: Addison Wesley Longman.

Wenglinsky, H. (2000). *How teaching matters: Bringing the classroom back into discussions of teacher quality.* Princeton, NJ: Milken Family Foundation and Educational Testing Service.

Yackel, E., Cobb, P., Wood, T., Wheatley, G., & Merkel, G. (1990). The importance of social interaction in children's construction of knowledge. In T. J. Conney & C. R. Hirsch (Eds.), *Teaching and learning mathematics in the 1990s, 1990 yearbook of the National Council of Teachers of Mathematics* (pp. 12–21). Reston, VA: National Council of Teachers of Mathematics.

CORWIN

A SAGE Company

The Corwin logo—a raven striding across an open book—represents the union of courage and learning. Corwin is committed to improving education for all learners by publishing books and other professional development resources for those serving the field of PreK–12 education. By providing practical, hands-on materials, Corwin continues to carry out the promise of its motto: **"Helping Educators Do Their Work Better."**